STANLEY CAVELL
AND THE
EDUCATION OF GROWNUPS

AMERICAN PHILOSOPHY

Douglas R. Anderson and Jude Jones, series editors

STANLEY CAVELL
AND THE
EDUCATION OF GROWNUPS

Edited by
NAOKO SAITO AND PAUL STANDISH

FORDHAM UNIVERSITY PRESS   NEW YORK   2012

B
945
.C274
S74
2012

694832835

Copyright © 2012 Fordham University Press

Fordham University Press has no responsibility for the persistence or accuracy of URLs for external or third-party Internet websites referred to in this publication and does not guarantee that any content on such websites is, or will remain, accurate or appropriate.

Fordham University Press also publishes its books in a variety of electronic formats. Some content that appears in print may not be available in electronic books.

Library of Congress Cataloging-in-Publication Data

Stanley Cavell and the education of grownups / edited by Naoko Saito and Paul Standish.—1st ed.
p. cm.— (American philosophy)
Includes bibliographical references (p.   ) and index.
ISBN 978-0-8232-3473-8 (cloth : alk. paper)
ISBN 978-0-8232-3474-5 (pbk. : alk. paper)
1. Cavell, Stanley, 1926–   2. Philosophy.   3. Education—Philosophy.
I. Saito, Naoko.   II. Standish, Paul, 1949–
B945.C274S74   2012
191—dc23
2011026662

Printed in the United States of America
14 13 12   5 4 3 2 1
First edition

Contents

STANLEY CAVELL
AND THE
EDUCATION OF GROWNUPS

INTRODUCTION
Paul Standish and Naoko Saito

Our lives require of us change. How are we changed? And how far is this change education? We learn far more than we are taught, and we learn inevitably, in spite of ourselves. Yet sometimes we fail to learn *because of* ourselves. We can seek out our education, and education can be thrust upon us. We can accumulate knowledge, skills, and aptitudes, and we can chart our own path of development and progress (though others more likely will do this for us), but we can also be transformed, in ways that we cannot anticipate. The societies in which we find ourselves can, given our compliance in some way or other, perpetuate themselves, but their daily renewal requires something more of us in the return we make, a return in the words we have learned. It is a particularly poignant evocation of thoughts such as these that is found in the now celebrated passage from *The Claim of Reason* in which Stanley Cavell writes:

> In the face of the questions posed in Augustine, Luther, Rousseau, Thoreau . . . we are children; we do not know how to go on with

them, what ground we may occupy. In this light, philosophy becomes the education of grownups. It is as though it must seek
perspective upon a natural fact which is all but inevitably misin-
terpreted—that at an early point in a life the normal body reaches
its full strength and height. Why do we take it that because we
then must put away childish things, we must put away the prospect of growth and the memory of childhood? The anxiety in
teaching, in serious communication, is that I myself require education. And for grownups this is not natural growth, but *change*.
Conversion is a turning of our natural reactions; it is symbolized
as rebirth.[1]

Cavell is, as the tone of these words indicates, very far from the writing of anything like "educational theory," yet his concern throughout
his work *is* with a kind of education, and he has been inclined sometimes to name it as such. It is there as a theme in multiple ways, ex-
tending from his Emersonian moral perfectionism to his response to
skepticism, with deep resonances in his writings on ordinary language
philosophy, Wittgenstein, politics, and aesthetics; it goes to the heart
of *The Claim of Reason*. He has sometimes been struck by the thought
that this, in one way or another, is what his work is always about. Yet
education has received only passing attention in the various commentaries and critiques of his work. While the response to his writings in mainstream philosophy has given insufficient attention to its
educational preoccupations, among educators his thought is very
much still to be received. Acknowledgement of this theme is necessary to an understanding of Cavell's work as a whole and invaluable
as a means of advancing thinking about philosophy and education.

If we are to give this a sharper accent, it is worth attending to Hilary Putnam's remark that Cavell is one of the few twentieth-century
philosophers to explore the territory of "philosophy as education."
In many ways, this might be an apt assessment of Cavell's conception
of philosophy. But Cavell's own somewhat enigmatic emphasis on the
phrase is not to be understood from one side alone. It is not only that
he engages in a sustained exploration of the nature of philosophy that
takes teaching and learning (and the anxiety inherent in these) to be

at its heart; it is also that he is preoccupied with *what it is to teach and learn*, with the kinds of transformation these might imply and with the inseparability of these from what a human life is. In his considerations of the ordinary and the social world, questions of teaching and learning recur.

But if philosophy becomes the education of grownups, what is it that a grownup is? Cavell's naming of the condition that we aspire to deserves studying. If, in respect of its canonical questions, philosophy sometimes tends toward pomposity, this child's word certainly serves to deflate its pretensions. But it does much more. "What is truth?" "What is beauty?"—these are questions that strut the philosophical stage. "What is a grownup?" by contrast, would likely provoke a ripple of laughter.[2] If we think we do not need this perspective of the child, that because we have reached a certain size we must be adults already, this only goes to show how far "our education is sadly neglected."[3] As possible grownups, our need of education is inseparable from why we need to revise our philosophy, to see it again, revisiting the very idea, and this helps in the process to define this "we," to show us something of who we are.

Hence, the idea of philosophy as education disturbs the question of what philosophy is. Such a phrasing is hardly likely to appeal to anyone anxious to shore up the subject in its professionalized academic form. Cavell's own style is itself a foil to a dominant conception of academic writing. His work does not fit into any familiar philosophical idiom, and it is difficult, in style and substance, in ways that are difficult to name. The upshot of this is that in many circles his work tends to be referred to rather than read. It is not that he writes in an especially technical way. It is certainly not that he writes in any kind of specialized jargon—say, like Heidegger—nor that his prose is technically demanding—like, say, John McDowell. On the contrary, the often conversational register of his writing embraces high theory, abstract argument, concrete examples, anecdotes, autobiographical reflection, film and literature, baseball, jazz, and jokes. Were he to have written in a more technical way, this might have provided the kind of challenge to which the more muscular philosophical reader would have felt compelled to rise, and a reputation would have been more easily won. Not surprisingly, there are those in the professionalized philosophical establishment who have found his approach not to be good form. We move in this book beyond such appropriations and proprieties.

Further, the idea of philosophy as education, we shall find, is inseparable from the question of how one should read. So what does it mean to read *philosophically*? Reading philosophically will not be a technique that is the preserve of that academic institution called "philosophy" but rather something closer to what we are all, as inevitable readers, enjoined to do. Can reading indicate something of the nature of our education as (potential) grownups? Let us for the moment, however, preempt any immediate response to this question by raising another: what does it mean to read Cavell? Given the commitments of his writing, this difficulty comes to the reader with a kind of inevitability. Hilary Putnam, recalling earlier remarks of his own, captures this when he writes:

> When I was invited to write a "Nachwort" to a collection of Stanley Cavell's writings that was recently published in Germany,[4] I opened my essay by saying that Stanley Cavell is one of the great minds of our time, but he is not a founder of movements or a coiner of slogans or a trader in "isms." I described him as "a writer who always speaks to *individuals*—and that means, one at a time." To read Cavell as he should be read is to enter into a conversation with him, one in which your entire sensibility and his are involved, and not only your mind and his mind.[5]

There is, then, no easy entry into Cavell's writing. His texts are impervious to easy summary; they admit no quick, formulaic response; and any readers hoping that a skim through the pages of his work will give the general gist are best warned off before they start. This will undoubtedly deter some. And if such readers should come across Cavell's own provocative comment, regarding *The Senses of Walden*, that he wrote the book to make Thoreau's *Walden* more difficult,[6] they may imagine themselves justified in going no further. This willfully

difficult—because assiduously attentive—investment in language results in writings that both frustrate readers too sure of what they are
after and provoke the more sympathetic to strikingly different interpretations: different interpretations and tensions become active
within the reader herself, in her ambivalence and hesitancy over how
to weigh the writer's words. Always itself a response to other texts,
Cavell's own writing can realize such tensions, functioning in an exemplary way for the kind of reading that is his theme. Reading like
this tells us something of what our education as grownups can be.

In the face of these texts, experience of a kind of disturbance is of
the essence. Attentive readers of Emerson or Thoreau or Wittgenstein
are likely to find themselves not merely the adjudicators of argument
but, as it were, "convicted" by every word. Philosophers have typically been preoccupied with how their enquiries can lead to conviction, and they have sought to achieve this, in the analytic tradition
especially, not by entrusting their thought to language but through
the precision of their argumentation; the rigor of this other writing,
by contrast, is that it leads the reader to feel conviction, where this
word carries the sense both of being convinced and being convicted.
The reader is tested or put on trial. (Thoreau tries his readers with
his questions.) So too philosophers have typically been preoccupied
with necessary and sufficient conditions, but the embedded sense
within that term of our saying (-dit-) of things together (con-) needs
to be heard here to resonate, as we shall see, with the insights of ordinary language philosophy. The reader's inclination to acquiesce in the
imagined authority of a given text or to accommodate it to the culture she comes from are defenses that such writing undermines.
Moreover, the reader must leave behind the persona of the writer, the
better to find her own words. Such writing does not set out to recruit
disciples or found schools. On the contrary, it incites a kind of detachment; it invites neutrality, therapeutic as this sometimes may be.
In reading Cavell, in "reading in a high sense,"[7] there is a pressing
challenge not to assimilate the text into any established framework,
while at the same time avoiding that other assimilation, into the work
of the writer that confronts us.

One approach to the question "What does it mean to read Cavell?" is to consider Cavell's way of reading Dewey, and, given the latter's central presence in philosophical enquiry into education, the comparison here is a particularly edifying one. Cavell has registered his sense of "Dewey's distrust of language."[8] For Cavell, language is significant not so much because it serves in the verification of our experience as because it realizes experience's depth. Hence, although Dewey sees language as both instrumental ("the tool of tools")[9] and consummatory ("This community of partaking is meaning"),[10] there remains a tendency for it to be subordinated in his work: he seems unwilling to release his thought to language's inherent productive tensions and stresses. Cavell's preoccupation with language manifests his distance from Dewey's pragmatism, simultaneously revealing something of his own investments in ordinary language philosophy. Yet to measure the burden of these senses of distrust and distance remains difficult. Is Cavell merely preoccupied with textual activity and missing the practical engagement with life that is pragmatism's hallmark?[11] Or is he, as Putnam has suggested, too harsh on Dewey and inclined thus to overplay the differences?[12]

In a sense, as Putnam points out, Dewey "anticipated Cavell's identification of philosophy with education."[13] Yet what turns on this phrase for each of them is really rather different. Experience, for both writers, is troubled by events, but whereas for Dewey these require the adaptation of the individual in order to open new possibilities of growth, for Cavell they are indicative rather of the way that the human is always in some sense riven. Undergoing conflict, external and internal, is the very process of our education as grownups: we are destabilized and, in the process, convicted by our every word: "If you can stand right fronting and face a fact," Thoreau writes, "you will see the sun glimmer on both its surfaces, as it were a cimeter, and feel its sweet edge dividing you through the heart and marrow, and so you will happily conclude your mortal career."[14] And growing up, it turns out, is also a movement down. Readers of Cavell, whether native speakers of English or not, may be struck by something like the sense of "bottomlessness" that Walter Benn Michaels finds in Thoreau.[15] Yet, paradoxically, and as Cavell himself puts this, quoting Thoreau: "There is a solid bottom everywhere."[16] Education leads not so much upward, toward some kind of ethereal transcendence, as downward and back to the rough ground, with each new step we take, each moment of crisis, affording a new *point d'appui*. And these steps on the way suggest, at each point, a potential turning of our efforts, where the turning of philosophy as education begins to suggest a "secular version of conversion"[17]—say, transcendentalism without the supernatural.[18]

In order to understand that Cavell's suspicions of Dewey's distrust of language do not reflect a preoccupation only with linguistic activity, it is necessary to understand Cavell's approach to skepticism, which is at the heart of what he draws from ordinary language philosophy. Cavell's distance from Dewey's pragmatism is caused not simply by what Dewey says about ordinary experience but also by *how* he describes this through language. In contrast to Emerson or Thoreau, Dewey's language does not acknowledge that people may not know they have an experience and that this may itself involve forms of denial. Recognition of our failures of acknowledgment may be the beginning of our education as grownups—where we come to acknowledge that others are real and separate from ourselves, that they have their own aspirations, are wholly responsible to themselves.[19] This is something we have to learn, and it does not require access to new information. Simultaneously, this means recognizing that this "I" is also among those others who need to discover the right to speak.[20]

This right is crucially related to the question of authorship in Emersonian perfectionism and the theme of finding one's voice in Cavell's account of philosophy as autobiography.[21] Perfectionism here is to be contrasted, to be sure, with any notion of the perfectibility of realizable ends (with the sinister connotations this obviously has), but nevertheless the term may signal a difference from any doggedly insistent, "cash-value" version of pragmatism. But Cavell's sense of distance from Dewey is also related to how we face the unknowable and the unintelligible in our experiences. For Dewey, the emphasis is on problem solving; Cavell's Wittgensteinianism points rather to *dissolution.*

Cavell's emphasis on reading bears some relation to his sustained preoccupation with skepticism, which has reverberations throughout his work. So what then of skepticism? Cavell's interest was shaped particularly by his encounter, in the 1950s, with the ordinary language philosophy of J. L. Austin and with the writings of the later Wittgenstein. The *Philosophical Investigations* has been widely read as an attempt to refute the skeptic—that is, to show that the skeptic's questions (Is this a table in front of me? Are there other minds? How do I know that I exist?) always presuppose a background in which, in effect, these items of doubt are taken for granted. In epistemological terms, these skeptical questions involve a kind of circularity, with the conclusions of enquiry embedded in the premises. Cavell's reading of Wittgenstein, however, finds rather more to be at stake here, and in the process it exposes the inadequacy of the idea that skepticism is hereby *refuted*. It is not so much that this is wrong (and not that this is exactly something one would want to *deny*) as that it partly misses the point. That the *Investigations* is something other than an epistemological refutation can be seen, as Cavell eloquently shows, in the way that Wittgenstein "dissolves" the problem only to allow it to start up again—and this Wittgenstein does repeatedly. The itch returns. The question will not go away. This is tantamount to an acknowledgment not of the truth of skepticism but of the truth *in* skepticism (a disturbing expression, as Putnam has said),[22] and this is not an epistemological but an existential truth. It testifies to something deep in the human condition: our compulsion to doubt; our inclination to demand a reassurance greater than the circumstances allow or a verification more robust than they could reasonably bear; and, as Cavell—attending to the mild deflation of the Wittgensteinian claim that explanation must come to an end somewhere, that there must be an end to justification in acknowledgment of our "form of life," and hence in acceptance that ultimately "This is simply what I do"—as Cavell nicely puts it, our disappointment in criteria. It is such denial that is at the heart of Shakespearean tragedy and is the stuff of our more everyday meanness of spirit.

Wittgenstein's "This is simply what I do" is sometimes taken to be evidence of his cultural conservatism, and, as if in support of this, it is not uncommon to hear it misquoted as plural ("This is what we do"). The context of the remark bears some attention: "If I have exhausted the justifications I have reached bedrock, and my spade is turned. Then I am inclined to say: 'This is simply what I do.' "[23] What are the implications of reaching bedrock here? Does this symbolize the foundation of our lives as human beings, their authentication in the cultural practices from which we come? The uncomfortable, sometimes unhandsome twisting of the hand as the spade turns carries, by contrast, a note of frustration: there is nothing more I can say to the other, and, as for further explanation to myself, I find myself at a loss, disappointed. This turning also is characteristic of my daily conversion, by which I may not always be uplifted but through which I may continually learn.

A part of Wittgenstein's purpose is to undo the knots that develop in our thinking, knots for which philosophy has often been responsible. The untying of these knots, sometimes requiring movements more elaborate and more difficult than those that constructed them, is part of the "therapy" of philosophy that Wittgenstein seeks to provide. In doing this, he repeatedly returns philosophy to the ordinary. In the flights of philosophy to which the skeptic is drawn, language goes "on holiday." One articulation of this in Cavell's thought is that the philosopher's problems tend to be expressed in a context that is "non-claim"—in contrast to the way that our ordinary language does involve making claims about the world. Hence, the title *The Claim of Reason*, whose genitive doubles to encompass our claiming of reason *and* reason's claim on us, our finding of reason through the voicing of our claims, is a challenge as to how far philosophy allows reason to make its claim.

Cavell is struck especially by the way that the characteristic procedure of the ordinary language philosopher, its characteristic mode of appeal, takes the form of "When we say . . . , we mean. . . ." This is an appeal to ordinary use not as some kind of empirical generalization about the behavior of a particular people; a survey of usage would be beside the point. Two things should be noted especially: the statement is in the first person, and it is plural. That it is in the first person shows the significance of voice; the authentication of the statement has to do with the speaker's sincere assent, with how things seem to her, and with her desire or responsibility to express this. That it is plural testifies to her desire or responsibility to speak *for* others, to find community of some kind with them. This is by no means to impose on their views, nor is it simply to align herself with them in terms, say, of shared characteristics (a community of the same); it is rather to offer her assertion as exemplary in some way, testing this against the responses of others and testing her own responses against what those others themselves say—where, if she does not do this sincerely, her claim will itself be void. Here is reason making its claim. That this relation to others does not spring from a fully fledged personal autonomy is evident in the importance attached to reading, hence reception, but that this is not merely conservative is seen in the importance attached to voice. This, then, is to see her autonomy as inevitably tied to the political (the creation of the *polis*)—as two sides, so it might be said, of the same coin—and to see it as inextricably linked to the conditions of response within which she finds herself. The political is to this extent internal, and the words in which we find ourselves condition political participation.

It is Cavell's claim that ordinary language philosophy is underwritten by American transcendentalism.[24] And his pondering of conditions finds expression in a number of iterations of the moral perfectionism that he associates with Emerson's name. While, in view of its very nature, this could scarcely be expressed in comprehensive or definitive terms, the following sketch, whose lines are abstracted from *Conditions Handsome and Unhandsome*, is helpfully suggestive:

> Each self is drawn on a journey of ascent . . . to a further state of that self, where . . . the higher is determined not by natural talent but by seeking to know what you are made of and cultivating the thing you are meant to do; it is a transformation of the self which

> finds expression in . . . the imagination of a transformation of
> society into . . . something like an aristocracy where . . . what is
> best for society is a model for and is modeled on what is best for
> the individual soul.[25]

Far from any crude individualism, any individualism complacent in
itself, this suggests aspiration toward our own best selves. What is as-
pired to is typically understood in terms of a new reality—the good
city, the good society, with the recognition that our city is necessarily
a "city of words."[26] It involves thinking how our world should be
constituted, what words we can find for it, what practices might give
it substance, and what standards sustain it; for Emerson, this involves
questioning what America might be—where "America" does not
stand primarily for any particular landmass, any more than does, in
a sense, "Israel." It is not a matter of mere circumstantial detail that
this is American philosophy, for what might constitute American philosophy is taken by Cavell to be inextricably linked to the question of
what America is or can be, which is itself a version of the question of
how democracy might be attained. These concerns are most explicitly
played out in Cavell's writings on Emerson, where he claims that the
repression referred to above has also led to an underappreciation of
the extent to which Emerson's work was influential for Nietzsche. Cavell has written also of Thoreau and Heidegger. For all the apparent
differences between these thinkers, it is difficult not to see Thoreau's
experiment in living and his lightness of touch in writing this experiment as in some ways anticipating so much of the profundity in Heidegger (though Thoreau's practice of building, dwelling, and thinking
becomes sonorous and ponderous, to be sure, in Heidegger's *Bauen
Wohnen Denken*)—unappreciated though these connections may remain. And Cavell has written more recently of what it is concerning
the relation of land and belonging that separates Thoreau from
Heidegger.[27]

We are not to gravitate to any particular landmass, for it is in the
lighter conditions of sociality that we can be "educations for one another."[28] But while it is true that "friendship" is a critical condition
for the education of grownups, especially in the sway of Emersonian

moral perfectionism, Cavell's ordinary language *philosophy* neither mystifies the unknown other nor, in turn, identifies and immobilizes the other in what purports to be "mutual understanding," in a politics of recognition. The import of friendship here is to be distinguished also from the face-to-face, immediate relationship with the concrete other. Cavell's perfectionism can never fully cohere with that familiar story of the self's recovery from loss and achievement of holistic integrity through its interaction with the other as a friend: rather, there will an opening to excess, which cannot be contained in the economy of exchange. The presence of the lunatic child in Cavell's writings symbolizes a kind of madness inherent in the language game. Cavell's ordinary language philosophy thus both desentimentalizes and de-moralizes the language of education, disturbing its developmental confidence by unsettling its familiar mother tongue.

We have moved, as it were in spite of ourselves, from that secondary question of what it means to read Cavell to the prior matter of what it is to read *philosophically*. The substance of this book will take us further in this in a way not thematic but rather exemplary, for each of the chapters enacts its own process of reading. Let us explain how we have presented this work.

We began by pointing out that, in the many volumes that have recently been published on Cavell's work, relatively little attention is given to education, and so it is a unique feature of this book that it does just this. This is by no means a matter of taking Cavell's thought and "applying" it to education. Education does not intrude into his writings as an outside concern but is there at the heart of what he most wants to say. This is more clearly a feature of Cavell's work than it is of other leading philosophers today whose success is embedded more obviously in the professionalized (and sometimes technical) traditions of the discipline. But this by no means makes him eccentric. It is not as if education were a side issue to which philosophy might be applied; rather, questions of teaching and learning, as of what it is to progress toward the good (and what that good life is), are internal to philosophy in its most characteristic and perhaps central endeavors, as even a glance at the work of Plato makes abundantly clear. In consequence, the idea of philosophy of education as a branch or as an applied field of the pure discipline of philosophy misunderstands the nature of both. Hence, the truth of philosophy as education. Hence, the importance of the education of grownups.

Our collection begins with a paper entitled "Philosophy as the Education of Grownups," in which Cavell himself revisits this signature phrase. This brings together thoughts, prompted by the recent preparation for publication of his autobiography, of a return to the opening of the *Investigations* and a pondering of how children and grownups figure in that text. In particular, he considers the ways that our natural history, unlike that of the animals, is one in which nature and convention intersect, a history of initiations and becomings and inventions in the countless different things human beings do. In this ongoing process, we depend upon our being, as it were, teachers to one another, and this in turn reflects the ongoing possibilities of our community—in short, our politics, our life together, an idea to which the education of grownups is singularly pertinent. The receptiveness that is necessarily involved in this evokes the idea of philosophy as a kind of reading. As a supplement to these thoughts and as a coda to the collection as a whole, we publish Cavell's short text "Philosophy as Education," of which we shall say more shortly.

The intervening chapters of the book are presented in three parts, and between them we insert remarks from Cavell and Putnam from the discussion that contributed to the development of this work. In each case the remarks resonate with the chapters that precede them, but they draw out threads of thought that run through the collection as a whole.

Part I, entitled "Entries in the Education of Grownups," begins with Hilary Putnam's exploration of the persistence of the fact/value distinction, a matter about which many who think themselves grown up in fact need education. Cavell's distinctive place in the story of resistance to this dichotomization is located by Putnam in part 3 of *The Claim of Reason*, where Cavell is reacting, among other things, to the emotivism of C. L. Stevenson. Thus, for example, Cavell denies that what makes science rational is that it consists of beliefs about matters of fact—and hence consists of methods that rationally settle disagreements. But Putnam finds Cavell's special depth in these matters to lie not only in his sense of the entangled nature of our concepts but in the centrality of disagreement, the former point aligning him with John McDowell, the latter showing how far apart they are. Against philosophy's tendency to divide into countless specializations, Putnam seeks to show that it is when different sources are connected with one another that philosophy truly becomes the education of grownups.

The autobiographical turn in Russell Goodman's "Encountering Cavell" provides an account of his own "education as a grownup." Goodman explains the importance of "vantage points" in the work of Cavell for his own passage from Wittgenstein's fertile explanation of "seeing aspects" to Emerson's call for the intellect to yield itself to the will. Goodman admires Cavell's insight in drawing out connections between what Wittgenstein means by "grammar" and what Kant means by "transcendental knowledge," while a further fruitful congruence or contiguity is found with Freud, implicit in Wittgenstein's philosophy as therapy. All three are connected in their concern with self-knowledge, and this, it turns out, is also at the heart of the motivation of ordinary language philosophy, the procedures of which are intimately bound up with a certain kind of education. Via a consideration of the theme of skepticism, Goodman returns to pragmatism but concludes with a note of regret (whose acceptance of or proximity to Cavell's aversion to calling Emerson a pragmatist remains equivocal): this is to the effect that the term has become so loosely used and burdened that there are times when it is better left behind.

Part II, entitled "Skepticism and Language," begins with a turn more directly to the practices of educational institutions. Paul Standish, in "Skepticism, Acknowledgment, and the Ownership of Learning," considers various ways in which claims of ownership have been made in contemporary education and the connections of these with a commodification of knowledge. This is discussed in the light of Cavell's examination of the extension of skepticism through various forms of the relation to the other, not least in his consideration of Shakespearean tragedy. The pivotal distinction between knowing and acknowledging, elaborated originally in the paper of that name collected in *Must We Mean What We Say*,[29] is used to reveal the consequences for educational practice of certain kinds of denial. Standish points to Cavell's suggestion that there is a "stratum of symmetry" linking *acknowledgment* in relation to others with *acceptance* in relation to objects such that failure in these respects is significantly connected with an inability to accept the human condition.

Gordon Bearn's "Sensual Schooling: On the Aesthetic Education of Grownups" begins by considering what Alfred North Whitehead called the "public dangers" inherent in the tendency of educational institutions to preserve the fixed ways and sometimes the errors of the past, a danger made worse, in Bearn's view, by the "professional" turn of higher education in recent times. This is a problem that cannot be laid exclusively at the door of, say, government or commerce, for among ourselves as educators there is the persistent inclination to enshrine our favorite abstractions and to force them upon our students or readers. A return to "great books" or a reaffirmation of "general education" cannot by themselves constitute any kind of solution to this problem. It is against this background that Bearn admires Cavell's reading of Wittgenstein but worries that the interpretation this yields, with the intermittent stability that it seeks, stands in the way of the aesthetic appreciation that is crucial to the education of grownups. This carries the surprising and disconcerting implication that Cavell's reading may contribute to a suppression of the aesthetic and, hence, frustrate the sensual schooling that Bearn advocates.

Part III focuses on Cavell's idea of Emersonian moral perfectionism and its implications for education. How we should interpret the relationship between initiation into culture and deviation from it is one of the common themes running through this part of the book. In Chapter 6, "Voice and the Interrogation of Philosophy: Inheritance, Abandonment, and Jazz," Vincent Colapietro, writing partly from a

Freudian psychoanalytical perspective, discusses the necessity of inheritance, which, in Cavell's view, already carries the "conflict of voices and generations" and the simultaneous necessity of improvisation represented by jazz. He also reveals the amorphous, multifaceted nature of Cavell's approach to skepticism. With regard to philosophy as the education of grownups, Colapietro lays emphasis on the work of mourning and recollection, with the voice of the child coming to be recognized as a forgotten voice from the past.

In Chapter 7, "Perfectionism's Educational Address," René Arcilla draws out from Emersonian moral perfectionism the idea of the "perfectionist text" as an avenue through which the person who has lost her way has a chance of regaining that way. This is understood to involve self-cultivation and friendship, where the encounter with the perfectionist text exemplifies the provocation from the friend that the receptive reader most needs. This requires humbling acceptance that one's work is destined to be grist to the mill of critical departure, such that the aim of becoming intelligible to oneself is conjoined with the cultivation of a democracy based on mutual learning. Arcilla's discussion examines the moral necessities of perfectionism in relation to major currents in modernism and existentialism, and he raises tentative doubts about the connotations of selflessness that Cavell's favored term may carry. The quest for self-understanding has historically been in tension with learning as the gratification of curiosity. It is the emphasis on the former, which Arcilla finds richly elaborated in Cavell, that offers a promising course for the future of liberal learning.

In Chapter 8, "The Gleam of Light: Initiation, Prophesy, and Emersonian Moral Perfectionism," Naoko Saito explores the prophetic dimension in Cavell's idea of philosophy as the education of grownups, which she interprets in terms of the necessity of the renewal of self and language. The idea of mutual education is examined in the light of the apparent tension it raises between self-cultivation and the need for the other. Taking its lead from Cavell's politics of interpretation, the chapter eases this tension by demonstrating the intricate relation between initiation into and departure

from one's language community. It is in Emerson's assertion that
"A man should learn to detect and watch that gleam of light which
flashes from his mind from within"[30] that Saito finds her title phrase
and from which she draws the idea of the other as teacher attesting
to the prophetic renewal of language. This opens a path from the
inmost to the outmost, demonstrating the inseparability of democracy and education. In the course of her discussion, she is at pains
to stress Emerson's American voice and hence to evoke the idea of
a democracy always still to come.

In Chapter 9, "The Ordinary as Sublime in Cavell, Zen, and Nishida: Cavell's Philosophy of Education in East-West Perspective,"
Steve Odin sheds light from a different angle on Emersonian moral
perfectionism, here with a particular focus on the idea of the ordinary. In Odin's discussion, the ordinary is the home to which we
must return, and skepticism is treated implicitly as the object of overcoming in the process of perfection, as in the case of the Great Doubt
in Buddhism. Back through tributaries of ordinary language philosophy, American transcendentalism, British romanticism, continental
philosophy, and Freud, Odin follows the current of Cavell's writings
on the ordinary in order to lay the way for an account of the ordinary
as Tao in Sino-Japanese philosophy. Points of contact are found between Cavell and Zen in their response to skepticism, the nihilistic
aspects of which are to be overcome by a recovery of the aesthetic,
artistic, and poetic value of ordinary life in its beauty and sublimity.
The Confucian tradition, deeply influenced by Zen/Chan Buddhism,
aims at realizing the unity of Tao with ordinary life through a dynamic *educational* process, described in terms similar, Odin tries to
show, to Emerson's perfectionist image of ever-expanding concentric
circles.

The coda provided by Cavell's short paper "Philosophy as Education" echoes themes that run through this collection. If philosophical
problems are solved by rearranging or putting together again what we
have always known, this will sometimes be a matter of remembering
what we have forgotten. This will perforce include what we have forgotten as a result of denials that prevail in the sometimes oppressive

institutions of contemporary education. Overcoming such forms of denial will not be a matter of acquiring new facts, and it will not be well described in terms of natural growth; rather, it will require a kind of conversion, for this will be a condition of the autonomy of the grownup. It is reference not just to Wittgenstein and Augustine but to Thoreau that leads Cavell back to thoughts of America and specifically to the thought that the public language of America is inadequate to the promise that is implied in its name. Finally, there is the thought that philosophy, as realized in Wittgenstein at the least, requires the kind of self-criticism that moves the education of grownups.

PHILOSOPHY AS THE EDUCATION
OF GROWNUPS

Stanley Cavell

The text that follows has turned out to become something quite different from what I thought I was preparing for this occasion. This is anything but unique in my case or, I believe, to my case. But the reason for it is, in my case, unique. Having within the past month completed the first thorough editing of the autobiography I have been working on, off and on, for the past several years, I found I was particularly struck by the amount of attention I had given in it to moments and conditions of my education, or lack of it, at every stage of my life. This is, in a sense, hardly surprising, given that I have lived as a grownup mostly an ordinary academic life and that I describe as a subgoal of the autobiography the articulation of some understanding of how *The Claim of Reason* was written, particularly why its longest, concluding part, part 4, sounds as it does, something for which I have been over the years perhaps equally rebuked and complimented. (I believe the balance between these responses may in the past few years have begun to tip in my favor, but I cannot count on it.) As I began riffling through those hundreds of pages of memories with the idea of selecting passages to read to you, I realized that I wanted to introduce them briefly by going back yet again over the opening paragraphs of Wittgenstein's *Philosophical Investigations*, to provide a new thought or two concerning their emphasis on education, or early learning, as well as to provide an orienting reminder of past work of mine touching on philosophy as education and my sense of luck in having continued my education, inspired by a series of colleagues and students through all the decades of my life. My brief introduction has, however, become essentially my entire text, though I will say something in closing about why that has happened and why it is a good if not inevitable thing. (I might say that the concept of luck, or of accident, is one of the continuous themes of the autobiography, one of the earliest events in which is the description of six-year-old Stanley being knocked unconscious by an automobile as he exuberantly ran after a kicked ball into the public street, an event that has had fateful consequences to this day.)

My title phrase comes at the end of part 1 of *The Claim of Reason* and forms part of what is in effect a response to, or is a kind of brief commentary on, the opening line of the first of Wittgenstein's paragraphs in *Philosophical Investigations*. It is the line in which Wittgenstein expresses his response to his citation from Augustine's *Confessions* as follows: "These words, it seems to me, give us a particular picture of the essence of human language."[1] Let me remind you afresh of those cited words of Augustine which begin the *Investigations*:

> When they (my elders) named some object, and accordingly moved towards something, I saw this and I grasped that the thing was called by the sound they uttered when they meant to point it out. Their intention was shown by their bodily movements, as it were the natural language of all peoples: the expression of the face, the play of the eyes, the movement of other parts of the body, and the tone of voice which expresses our state of mind in seeking, having, rejecting, or avoiding something. Thus, as I heard words repeatedly used in their proper places in various sentences, I gradually learnt to understand what objects they signified: and after I

had trained my mouth to form these signs, I used them to express my own desires.[2]

Now, if I ask myself what aspect of language these words give us a picture of, I do not find that I am inclined to speak, as Wittgenstein reports of himself, of the *essence* of language but rather to speak of the *learning* of language. Wittgenstein does speak in his second paragraph of Augustine as "describing the learning of language," and he goes on in his third paragraph—so I suppose—to test this picture:

> Now think of the following *use of language*: I send someone shopping. I give him a slip marked "five red apples." He takes the slip to the shopkeeper, who opens the drawer marked "apples"; then he looks up the word "red" in a table and finds a color sample opposite it; then he says the series of cardinal numbers—I assume he knows them by heart—up to the word "five" and for each number he takes an apple of the same color as the sample out of the drawer.[3]

And so on. What is the point of this surrealism—unreal even to the point of narrating from the shopkeeper's point of view his taking out apples "up to the *word* 'five,'" stopping there not because he knows this word is a number word (that is, not because he has *counted*) but simply because it is the last of a memorized list, specifically the last of a list containing what we call four other words?

In the following paragraph, the first paragraph of §2 of the *Investigations*, Wittgenstein opens by speaking of "That philosophical concept of meaning" (namely, the concept according to which individual words of a language name objects and according to which sentences are combinations of such names), saying of that concept that it "has its place in a primitive idea of the way language functions." I have two brief suggestions about this. First, I take the idea of the primitive here to be the result of the experience conveyed by the primitive or the somewhat mechanical or inflexible manner of the shopkeeper in this portrait of him. This is confirmed, I find, by the ensuing example of the builders who possess only four words and who seem to exist in an unspecified, perhaps unspecifiable, environment. What are we to imagine the builder is building? What determines the "order in which he needs" the stones? Second, the shopkeeper's primitiveness seems to be an effect of trying to imagine that he seeks an independent object or an independent routine for each word he is given. This points to the array of unspecified sources of understanding of the terms in which he is described. For example, how does he know what a "table" of color words is and what the point is of a mark on a drawer? Perhaps the question before all, to my mind, is what could count as "sending" my interlocutor "shopping"? An air of puzzlement is created in which, to my mind, we are being prepared for what we might call the paradox of acquiring language: namely, that to "learn" language we have already to "have" it.

And I take it as part of this paradoxical air that Wittgenstein insinuates the concept of philosophy into the opening of this second section. Why does he identify as "philosophical" what he calls the primitive idea of the functioning of language? An obvious answer is that he had begun expressing his reaction to his citation from Augustine by describing it as giving a picture of the essence of human language. "Essence" is a philosophical term if any term is. Sometimes Wittgenstein uses the terms "philosophy" and "philosophical" shaded in a negative tone, sometimes in a positive tone, as if philosophy is essentially in struggle with itself. (Hardly a surprising idea, as it occurs explicitly as early as in Plato's fundamental struggle with the teaching of the Sophists.)

Is the term "philosophical" at the opening of the *Investigations* used negatively or positively? It can seem negative both because we know that Wittgenstein's speaking of Augustine's description as giving us a "picture" is a Wittgensteinian term of criticism that puts us on philosophical alert and because Wittgenstein will soon invite us to "imagine a language for which the description given by Augustine is right," hence implying that the description is wrong. Actually, the German does not strictly say that Augustine's description is not "right" but something closer to not "exact" (*stimmt*), so that while something about it may not be completely wrong, the philosophical stake is one in which being exactly right is decisive.

Then what about it might not be completely wrong, or, in other words, what about the modifier "philosophical" might be positive? Here I offer a speculation that you may feel reads too much into the *Investigations'* early words. I am impressed, as I have said, with the shift from Wittgenstein's speaking in his first paragraph of Augustine's words as giving a picture of the essence of human language to his characterization in his second paragraph of Augustine's description as of the learning of language. It is the connection of *essence* with *learning* that I am calling philosophy in a positive sense. A further word about this.

Recall Wittgenstein's announcing that "Our investigation [hence the work of *Philosophical Investigations*] is a grammatical one,"[4] that "*Essence* is expressed by grammar,"[5] and that to give what he calls "the concept of a perspicuous presentation" of our otherwise unperspicuous grammar "is of fundamental importance to us. It earmarks the form of presentation we give, the way we look at things." And he then suggests parenthetically that he wouldn't mind calling this a "Weltanschauung,"[6] namely, the kind of world outlook that philosophy is characteristically or popularly taken to provide. (I surmise that Wittgenstein will not there call this philosophy because, as I believe Kant was the first to say, philosophy cannot be taught; only philosophizing can be taught.) The implication I draw, phrased in full-blown late Wittgensteinian parlance, can be put this way: "It is part of the grammar of 'human language' [that is, part of its essence, hence part of, a path to, what philosophy seeks] that *this* is what we call 'the learning of language.'" (Already in the *Blue Book*: "It is part of the grammar of the word 'chair' that *this* is what we call 'to sit on a chair.'")[7] It is, in other words, the internal connection between what Wittgenstein proposes as the signature practice of philosophizing (eliciting and making perspicuous the grammar of our utterances) with the most fundamental of the matters we can be said to learn (namely, the learning of speech, the ordering and reordering of words, the power of unending exposure and responsiveness to the new and to self-reflection, which marks our capacities with the tinge of the human) that I am calling the positive sense Wittgenstein gives to the concept of philosophy.

By the way, it is by now so easy to say that Wittgenstein is concerned with grammar that we forget how very strange it is, or was, for him to speak of "the word 'chair'" as "having a grammar." No one else I have encountered had said, or would have cause to say, such a thing. The grammar of the word "chair," if we are to speak so, would simply seem to be the grammar of a (kind of) noun (infrequently as a kind of predicate), a word that is fated to occupy different particular positions, serve different functions (say, as subject or as object), in different structures of sentences. Whereas Wittgenstein attributes to this particular noun (and proposes that there will be a similar exercise for each other noun in the language) a structurally essential, or essentially structural, articulation of its own, bound up with the human life form, something he also characterizes as the natural history of the human. The articulation recalls that the family of things we call chairs, hence the family of postures we describe as sitting on a chair, plays a distinct family of roles in human existence, essentially related to (what we call) sitting on a canvas camp stool or on a fence or a swing or on a bottom step and hence related to getting up and standing still and walking and resting and chatting and dining and presiding and squatting and kneeling and cushioning and leaning and stretching out and writing alone for hours at a table. Every step we take across the web of speech makes the entire web tremble, as if to remind us that it requires the entirety to sustain us. Wittgenstein seems indifferent to the distinction between syntax and semantics.

But an essential matter concerning what Augustine's description is wrong about, or how it is wrong, has still to come out. This is noted when, in §2, Wittgenstein shifts from speaking of a primitive idea of language to specifying that it is "the idea of a language more primitive than *ours*." This emphasis is continued, in §3, when Wittgenstein says that Augustine's description of a system of communication is "not everything *we call* language." That is, Augustine is wrong, falsifies something, not alone about the child and its relation to words but about himself, that is to say, about us, about our relation to our words. And Wittgenstein goes on to suggest that such falsifications are chronic in human exchange, with the implication that it is we who continue to stand in need of education and that there is no one to educate us but others not relevantly different from ourselves. It is this circumstance that necessitates the mode of instruction Wittgenstein wishes to call philosophy. He describes Augustine as conceiving the child to be a small grownup; he can himself be seen to treat grownups as large children.

I have in recent years emphasized my sense—perhaps it could be called my world outlook—that in our exchanges with each other we are incessantly teachers of each other, good or bad, strong or bland, assaulting or liberating, examples of what can or might or should or thoughtfully or mindlessly be said and be done. This has gone with what I have wished to call the search for community. This approach to the idea and the fact of community has been centrally taken up in a book recently published under the title *The Claim to Community: Essays on Stanley Cavell and Political Philosophy*, most of the contributors to which, including the book's editor, identify themselves as political theorists.[8] This exploration of the intersection of the concepts of education and the political is the most recent departure I am aware of in the path of reception of my writing. I am the more pleased by it because the earliest reactions I received to my first book, *Must We Mean What We Say?*, especially those that focused on my concluding reading of *King Lear*, insisted that I had missed the politics of the play. I did not feel I understood the criticism, because, as I tried to explain in my defense, I took the play itself to be about the missing, or destruction, or freezing of the possibility of politics (for example, by making the public private). This suggests to me that a step perhaps not, or no longer, sufficiently stressed in considering the intersection of politics and education is the articulation of ways in which the possibility of education is destroyed or missed or frozen (for example, by making education indoctrination or, I would like to say, not sufficiently philosophical, perhaps discovering at what age it is illuminating to ask, for example, "What is a chair?"). (Here am I prompted by the memory of perhaps the most impressive class I took during my

college years, as a major in music at Berkeley, given by the aging composer Ernest Bloch. At a certain point he interrupted himself—a signature feature of his teaching I came to recognize—and asked, "By
the way, do you know what a triad is?" He might as probingly have
asked, "Can you spell 'cat'?" He would not continue until someone
obligingly responded, "Well C, E, G, for example." "Excellent," cried
Bloch. Perhaps he added, "And your caution 'for example' suggests
that this is a major triad and that there are in traditional harmony
eleven other such triads, for example." What is unforgettable is that
Bloch thereupon turned to one of the two solid—that is, window-
less—black walls of the music room, each bearing musical staves per-
manently painted along the length and covering the height of them,
accommodating the reach at least of the normal human arm, and,
beginning with a simple chord of C, E, G, began filling the board with
different dispositions of spacings, doublings, inversions of simultaneous C's and E's and G's, and eventually turned back to say, "You see,
I could fill the other board with indications of dynamics and with
orchestral textures of each of these, and another board with contexts
leading up to and away from these sonorities as may be needed, and
so on. So now you have some idea of what a major triad is." Did he
add: "And didn't you already know this?" But the class, audited by
a number of musicians of considerable musical experience, seemed,
judging by the appreciative hubbub following this demonstration, illuminated by the experiment.)

The incessancy and absence of education is, to my mind, further
allegorized by the scene from Augustine that opens the *Investigations*.
I have elsewhere described that scene as one in which it can be con-
ceived that the child is invisible to or unnoticed by its elders (as if it
is not spoken *to*) and hence can be felt to steal what it is learning
from them, as though something illicit is in play. (How indeed *could*
it be spoken "to" if it lacked speech? One thinks of the ways it could
be sung to. This sense of isolation in learning seems to be brought
out in the opening of the paragraph-length chapter of Augustine's
Confessions from which Wittgenstein takes his first words: "I remember . . . how I first learned to speak, for my elders did not teach me

words in any set method, as they did letters afterwards; but I myself, when I was unable to say all I wished and to whomsoever I desired, by means of the whimperings and broken utterances and various motions of my limbs, which I used to enforce my wishes, repeated the sounds in my memory by the mind, O my God, which Thou gavest me.") One might understand this moment of invisibility or mystery of origin in speech as an interpretation of the fact that in acting we necessarily teach, as in speaking we inevitably say, less than we mean and more than we intend, or know we intend, that we cannot humanly be everywhere in command of the implication of our utterances, their tone or mood and their timing and point (Augustine cites "the expression of the face, the play of the eyes, the movement of other parts of the body"), so that something I am perpetually learning takes the form of secrets. (Here I would like to mention my recent expansion of my thoughts on Austin's work on the performative utterance and my effort to extend or supplement the analysis to include passionate utterance.)[9] What I mean by speaking of allegorizing here is simply that I take Augustine's quasi-memory of his acquiring speech as a projection of a continuing present sense of our participation with others, of any age, not alone those we call strangers; a sense of my invisibility to them, of my doubts about my standing with them, about the range of my right to intervene in their consciousness, of my wavering attention and interest in what they seem waveringly attentive to and interested in.

The allegory comes to rest with the child, who has taken language upon himself/herself—this unshiftable individual necessity, or necessity of individuality (emphasized in both Plato and in Aristotle as eventually my having to choose my life, take it upon myself), is the sense I get from Augustine's saying that he had "trained [his] mouth" to repeat the sounds he heard. And the purpose of all this energy and theft (I am vividly, even graphically, on my own in training my mouth) is that it allows him to "express [his] own desires." Here Augustine's description of taking on language gives us a further picture of the essence of human language, namely that it perpetually exposes our desires to those able and willing to understand them. This would enter into the sense I express of the illicit in play.

The observant or, say, speculative child raises to my mind the question of how we understand or explain the child's interest in our namings and gestures and intentions and eyes and tones. If I say that we understand the child to care about us or to recognize its dependence upon us, does this provide an answer, or does it only rephrase the question? Still within the initial momentum of investigating the relation of naming to something named and of stressing the variousness of the uses of words and the points of sentences, Wittgenstein remarks: "It is sometimes said that animals do not talk because they lack the mental capacity. . . . But—they simply do not talk . . . do not use language—if we except the most primitive forms of language.— Commanding, questioning, recounting, chatting, are as much a part of our natural history as walking, eating, drinking, playing."[10] Is this an explanation of our capacity for speech, or is it a rejection of the call for explanation?

Our natural history, as opposed to that of the beasts, contains our coming into what Wittgenstein emphasizes as *countless* different kinds of use of what we call symbols, words, sentences.[11] This emphasis on the natural seems clearly to reject any "because" or "explanation"; these phenomena are simply, just, quite exactly, after all, indeed, the way we are, what we do. Yet a sense of explanation, anyway, some intellectual step, seems to have been taken. After all, what does it mean to think of the human—anyway, of us, us moderns, builders of cities, no longer divisible into species—as having a natural history, something invoked whenever Wittgenstein speaks of our "form of life"?

In a contribution to the volume I mentioned earlier, *The Search for Community*, Sandra Laugier takes up the phrase "philosophy as the education of grown-ups" as the pivotal point in showing the political drive of *Philosophical Investigations*. What she is pointing to is my emphasis on the inheritance of language by the human child (Wittgenstein, in this connection, speaks of commanding, questioning, recounting, chatting) as something natural—as natural, in Wittgenstein's words, as walking, eating, drinking, playing. The difference of these registers is that one person's mastery of walking, eating, playing, etc. does not naturally come to contest the walking, eating, playing, etc. of others, whereas commands are inherently subject to countercommands, to questioning, to various recountings, to denials. In offering language to us, human society creates critics as well as conformists, and in the same persons. In chapter 5 of *The Claim of Reason*, which concludes with the definition of philosophy as the education of grownups, I picture this inheritance as the intersection of nature and convention in principle unendingly questioning, or countercommanding, each other. Subsequently, I have begun epitomizing this picture by stressing the two directions implied in Wittgenstein's idea of human beings and their language agreeing in form of life (*Lebensform*), which I name as a horizontal and a vertical direction. Horizontally, we share conventions that distinguish human groups from one other, eating different things, shaped by different etiquettes and taboos, etc.; vertically, our social and emotional bonds distinguish human families and societies from those of other orders, call them animal and (should there be any) angelic orders. The idea of the human *polis* is of the order whose conventionality and whose naturalness are in intercourse and contest with each other from beginning to end. Such is the fate of comfort and of conflict opened to the human life form bequeathed to it by the possession of human language, hence the fate of self-reflection, of self-definition through exclusion, learning to say "I." Community is always partial, always to be searched for, as individual integrity is, always within circumstances of false unities, misplaced desires.

I end abruptly with the suggestion of a kind of philosophical joke arising from the ground of what I have been led to cover in these remarks.

The joke is derivable from Wittgenstein's opening examples of the shopkeeper and the builders. Its background is a remark reported during the years I was in graduate school to have been made by Bertrand Russell in response to the later Wittgenstein's turn to the ordinary or everyday, reported, for example, in Austin's "A Plea for Excuses," near the end of its opening half, where Austin has been defending so-called ordinary language philosophy (not, of course, Wittgenstein's version and practice of it), at this moment defending it against certain of what he takes to be inept charges. Austin's defense opens with a paragraph whose second and third sentences read as follows: "Certainly ordinary language has no claim to be the last word, if there is such a thing. It embodies, indeed, something better than the metaphysics of the Stone Age, namely, as was said, the inherited experience and acumen of many generations of men."[12] Its allusion to the metaphysics of the Stone Age has been attributed to Russell; Austin's invoking it clearly takes the attribution as something well known. Even allowing for the academic humor of Russell's using an uneducated phrase, presumably to imply the uneducated view he is dismissing, what can Austin mean by accepting it as though they understand each other—or is he tossing it back at Russell as patently empty, undeserving of attempting to specify and answer seriously? This aside, Austin's slap at Russell has from the first time I read it seemed to me defensive and disappointing, saying no more than that ordinary language has proven to be quite useful in human affairs, a proposition it is hard to imagine anyone seriously wishing to doubt. He is not even saying what his knack with examples at a minimum shows: that we have little idea just how deep and systematic the usefulness of having ordinary language is. (I might say that it is roughly as useful as having a human body.)

The joke I see here essentially consists in taking Wittgenstein's early language games in the *Investigations* with the primitive builders who build only with stones in connection with Russell's dismissive remark about the age of stone. Let's first assume that Russell made the remark after reading Wittgenstein's manuscript called *The Blue Book* (a copy of which Wittgenstein had sent Russell in 1934 or 1935) and that Wittgenstein had heard of the remark before composing the manuscript called *The Brown Book* some two years later (which opens with a draft of the eventual opening of *Philosophical Investigations*, a manuscript that I gather Wittgenstein did *not* send Russell). Then we can take Wittgenstein's opening as a rebuke simultaneously to Russell and to Austin. Instead of, in effect, dismissing the builders as Austin apparently does in his response to Russell, Wittgenstein, in a signature fashion of his later manner, asks, in effect: What strikes Russell as primitive in thinking about language? About what kind of language would it be right to call it primitive (colloquially "Stone Age"), to embody in the lives of its users a primitive language and (hence) a primitive idea of what language is, of what its work is? The cream of the jest is the gradual revelation as the *Investigations* unfolds that Wittgenstein thinks this primitive idea of language is endemic in philosophy, in our philosophical thinking—for otherwise why would he go on painstakingly and interminably to get his reader to see that language cannot be understood as functioning everywhere as if each of its words named some concrete thing, or named anything? It is we, including Russell, in philosophical moods, who are the primitives—in Russell's case, a primitive of genius.

If, on the other hand, Russell had seen the passages about the builders with stone, and if his remark was directed to them, then his remark is beautifully pertinent but more perfectly uncomprehending.

I said I wanted also to end with an autobiographical note, indeed, a double such note. With my publication of *The Claim of Reason*, at the age of fifty-three, I first knew I would, if I lived, go on writing and publishing. I liked the earlier three books I had published, but none of the three promised a continuation. *Must We Mean What We Say?* was as full a defense of what I had learned from Austin and as full a demonstration of the fruitfulness of thinking of philosophy and literature in light of each other as I then felt capable of, and the following books on film and on Thoreau also felt to me like statements of their material that I was glad to live with. And none had achieved any significant and positive notice that I was aware of, except of course from friends. But one does not write, anyway publish, for friends alone. With the appearance of *The Claim of Reason*, such considerations seemed to fall away. I might say that I felt I had learned to articulate my ignorance as well as my knowledge, poor thing, and that I had accordingly uncovered for myself unnumbered paths to follow.

An obvious question is then why I felt that yet another analysis from my hand of the opening of *Philosophical Investigations* was required in order to justify, or to orient, what in my memoir I repeatedly describe, from various angles, as the craving for knowledge and as the authorization of the right to know as grounding a human life and, in one of its transmutations, motivating philosophy. My first answer is that philosophizing for me is possible and necessary as the contesting of a natural language by itself, a dramatization of the mind's self-reflection. My second answer is that a text—a phrase, a sentence, a volume, one's own or another's—is fruitful only when it is alive, which in practice means that it is shown to yield fresh results. My third answer is that while this puts a certain kind of pressure on one's own writing, I do not conceive philosophy, as it has been put, as a kind of writing (for there are many kinds) but as a kind of reading, say a kind of responsiveness, a kind that understands itself to be endless.

REMARKS FROM DISCUSSION

PUTNAM: Philosophy is educational only when the educator, the teacher of philosophy, draws connections.

ONE

ENTRIES IN THE EDUCATION
OF GROWNUPS

TWO

THE FACT/VALUE DICHOTOMY
AND ITS CRITICS

Hilary Putnam

My favorite definition of philosophy is Stanley Cavell's: "education for grownups."[1] In this essay, I shall discuss an issue that is obviously a philosophical one and, at the same time, one on which many who certainly consider themselves "grownups," including many philosophers, economists, lawyers, and policymakers of all kinds, unquestionably *need* "education." That is the issue that I described in a recent book as "the fact/value dichotomy."[2]

The Fact/Value Dichotomy

The book I just mentioned begins thus:

> Every one of you has heard someone ask, "Is that supposed to be a fact or a value judgment?" The presupposition of this "stumper" is that if it's a "value judgment" it can't possibly be a [statement of] "fact," and a further presupposition of this is that value judgments are subjective.[3]

I illustrated the way in which this idea can affect policy by citing the views of Lionel Robbins during the depths of the depression. At that time, Robbins argued against the whole idea of income redistribution on the philosophic ground that value judgments are (according to him) outside the sphere of reason altogether. I quote:

> If we disagree about ends it is a case of thy blood or mine—or live or let live according to the importance of the difference, or the relative strength of our opponents. But if we disagree about means, then scientific analysis can often help us resolve our differences. If we disagree about the morality of the taking of interest (and we understand what we are talking about), then there is no room for argument.[4]

Other influential economists in the 1930s, 1940s, and 1950s, while no less respectful of logical positivism and its insistence that value judgments totally lack what the positivists called "cognitive meaning," were not willing to follow Robbins in jettisoning welfare economics. Instead, they allowed the economist to appeal to values, *provided it was made clear* that all that she was doing was making means-ends judgments of the form "if you have such and such values, then such and such is the most feasible economic policy." That values themselves did not admit of rational argument was not challenged. Thus, for example:

> It is fashionable for the modern economist to insist that ethical value judgments have no place in scientific analysis. Professor Robbins in particular has insisted upon this point, and today it is customary to make a distinction between the pure analysis of Robbins *qua* economist and his propaganda, condemnations, and policy recommendations *qua* citizen. In practice, if pushed to extremes, this somewhat schizophrenic rule becomes difficult to adhere to, and it leads to rather tedious circumlocutions. *But in essence Robbins is undoubtedly correct.*[5]

In this way, the logical positivist claim that "Why people respond favorably to certain facts and unfavorably to others is [merely] a question for the sociologist"[6] came to be regarded as "undoubtedly correct" by a policy science whose recommendations affect the lives of literally billions of our fellow human beings. Ethical questions are the questions that most of us think it most important to discuss rationally and not irrationally. But if the logical positivist view that economists deferred to for such a long time were indeed correct, then the very idea of discussing value questions rationally would be ("cognitively") *nonsense*.

Cavell's Place in This Discussion

I mentioned Stanley Cavell's definition of philosophy as "education for grownups," and one reason I did that is that he has an important place in the debate concerning facts and values. If this is not obvious at once, the reason, I believe, is the strange way in which one of Cavell's most important contributions has been neglected, by his admirers as well as by his critics.[7] I am referring to the four chapters that make up part 3, titled "Knowledge and the Concept of Morality," of Cavell's *The Claim of Reason*.

I just said that if the logical positivist view that economists deferred to for such a long time were indeed correct, then the very idea of discussing value questions rationally would be *nonsense*. But in my time and Cavell's, many analytic philosophers became acquainted with (and, alas, often embraced) that idea as the result of reading Stevenson's *Ethics and Language* rather than the logical positivists, and although Stevenson's affinity to logical positivism was recognized immediately, the irrationalist consequences of emotivism are intentionally played down in that work.[8] In "Knowledge and the Concept of Morality," Cavell is concerned from the beginning to expose the points at which that irrationalism is nonetheless visible in Stevenson's book. Indeed, it is not very *well* hidden, since Stevenson devotes a whole chapter (chapter 7) to telling us that there is no such thing as a valid argument in ethics.[9] Stevenson's "first question," as he calls it, is this: "What is the nature of ethical *agreement* and *disagreement*? Is it parallel to that found in the natural sciences, differing only with regard to the subject matter; or is it of some broadly different source?"[10]—and his well-known answer is that "the disagreements that occur in science, history, biography" are "disagreements in belief," whereas "it is disagreements in attitude . . . that chiefly distinguish ethical issues from those of science."[11] Where a disagreement is in attitude, Stevenson does say that "reasons" can be offered for and against, but he says that these "reasons" are related (only) *psychologically* (because not deductively and not inductively) to the judgments they support.

Stevenson assumes (as is too often assumed today) that all disagreements in "science" (or disagreements about "facts"—these notions are often simply equated) can be settled either deductively or inductively and that such settlement results in agreement.[12] That not all moral disagreements can be so settled is another of Stevenson's reasons for concluding that these are not disagreements in "belief." For he argues that only on the assumption that "All disagreement in attitude is rooted in disagreement in belief" can moral disagreements be settled by rational proof, and this he calls a dubious "psychological generalization."[13]

One of Stevenson's early examples of "the methods used in moral arguments" is the following:

> A (speaking to C, a child): To neglect your piano practice is naughty.
> B (in C's hearing): No, C is very good about practicing. (Out of C's hearing): It's hopeless to drive him you know, but if you praise him he will do a great deal.[14]

As Cavell remarks, one wonders why such examples "as much as seem to be examples of *moral* encounter."[15] In fact, the possibility that morality has characteristic modes of *argument*, which distinguish it from, inter alia, mere rhetoric and propaganda, is (as we shall see) explicitly ruled out by Stevenson. But the investigation of such modes of argument (and the modes of description that they presuppose) is precisely what has always concerned the best moral philosophers, up to and including Cavell.

In addition, Cavell writes,

> But suppose that it is just characteristic of moral arguments that the rationality of the antagonists is not dependent on an agree-

ment emerging between them, that there is such a thing as a *rational disagreement* about a conclusion. . . . Without the hope of agreement, argument would be pointless, but it doesn't follow that without agreement—and in particular, apart from agreement arrived at in particular ways, e.g. apart from bullying, and without agreement about a conclusion concerning what ought to be done—the argument was pointless.[16]

But if, as Cavell suggests here, there is such a thing as a rational argument that cannot be conclusively settled, then the whole argument from the existence of "irresolvable" disagreements in ethics to the absence of "cognitive meaning" in ethical judgments collapses. (In fact, as I point out elsewhere,[17] there are "factual" issues, especially in the social sciences, on which it is difficult and perhaps impossible to get agreement.)

Summing up these opening observations in "Knowledge and the Concept of Morality," Cavell already lists four points on which he disagrees with Stevenson:

1. That all disagreement in attitude is *moral* disagreement;
2. that all disagreements which cannot be (rationally) *settled* (end in a conclusion which all parties agree is the right one) are irrational;
3. that a reason which is neither deductively nor inductively related to a judgment is "therefore" "only" "psychologically" related to it;
4. that what makes science rational is that it consists of beliefs about matters of fact—and hence consists of methods which rationally settle disagreements.[18]

Cavell remarks that

> Stevenson's view requires, or contains, all of these ideas, and he must obviously take them to be obvious in themselves or to follow, obviously, from the fact that there are different "kinds" of disagreement. Given what I take to be the remorseless paradoxicality of his view, its wide acceptance—despite criticisms of *pieces* of his view which would have seemed essential to it (e.g., of his causal theory of "meaning," and in particular of emotive "meaning," and still more particularly of his analysis of the word "good")—must mean that these assumptions . . . are widely shared.

They are indeed widely shared assumptions. In fact, they have become a sort of cultural institution—a most unfortunate one, which is why I have devoted a good deal of my writing in the last quarter of a century to attacking it. That is why I began this essay by describing this as an issue where "education for grownups" is desperately needed. I have argued (sometimes in concert with the economist/philosopher Vivian Walsh) that the intellectual legs on which the fact/value dichotomy stood are now in ruins. But to see that that is the case, one needs to bring together results from different parts of philosophy. Specifically, one needs to bring together the observations (by different philosophers) of the way in which so-called factual and so-called evaluative predicates are mutually "entangled"—the way in which it is a fantasy to suppose that the predicates we use to give sensitive and relevant descriptions of human beings and human interactions can be "disentangled" into two "components," a "purely descriptive component" and an "evaluative component"—and the point, first argued at length by Morton White,[19] that Quine's demolition of the logical positivist dichotomy of theory and observational fact (or "fact" and "convention," as Quine sometimes put it) also destroyed the logical positivist arguments for the fact/value dichotomy. It was the prestige of those arguments that had exerted such a powerful influence on social scientists such as the economists mentioned at the beginning of this chapter.

The logical positivist arguments in question depended on a *serious* effort, one continued over many years, to draw a clear line between factual propositions, theoretical postulates (which they eventually came to regard as only "partially interpreted"),[20] mathematical-logical propositions (which they took to be analytic), and "pseudopropositions" (or "nonsense"), which latter included, according to Carnap, "all statements belonging to Metaphysics, regulative Ethics, and (metaphysical) Epistemology."[21] The sequence of attempts to do this was summed up in Hempel's "Problems and Changes in the Empiricist Criterion of Meaning,"[22] a famous paper that closed with an idea proposed in "The Foundations of Logic and Mathematics"[23] and later developed more fully in "On the Methodological Character of Theoretical Concepts."[24]

In brief, the idea was that "cognitively meaningful" language could contain not only observation terms (and terms defined in terms of these) but also "theoretical terms," terms referring to unobservables and introduced by systems of postulates, the postulates of the various scientific theories. As long as the system as a whole enables us to predict our experiences more successfully, such "theoretical terms" were now to be accepted as "empirically meaningful."

However, the acceptance of this idea led to a serious problem: to *predict* anything means (on the logical positivists' account) to *deduce observation sentences from a theory*. And to deduce anything from a set of empirical postulates, we need not only those postulates *but also the axioms of mathematics and logic*. And, according to the logical positivists, these do not state "facts" at all. They are *analytic* and thus "empty of factual content." In short, "belonging to the language of science" was (after the acceptance of Carnap's idea) a criterion of *scientific* significance, but not everything *scientifically* significant was regarded by the positivists as a statement of *fact*: within the scientifically significant there are, according to Carnap and his followers, *analytic* as well as *synthetic* (i.e., factual) statements. Thus the search for a satisfactory demarcation of the "factual" became the search for a satisfactory way of drawing "the analytic-synthetic distinction."

At this point, Quine demolished the positivists' metaphysically inflated notion of the "analytic," to the satisfaction of most philosophers.[25] But Quine did not suggest that every statement in the language of science should be regarded as a statement of "fact" (i.e., as "synthetic"). Instead, he argued that the whole idea of classifying such statements as the statements of pure mathematics as "factual" or "conventional" (which the logical positivists equated with "analytic") was hopeless. As he later put it:

> The lore of our fathers is a fabric of sentences. In our hands it develops and changes, through more or less arbitrary and deliberate revisions and additions of our own, more or less directly occasioned by the continuing stimulation of our sense organs. It is a

pale gray lore, black with fact and white with convention. But I
have found no substantial reasons for concluding that there are
any quite black threads in it, or any white ones.[26]

But if we lack any clear notion of "fact," what happens to the fact/
value dichotomy? As Vivian Walsh has written: "To borrow and
adapt Quine's vivid image, if a theory may be black with fact and
white with convention, it might well (as far as logical empiricism
could tell) be red with values. Since for them confirmation *or* falsifi-
cation had to be a property of a theory *as a whole*, they had no way
of unraveling this whole cloth."[27]

If the logical positivists' arguments are now generally regarded as
failures (which does not mean that the *conclusions* they drew from
those arguments have ceased to exert a powerful influence), it must
be said to their credit that those arguments were the product of years
of careful effort, as the successive reformulations of "the empiricist
criterion of meaning" charted by Hempel testify. Although it was his
high regard for logical positivism that inspired Stevenson to defend
their "emotivist views," his own arguments for a fact/value (or "be-
lief/attitude") dichotomy rest on no such hard work. For him it is
self-evident, as Cavell pointed out in his list of Stevenson's assumptions, that genuine "beliefs" can be proved or refuted by deduction
or induction, and that is the only criterion of cognitive meaning that
he thinks he needs.

Fact/Value Entanglement

Facts and values are entangled in at least two senses. First, factual
judgments, even in physics, depend on and presuppose *epistemic* values. One would think this ought to be uncontroversial, but, in fact,
all the leading positivists—joined here by Popper, in spite of his frequently touted disagreements with Carnap and Reichenbach—made
what I regard as pathetic attempts to evade this fact.[28] What the logical positivists were shutting their eyes to, as so many today who refer
to values as purely "subjective" and science as purely "objective"
continue to shut their eyes to, is obvious: that judgments of coher-

ence, simplicity (which is itself a whole bundle of different values, not just one "parameter"), "beauty," "naturalness," etc. are presupposed by physical science. Yet *coherence* and *simplicity* and the like are *values*. All of the standard arguments for noncognitivism in ethics could be repeated without any change whatsoever for noncognitivism in *epistemology*; for example, Hume's argument that ethical values are not "matters of fact" (because we don't have a "sense impression" of goodness) could be modified to read: "epistemic values are not matters of fact because we do not have a sense impression of simplicity or a sense impression of coherence." Certainly, disagreements about the beauty or "inner perfection" (Einstein's term) of a theory could certainly be described as "differences in attitude." And when it comes to fields less subject to experimental control than physics, fields such as history or economics, for example, it is utterly simplistic to suppose that such disagreements can always be settled by "induction and deduction." In fact, after the publication of Nelson Goodman's "The New Riddle of Induction,"[29] the idea that there is such a thing as *the* method of "induction" has been seen by philosophers of science to be extremely problematic.

A second way in which values and facts are entangled might be described as "logical" or "grammatical." What is characteristic of "negative" descriptions like "cruel" as well as of "positive" descriptions like "brave," "temperate," "just" (note that these are the terms that Socrates keeps forcing his interlocutors to discuss!) is that to use them with any discrimination one has to be able to understand an *evaluative point of view*. That is why someone who thinks that "brave" simply means "not afraid to risk life and limb" would not be able to understand the all-important distinction that Socrates kept drawing between mere *rashness* or *foolhardiness* and genuine *bravery*. It is also the reason that, as Murdoch stressed, that it is always possible to *improve one's understanding* of a concept like "bravery" or "justice."[30] If one did not at *any* point feel the *appeal* of the relevant ethical point of view, one wouldn't be able to acquire a thick ethical concept, and the sophisticated use of it requires a continuing ability to identify (at least in imagination) with that point of view.

My description of this phenomenon as "entanglement"[31] was suggested to me by John McDowell's use of the phrase "disentangling manoeuvre."[32] He described a move made by emotivists somewhat more recent than Stevenson thus:

> Typically, non-cognitivists hold that when we feel impelled to ascribe value to something, what is happening can be disentangled into two components. Competence with an evaluative concept involves, first, a sensitivity to an aspect of the world as it really is (as it is independently of value experience), and, second, a propensity to a certain attitude—a non-cognitive state that constitutes the special perspective from which items in the world seem to be endowed with the value in question.[33]

and he remarks,

> Now, it seems reasonable to be skeptical about whether the disentangling manoeuvre here envisaged can always be effected; specifically, about whether, corresponding to any value concept, one can always isolate a genuine feature of the world—by the appropriate standard of genuineness: that is, a feature that is there anyway, independently of anyone's value experience being as it is—to be that to which competent users of the concept are to be regarded as responding when they use it: that which is left in the world when one peels off the reflection of the appropriate attitude.[34]

To appreciate why McDowell believes that this claim is so dubious, he asks us to consider any specific conception of a moral virtue. And he continues,

> If the disentangling manoeuvre is always possible, that implies that the extension of the associated term, as it would be used by someone who belonged to the community, could be mastered independently of the special concerns that, in the community, would show themselves in admiration or emulation of actions seen as falling under the concept. That is: one could know which actions the term would be applied to, so that one would be able to predict applications and withholdings of it in new cases—not merely without oneself sharing the community's admiration

(there need be no difficulty about that) but *without even embarking on an attempt to make sense of their admiration.*[35]

Later in this essay, McDowell connects this discussion with a discussion of Cavell's views, and of Wittgenstein's views, as interpreted in Cavell's *Must We Mean What We Say,* an interpretation that McDowell likes.[36] (Cavell expands upon that interpretation in part 2 of *The Claim of Reason.*) And indeed, "entangled" terms are spoken of repeatedly in "Knowledge and the Concept of Morality." One of the earliest such places is the following:

> If . . . we take the case of some specific action, then we might take a case in which the "action" in question is described in ethically prejudicial terms (e.g., "Ought he to have murdered him" rather than ". . . killed him?", or "Was he wrong to betray him?" rather than ". . . to refuse to do what he said?"), or else we might feel that any agreement about the morality of an act will turn on some agreement about how the act is to be described. Was it really breaking a *promise?* Is it fair *just* to say he lied when what he did was lie *in order to . . .* or *as a way of . . .* (Socrates: "Then [i.e. in moral disputes] they [i.e. mankind, men] do not disagree over the question of whether the unjust individual must be punished. They disagree over the question, who is unjust, and what was done and when, do they not?"[37]).

Apparently, what the "case" in question is *forms part of the content of the moral argument itself.* Actions, unlike envelopes and goldfinches, do not come named for assessment nor, like apples, ripe for grading.[38]

An Important Difference Between Cavell and McDowell

Yet, for all that I have just said, there is an important difference between Cavell's and McDowell's views. Although each of them accepts the idea that a competent use of what I have called "entangled" terms requires that one understand an evaluative point of view—a "Wittgensteinian idea" that dates back to Philippa Foot and Iris Murdoch in the 1950s, if not earlier[39]—their understandings of the nature and function of the moral life seem to me quite different. What makes

"Knowledge and the Concept of Morality" so important, in my opinion, is the originality and profundity of the picture of morality that
informs it.

McDowell, as is well known, defends a philosophical view of perception with Kantian roots, a view in which all perception, indeed all
experience, is conceptualized. His account of morality is dependent
on that view of perception. In McDowell's account, ethical judgments
are justified (as all judgments, in the end, are justified on his view) by
conceptualized experiences. The concepts involved are just the entangled concepts we have been speaking of, and with their aid we are
able to *perceive* that certain actions are cruel or considerate, honest or
morally dubious, etc. The possession of those concepts is a large part
of what McDowell calls (following Aristotle) our "second nature."
And that second nature is one we come to have via a proper moral
education.

One feature of that view that stands out is that moral *disagreement*
is far in the background. But what is most distinctive about Cavell's
description of morality in part 3 of *The Claim of Reason* is precisely
the centrality of disagreement.

In a passage I am especially fond of, Cavell describes the function
of morality thus:

> Morality must leave itself open to repudiation; it provides *one*
> possibility of settling conflict, a way of encompassing conflict
> which allows the continuance of personal relationships against the
> hard and apparently inevitable fact of misunderstanding, mutu-
> ally incomprehensible wishes, commitments, loyalties, interests
> and needs, a way of mending relationships and maintaining the
> self in opposition to itself or others. Other ways of settling or en-
> compassing conflict are provided by politics, religion, love and
> forgiveness, rebellion, and withdrawal. Morality is a valuable way
> because the others are so often inaccessible or brutal; but it is not
> everything; it provides a door through which someone, alienated
> or in danger of alienation from another through his action, can
> return by the offering and the acceptance of explanation, excuses
> and justifications, or by the respect one human being will show
> another who sees and can accept the responsibility for a position

which he himself would not adopt. We do not have to agree with one another in order to live in the same moral world, but we do have to know and respect one another's differences.[40]

This is a passage that demands many readings to be fully appreciated. What Cavell is "getting at" cannot be stated "in a nutshell." It has obvious points of connection with democratic theory. (Like morality, democracy is "a valuable way" because "the others are so often inaccessible or brutal.") It is Kantian in the emphasis placed on mutual respect, but Kant is criticized by Cavell because "the most serious sense in which Kant's moral theory is 'formalist' comes not from his having said that actions motivated only in *certain* ways are *moral* actions but in his having found too little difficulty in saying *what* 'the' maxim of an action is in terms of which his test of its morality, the Categorical Imperative, is to be applied."[41] And Cavell's obvious emphasis on knowing and respecting "differences" needs to be tempered by the reading of part 4 of *The Claim of Reason*, in which what he refers to as the "truth of skepticism, or what I might call 'the moral of skepticism,' "[42] turns out to problematize—problematize existentially, not just intellectually—the notion of "knowing" one another's differences.

But—in a sense this is the whole point of *The Claim of Reason*—to say that there is a truth *of* skepticism isn't to say that the skeptic is right or that skepticism is flat out "true." Entangled terms do have extensions, and we do often get their uses right.

On this point, the opposition between Cavell's view, which links evaluation, cognition, rationality, responsibility, and the inevitability of disagreement, and Stevenson's, which links evaluation, "feeling," "causing," and getting others to perform the actions we want them to, is stark. According to Stevenson, for example, the terms "propaganda" and "persuasion" have the *same* extension, if we discount the emotive meaning, and thus "when the terms are *completely* neutralized, we may say with complete equanimity that all moralists are propagandists, or that all propagandists are moralists,"[43] and he also tells us that "one may be sad to exert a peculiarly 'moral' influence if he influences only those attitudes which are correlated with a sense of guilt, sin, or remorse, and so on."[44] Cavell's response is biting:

> So, for example, a mother who plays upon ("influences") her child's sense of guilt in order to have him give up the girl he wants to marry is acting the role of a moralist; and Kate Croy, interpreting her project to attract a legacy from Millie Theale in ways which muddle and blunt ("influence") Merton Densher's perception of his guilt, is a spokesman for morality. I hope it will not be thought that I would deny that parent and Kate Croy the title of moralist merely on the ground that they are morally wrong; moralists can, with the best will in the world, take morally wrong positions, positions which they themselves, could they see their positions more fully, would see to be culpable. But in the case of that parent and of Kate Croy, there is not so much as the intention to morality. . . . To propagandize under the name of morality is not immoral; it denies morality altogether.[45]

In Closing

I sometimes imagine myself confronted with an objector who says to me: "I grant you that Cavell's work is education for grownups. But so is the work of any significant writer. And Cavell's work is hardly typical of what is called 'philosophy' by most professors and graduate students in philosophy departments. Can philosophy in this more conventional sense ever be what Cavell means by that phrase?"

I have approached this challenge indirectly, and I have done so by looking at what I have referred to as the "collapse" of the fact/value dichotomy and at Cavell's own contribution to that collapse. But—and this is important—I didn't *confine* my attention to that contribution, although I did describe it in some detail. (Nonetheless, I had to leave out of my account a great deal that is important, because discussing all of it would have made this essay much longer than it is). I also described what I see as Quine's contribution (even if he was willfully ignorant of the fact that he was undermining a dichotomy that he loved!). A metaphor that Vivian Walsh and I use in this connection is the following: One may think of the logical positivists' fact/

value dichotomy (and of the "emotivist" account of ethical language that goes with it) as the top of a three-legged stool. The three legs are (1) the postulation of theory-free "facts," leading to their dichotomy of fact and theory (or "experience" and "convention"); (2) the denial that fact ("science") and evaluation are entangled; and (3) the claim that science proceeds by a syntactically describable method (called "induction").[46] The fact that even theoretical physics presupposes *epistemic values* means that if value judgments were really "cognitively meaningless," all science would rest on judgments that are, in the language of Carnap, *nonsense*.[47] That is why both Carnap and Reichenbach tried so hard to show that science proceeds by an *algorithm*, and it is the reason that Popper tried to show that science needs only deductive logic. Thus the failure of the third leg is also a failure of the second leg. But the second leg also broke because, as we have seen, facts and values—ethical values—are entangled at the level of single predicates. And the first leg broke because the "two dogmas" on which it was based were refuted by Quine.

I wish to emphasize that the destruction of the fact/value dichotomy was a task that it took many brilliant women and men and many years of the last century to accomplish (I say "accomplish" and not "complete" because philosophical tasks are never really "completed"). Those women and men are associated in the textbooks (with their unfortunate love of such classifications) with many different kinds of philosophy. Quine was a high analytic philosopher if there ever was one, and he was close to the logical positivist movement, even if he turned out to be its severest critic. Morton White was sympathetic both to Quine's brand of analytic philosophy *and* to Oxford ordinary language philosophy as practiced by Gilbert Ryle, among others. That there is no "algorithm" for doing science was stressed by Ernest Nagel and also by the most celebrated "philosopher-scientist" Albert Einstein. The failure of the "disentangling manoeuvre" that was supposed to split up thick ethical predicates into a value-free "cognitive" component and a cognition-free "emotive" component was first seen by Philippa Foot and Iris Murdoch and then further discussed, as we have seen, by Stanley Cavell and more recently by John McDowell and myself.

The moral I wish to draw is a simple one. It is not from any one "type" or "school" of philosophy that enlightenment comes. Enlightenment can come from any type of philosophy. And further, it is important to see how the different sorts of enlightenment that come from different philosophical sources can be *related* to one another. In "Knowledge and the Concept of Morality," Cavell shows how a vision of the function of morality can be related, on the one hand, to all the issues I have just mentioned and, on the other hand, to the many other issues discussed in his book *The Claim of Reason*. Yet philosophy in "the more conventional sense" can also be "education for grownups." Philosophy only stops being that when it starts thinking of itself as a collection of "specializations" (like medical "specializations"). But philosophy, even in "the more conventional sense" need not and must not think of itself in that way. It is when different insights from different sources are connected with one another that philosophy truly educates us.

REMARKS FROM DISCUSSION

CAVELL: Wittgenstein looks like he is doing philosophy of mathematics, but sometimes it is not just that. It is everything. And it is precise. Thoreau presents a surface that so many readers can't dig into. It's a surface that keeps being unbroken. It seems to be naturalist writing, with good descriptions of the natural world, and to have no resonance except for a sentimentalism or religiosity. The idea that it is a precise language is hard to come by.

CAVELL: I do not understand why my writing has affected other philosophers with exasperation. And I see now that it is as if other philosophers, intelligent philosophers, are saying to me: "This is so obvious. How can you possibly think, as Wittgenstein seems to, that there is anything new that's being learned? You said that philosophy doesn't teach you anything new, and that's right! It's empty and it's boring." And there I am having to speak out of ecstasy, to people who are settled where they are. This is, I think, giving me some way to make progress with what debasement is in philosophy and with the sense of exasperation that comes from boredom.

I would also come back to something I have said before about philosophy as demanding change—what kind of change and how? How does that fit the classroom? Can you demand change from students? In elementary education, you don't have to demand change but to keep up with it and guide it as change is in the air. But when you are talking about college students . . . ? And I don't know about high school. High school was just a mystery when I was there, and now it seems clear to me that it is the absolute best time for education and completely the worst time for education. I ask myself whether and to what extent it is all right to break into students' lives. There are spellbinding teachers, and I distrust them deeply. I see how they behave and the way they create interest by enlivening and doing tricks with texts, and I have asked myself: "Is that what I do, when I get overly excited?" I was very relieved when a colleague talked some time ago about the course that eventually became *Cities of Words* and described my manner as very controlled and calm. I was extremely relieved to hear that. But how can one see that? I've never seen that. Maybe we should all undergo that experience of seeing ourselves in a classroom to see if we could survive the experience.

THREE

ENCOUNTERING CAVELL

The Education of a Grownup
Russell B. Goodman

The Idea of Stanley Cavell

I first heard the name of Stanley Cavell in Oxford, where I was studying philosophy, politics, and economics after graduating from the University of Pennsylvania. At Penn I had taken all the philosophy I could, Greek and Chinese, philosophy of science and philosophy of the social sciences, logical positivism and pragmatism, and had been disappointed only by a course in aesthetics, the main object of which seemed to be to show that R. G. Collingwood's *The Principles of Art* was mistaken in every respect. Where was the beauty of it all, I thought? And was I wrong to wish for that?

Looking over the lecture list for my first term in Oxford, I saw a course in aesthetics and thought that I would try again. So I began attending lectures in a small room in the High Street. Almost before I knew it, the class was down to ten, then to three students. It was dismal in its own particular way, and I can remember nothing of its content. One day after the lecture ended, I found myself talking with one of the remaining students, who, it turned out, was another disappointed American. We were discussing the prospect that soon there would be no one to hear the earnest but uninteresting lecturer and whether we had the responsibility for preserving at least some audience for him. Who were we, newly arrived Americans in the beautiful city of dreaming spires, to take responsibilities for a course of such dreariness? I was reassured by my companion's agreement about the quality of these lectures and by his reports of something much better, something exciting and alive that he had found in a class at Harvard with Stanley Cavell. So I had the idea of Stanley Cavell as a very good thing.

Reading Wittgenstein

It was not an idea I immediately filled in, however, for, once I decided to stay with philosophy, I was not working in aesthetics or on Wittgenstein but on philosophy of language and Kant at Oxford and, in my Ph.D. dissertation at Johns Hopkins, on theories of perception. I made the decision to study and, as it were, to get certification in analytic philosophy, but I was reading—out of school, as Cavell says—Nietzsche, Gabriel Marcel, Huang Po, and Heidegger.

My entry to Cavell's work was through Wittgenstein, whom I began reading at Oxford. To my surprise, Wittgenstein was not part of the curriculum there, although he haunted the project of what was called "ordinary language philosophy." I remember asking Alan Montefiore, one of the more soulful philosophers on the faculty, whether it was worth reading Wittgenstein, whose books were in every bookstore but about whom no one on the faculty spoke. He told me: "Of course you should read Wittgenstein." That was good advice. So I read the *Blue and Brown Books* and the *Philosophical Investigations* in my little sitting room with the electric bar heater, high up in Jesus College. I don't think I understood much, but at least I became familiar with some of Wittgenstein's words and with the philosophical characters who inhabit his pages.

At Hopkins, I continued to read Wittgenstein and ended up writing a dissertation about the ambiguous figures, such as the duck-rabbit, which figure so prominently in part 2 of the *Philosophical Investigations*. I was interested in the differences and similarities between seeing aspects and seeing colors or shapes and particularly in the way our perception of ambiguous figures could be involved with our will. Wittgenstein writes: "Seeing an aspect and imagining are subject to the will. There is such an order as 'Imagine *this*,' and also: 'Now see the figure like *this*'; but not: 'Now see this leaf green.'"[1] It is a long way from this fertile observation of Wittgenstein's to Emerson's call, in the last paragraph of *Nature*, for the intellect to yield itself "passive to the educated Will," but it is a path I took—but only because I could find it from vantage points in the work of Stanley Cavell.

Because I had been at Oxford and because I had worked, however narrowly, on Wittgenstein, I was hired by the philosophy department at the University of New Mexico to teach Wittgenstein and other writers in "analytic philosophy." As I prepared for various versions of my course on Wittgenstein, I boned up on the *Tractatus* with the assistance of the standard commentaries by Max Black, Elizabeth Anscombe, and others, and I read the *Investigations* alongside a well-regarded collection edited by George Pitcher. It was there that I first read Cavell's "On the Availability of Wittgenstein's Later Philosophy."

People often talk about Cavell's style, for example, as something that attracts them or repels them or that is essential to his practice as a philosopher. At the beginning, it wasn't the style that struck me but simply the deep points about Wittgenstein that he makes. For Cavell is a great critic, one who helps us to see what is there in the text. In "The Availability," for example, Cavell considers Wittgenstein's statement:

> We feel as if we had to *penetrate* phenomena: our investigation, however, is directed not towards phenomena, but, as one might say, towards the "*possibilities*" of phenomena. We remind ourselves, that is to say, of the *kind of statement* that we make about phenomena. . . .

Our investigation is therefore a grammatical one.[2]

Cavell was the first commentator to appreciate Wittgenstein's affinities with Kant in this statement and others, specifically the connection between what Wittgenstein means by "grammar" and what Kant means by "transcendental knowledge." Whereas Kant speaks of transcendental illusion as the belief that we know "what transcends the conditions of possible knowledge," Cavell explains, "Wittgenstein speaks of the illusions produced by our employing words in the absence of the (any) language game which provides their comprehensible employment."[3] Students of Wittgenstein are now familiar with these comparisons through the work of David Pears, Ernst Konrad Specht, P. M. S. Hacker, and others, but in 1962, when "The Availability" was published, this was news. Cavell enabled us to see Wittgenstein's philosophy as deeply "critical" in Kant's sense: seeking not to give an account of the world as it is in itself but to restrain our intellect within the bounds of our human capacities.

Cavell's paper also broke ground in explicating Wittgenstein's statement that "There is not a philosophical method, though there are indeed methods, like different therapies."[4] Although the word "therapies" is used just once in the *Investigations*, this is not an offhand use of the term. The sentence concludes a crucial section (§109–133) where Wittgenstein discusses his method and is the climax to a paragraph that, in other ways as well, suggests the comparison with another Viennese thinker of the early twentieth century, Sigmund Freud. Wittgenstein writes:

> The real discovery is the one that makes me capable of stopping doing philosophy when I want to.—The one that gives philosophy peace, so that it is no longer tormented by questions which bring itself into question.—Instead, we now demonstrate a method, by example; and the series of examples can be broken off.—Problems are solved (difficulties eliminated), not a *single* problem.
>
> There is not a philosophical method, though there are indeed methods, like different therapies.[5]

Cavell follows the leadings of Wittgenstein's text in bringing Freud into his discussion, along with Kant, and in suggesting that the link among all three is their concern with self-knowledge. For Cavell, the procedures of ordinary language philosophy found in Wittgenstein (and J. L. Austin) rely on an understanding that all speakers of a language have and that they do not need anyone else to confirm:

> Such questions as "What should we say if . . ." or "In what circumstances would we call . . . ?" asked of someone who has mastered the language (for example, oneself) is a request for the person to say something about himself, describe what he does. So the different methods are methods for acquiring self-knowledge. . . . Perhaps more shocking, and certainly more important, than any of Freud's or Wittgenstein's particular conclusions is their discovery that knowing oneself is something for which there are methods— something, therefore, that can be taught (though not in obvious ways) and practiced.[6]

Reading this now, and as I remember reading it then, the excitement comes from Cavell's finding things that are unmistakably present in Wittgenstein's text and that connect it with wider currents in our culture and in our lives—not only with Freud and Kant but, for example, with the self-examination of Socratic philosophy. Cavell teaches us to see Wittgenstein as a kind of ethical philosopher—not a meta-ethical philosopher—but one for whom ethics is a concern at every point in his investigations, every point in his life. This makes him, Cavell will come to say, a moral perfectionist.

The third aspect of Wittgenstein's philosophy that Cavell illuminates in "The Availability of Wittgenstein's Later Philosophy" is its dialogical form. It is obvious that the *Investigations* contains dialogues, but it is not obvious how to take them. Cavell points out that they contain several voices or characters, one of which he calls the voice of temptation, another of which he calls the voice of correction. It is not clear, Cavell insists, that only one of these voices is Wittgenstein's. The analytic philosophers who were the first to appropriate Wittgenstein's work looked in it for theses and arguments, and they found some—for example, the so-called private language argument. Yet they did not take as seriously as Cavell does the clash between this approach to Wittgenstein and Wittgenstein's own admonition that "we must not advance any kind of theory"[7] and his claim that "[i]f one tried to advance theses in philosophy, it would never be possible to debate them, because everyone would agree to them."[8] Cavell notes that "there is virtually nothing in the *Investigations* that we should ordinarily call reasoning,"[9] and he reads Wittgenstein's dialogues as devices for drawing us into the philosophical problems. Working through these dialogues, accepting the counsel of the voice of correction, we learn techniques for putting the philosophical problems in their place (for example, as the result of natural but not reliable fantasies). We learn, as Wittgenstein put it in a well-known epigram, to show "the fly the way out of the fly-bottle."[10]

Romanticism

Reading Cavell on Wittgenstein had two beneficial results for me: I learned how to read Wittgenstein better, and I began to learn how to read Cavell, to get his tune in my ear. I had tried more than once to read *The Senses of Walden*—a book I thought I ought to like—but without success. A third attempt, on a week-long camping trip in the mountains of southern New Mexico, succeeded. I began to see how the book extended Cavell's work on ordinary language philosophy and on Kant. Cavell writes, for example, that "the saying of something when and as it is said is as significant as the meaning and ordering of the words said."[11] Kant makes an appearance late in the book as Cavell discusses Thoreau's description of a field in late winter, particularly his attraction to "the arching sheaflike top of the wool-grass." Thoreau writes about the wool-grass that "it brings back the summer to our winter memories, and is among the forms which art loves to copy, and which, in the vegetable kingdom, have the same relation to types already in the mind of man that astronomy has."[12] Picking up the Kantian sound of "forms" and "types in the mind of man," Cavell states: "Human forms of feeling, objects of human attraction, our reactions constituted in art, are as universal and necessary, as objective, as revelatory of the world, as the forms of the laws of physics."[13] I was prepared neither to defend nor to fully explicate this statement, which foreshadows Cavell's later work on romanticism, but I found it amazing, fascinating.

I was also reading *The Claim of Reason* in those days, particularly part 4, tracking Cavell's discussions of Wittgenstein on our knowledge of other minds. I was intrigued by Cavell's statement that he was trying to "discover the problem of other minds"—as if we hadn't quite seen it yet—and by his arguments that the structure of skepticism about others contrasted with the structure of our skepticism about the external world. These two forms of skepticism are typically thought of as parallel: the other's body hides her "inner" psychological reality, just as the "veil of ideas" in my mind hides, or intervenes between, me and the world that the ideas represent. Cavell challenges this picture, claiming that the skeptical problem in my relations with others does not stem from their hiddenness inside their bodies but from something about *me*, from my own barriers and failures to "acknowledge"—to use Cavell's term—their reality. In Descartes' recital of skepticism in the *Meditations*, if he is deceived, that would not be his responsibility but that of the malignant and powerful genius who deceives him. The terror and disorientation at the end of the First Meditation stems in large part from the fact that there is nothing *he* can do to avoid the skeptical abyss. Cavell's point is that my skepticism about other minds is precisely something I *can* do something about. Cavell finds models of such skepticism in Othello's lethal doubts about Desdemona; Lear's doubts about the love of his faithful daughter, Cordelia; and in the institution of slavery, where some human beings treat others as mere property, even while "they know, or all but know [them] to be human beings." In these cases, Cavell asserts, we *live* our skepticism concerning other minds. For Descartes and Hume, the everyday world is an alternative to skeptical thinking, whereas, Cavell argues, the everyday world is laced with skepticism about others: "there is no general, everyday alternative to skepticism concerning other minds."[14]

Cavell visited the University of New Mexico in 1981 to deliver early versions of *In Quest of the Ordinary* in a class taught by Michael

Fischer and Morris Eaves, and this was when we first met. I was enchanted by his new ideas and by the man, by the boldness and courage of his using Wordsworth and Coleridge for philosophical purposes, by his seriousness as a philosopher and his demands of and disappointments with "professional philosophy." Over coffee in the Frontier Restaurant after one of his talks, I found myself thanking him for making philosophy fun again.

In these new lectures, Cavell was turning back on his initial point that there is a fundamental difference between skepticism about minds and about the world—not in the direction of the orthodox view that they both respond to a fundamental structure or position for which we have no responsibility, but in arguing that external-world skepticism, and not just skepticism about other minds, is something for which we bear responsibility, something that we live. Coleridge's "Rime of the Ancient Mariner," Cavell argues, is a portrayal of such lived skepticism about the world, and romanticism as he proposes to understand it is the task of "bringing the world back, as to life."[15] This is a task Cavell finds taken up not only by Wordsworth and Coleridge but also in Thoreau's diagnosis of the "lives of quiet desperation" lived by most of his countrymen and in Heidegger's call for a "redemption of human nature from the grip of itself."[16] This all made sense to me, and I loved reading these texts again in Cavell's new ways. And I had an idea.

American Philosophy

The landscapes of thought illuminated by Cavell's visit and the new ways of writing philosophy that he was fomenting led me to the thought that romanticism in American philosophy extends not only through Emerson and Thoreau but through the work of William James and John Dewey—the "pragmatists." I knew enough about James to be confident that I would find much material in his writing to make my case. I soon concluded that what James calls "the sick soul" in *Varieties of Religious Experience* is a form of the lived skepticism that Cavell describes in his essays on Thoreau, Coleridge, and

Wordsworth. I found that, like Cavell and Heidegger, James searches for an "intimacy" between self and world. And I was intrigued by the thought that James is a great writer who, like Cavell and Wittgenstein, places the human subject at the center of his philosophy. It was James who wrote:

> The books of all the great philosophers are like so many men. Our sense of an essential personal flavor in each one of them, typical but indescribable, is the finest fruit of our own accomplished philosophic education. What the system pretends to be is a picture of the great universe of God. What it is,—and oh so flagrantly!—is the revelation of how intensely odd the personal flavor of some fellow creature is.[17]

Dewey was the harder case, in part because his work lacks the literary qualities of Coleridge, Emerson, James, and Cavell himself—qualities crucial for the conception of romanticism as a union of poetry and philosophy, the conception that Cavell favors. But I had this feeling about Dewey, whose *The Quest for Certainty* I regularly used in my courses on epistemology. My feeling was reinforced by Cavell's own reference to Dewey's "Empirical Survey of Empiricisms" in his paper "An Emerson Mood." Commenting on Emerson's condemnation of "a paltry empiricism," Cavell writes that "what is wrong with empiricism is its paltry idea of experience," adding that this "is the kind of criticism of classical empiricism leveled by John Dewey—who praised Emerson but so far as I know never took him up philosophically."[18] So Dewey shares with Cavell, and with Emerson and James, the project of *reconstructing* (as he puts it) both our experience and our conception of it. I found that Dewey's address for the Emerson Centenary of 1903, entitled "Ralph Waldo Emerson—Philosopher of Democracy," was in fact an account not only of Emerson's point of view on things but of Dewey's own.[19] Emerson, Dewey states, subjects "all the philosophers of the race, even the prophets like Plato and Proclus whom Emerson holds most dear, to the test of trial by the service rendered the present and immediate experience."[20] I knew that I had something equally powerful to go on when I read Dewey's

Art as Experience and saw how important Keats, Coleridge, and Shelley are for Dewey's argument that the aesthetic is a part, if a suppressed and degraded part, of all experience.

I poured these ideas out in a long letter to Cavell, and he replied with understanding and generous encouragement, which did me a lot of good. I spent part of a sabbatical visiting him at Harvard, and it was then that I began reading Emerson seriously, led along by Cavell's remarkable paper on "Self-Reliance," "Being Odd, Getting Even." I had read Emerson in college, but it made almost no impression on me. Now, reading "Self-Reliance" in preparation for Cavell's seminar, I found myself having the experience described in *The Senses of Walden*, of reading "words addressed to our condition exactly,"[21] words with the "power to divide [one] through."[22] Cavell was right to say, I found, that although Emerson's writing seems "vague and inflated" from the outside, from inside it acquires "a terrible exactness."[23]

That is how my career as a writer about American philosophy began. To use Wittgenstein's expression, Cavell allowed me to see some ways *to go on*. In the years since *American Philosophy and the Romantic Tradition*, I have continued to write about Emerson, James, Dewey, and Cavell, and I have even found a way to return to Wittgenstein in my book *Wittgenstein and William James*.[24] I have directed a summer institute and a summer seminar on Emerson for the National Endowment for the Humanities, at which Cavell was a principal visitor, and I am currently at work on a monograph about Emerson's philosophy.

In thinking about what it is I do with Emerson's essays and how it relates to what Cavell does with them, I often recall a remark I've heard Cavell make on more than one occasion, often in the face of some unappreciative or mistaken judgment about Emerson (those by John Updike come to mind). When someone writes, for example, that Emerson is vaporous and never comes to the point, or that he has no sense of tragedy, or that it goes without saying that Emerson is a pragmatist, Cavell will ask: "Has he *read* Emerson?"

I try to read Emerson, to see how his words work and, lately, how his individual essays offer points of view on a coherent system or vision. I have been thinking, for example, about "Spiritual Laws," a minor masterpiece among such essays as "Circles" and "Self-Reliance" in Emerson's *Essays, First Series*. A central concern of "Spiritual Laws" is the will—or, more accurately, how much of what is important in life is not a matter of will. The great epochs of our lives are *not* formed, Emerson states, "by the visible facts of our choice of a calling, our marriage, our acquisition of an office, and the like, but in a silent thought by the way-side as we walk; in a thought which revises our entire manner of life." What Emerson calls "self-reliance" appears sometimes as a forthright assertion or imposition of personality, but here in "Spiritual Laws" it appears rather as something we allow to happen. For each of us, Emerson argues, there is a direction where there is no block to our expansion, growth, or ascent. Each of us is "like a ship in a river," running "against obstructions on every side but one—on that side, all obstruction is taken away, and he sweeps serenely over a deepening channel into an infinite sea."[25] That serene sweeping is also found in society, where we find that "a person of related mind, a brother or sister by nature, comes to us so softly and easily, so nearly and intimately . . . that we feel as if some one was gone, instead of another having come."[26] "Spiritual Laws" is a meditation on the varieties of receptivity in friendship, education, and writing.

I thus find it easy to talk about Emerson without considering his relation to pragmatism or to any pragmatist, but my angle on the American tradition makes me alert to ways in which Emerson is a presence in the thought of such writers as James and Dewey. Recently, preparing to write an entry on "Emerson, Romanticism, and Classical American Pragmatism" for the *Oxford Handbook of American Philosophy*, I have been thinking about Emerson and William James. James's father, Henry James Sr., was a friend of Emerson's. In a letter from 1870, the elder James thanks Emerson for the present of his new book, *Society and Solitude*, but adds that he cannot read it to the family, for "just before the new volume arrived, we had got a handsomely bound copy of the new edition of the old essays, and I had been reading them aloud in the evening to Mama and Willy and Alice with such delectation on all sides, that it was vain to attempt renewing the experience."[27] Willy's continuing appreciation for Emerson is indicated in one of his first publications, "Some Remarks on Spencer's Definition of Mind as Correspondence" (1879), and in *The Principles of Psychology*, where he quotes from "The Over-Soul" in describing "the difference between one and another hour of life, in their authority and subsequent effect."[28]

I am particularly taken with the period during which James prepared his remarks for the centenary of Emerson's birth in 1903. James read or reread all twelve volumes of Emerson's writings, underlined passages, wrote quotations in the flyleaves, constructed indices, and wrote to his brother Henry:

> The reading of the divine Emerson, volume after volume, has done me a lot of good, and, strange to say, has thrown a strong practical light on my own path. The incorruptible way in which he followed his own vocation, of seeing such truths as the Universal Soul vouchsafed to him from day to day and month to month . . . seems to me a moral lesson to all men who have any genius, however small, to foster. I see now with absolute clearness, that greatly as I have been helped and enlarged by my university business hitherto, the time has come when the remnant of my life must be passed in a different manner, contemplatively namely, and with leisure and simplification for the one main thing, which is to report in one book, at least, such impression as my own intellect has received from the Universe.[29]

Mathias Girel argues that this book was *Pragmatism*, a suggestion that has considerable plausibility.[30] Whether *Pragmatism* is in any interesting way Emersonian and whether Emerson is in any interesting way close to pragmatism are further, separate questions. What is quite astonishing is that James thought that the answer to the last question is "yes." For among the headings under which James indexed passages from Emerson's works is "pragmatism," where he lists: " 'An action is the perfection and publication of thought'; 'Colleges and books only copy the language which the field and work-yard made'; and 'Nature is not fixed but fluid. Spirit alters, moulds, makes it. . . . Build therefore your own world.'"[31] James does not say, however, that Emerson "is a pragmatist." He doesn't name Emerson in the list of ancestors he sets out in *Pragmatism*'s second chapter, and he fails to mention pragmatism at all in his Emerson Centenary address.

I couldn't agree more with Cavell when, in his discussion of this paper, he complains of being told again and again that Emerson is a pragmatist, with no sentence of Emerson given and without any sense of the difficulties and dangers of seeing him this way. As in my essay "Cavell and American Philosophy,"[32] I grant his point about the repression of Emerson by American culture, including American philosophical culture, and I agree that the repression of Emerson continues even among the contemporary revival of Emerson to the degree that his affiliation with pragmatism is taken to be what is most original or important about him. James wrote in "What Pragmatism Means" that "if you follow the pragmatic method, you . . . must bring out of each word its practical cash-value, set it at work within the stream of your experience."[33] If we apply this test to the contemporary use of the word "pragmatism," we find that often little positive work is being done. Indeed, the word is frequently used indiscriminately of James himself, whose *The Principles of Psychology*, *The Will to Believe*, *A Pluralistic Universe*, and *Essays in Radical Empiricism* are hardly pragmatist works, each taking off in its own direction. It is at such times that I am happy to leave the word "pragmatism" behind.

REMARKS FROM DISCUSSION

CAVELL: I still feel somewhat defensive about my discomfort in calling Emerson a pragmatist. First of all, I can easily say, of course, that he is part of the story. . . . Dewey and James read him with infinite pleasure and have written tremendously complimentary things about him. So he is part of their story. There is no doubt in my mind. I have never denied it. But that that makes Emerson a pragmatist doesn't follow. Can you imagine Kant without Hegel? On the other hand, would you say that Kant is a Hegelian? And can you imagine Plato without Aristotle?

When I was turning fifty, and a little later, I was feeling tired of being told these things so often as though it was just sort of obvious. And when it was said that Emerson is a pragmatist, no sentence of Emerson was given. So the background of this is my sense of the repression of Emerson and Thoreau in American thought, in American philosophy, and what I thought is that there is another case of a man not being given his voice.

CAVELL: I would come back to a remark of Thoreau's when he talks about an experience he had in a field doing something repetitive, and he says: "An old-fashioned man would die of ennui." And I thought that how you distinguish the ecstasy of the ordinary from the ennui of the ordinary was a critical, pivotal point for me. When I first read *Walden*, it did strike me as exceedingly boring, and yet when I got around to getting into it, I almost found it hard to breathe I was so excited.

PUTNAM: I think American philosophy, and increasingly Oxford philosophy, is currently too much dominated by what I would call "positivism," meaning by that term not just Logical Positivism, but what was called "positivism" (with a small "p") in the nineteenth century, namely the idea that only the hard sciences represent knowledge that is worthy of the name, and the humanities need to ape the hard sciences. Unfortunately, instead of calling this "positivism," philosophers often call this attitude "naturalism" (which was a good Deweyan word, but did not connote positivism in Dewey's day). Of course, something is responsible for this reappearance of positivism—something about present-day culture.

CAVELL: The idea of the intergenerational, that struck me as something that I hadn't thought enough about, even though I talk about the child and the grownup, and the grownup and the child, and so forth. But still, and of course, it took me back to the opening of the *Investigations*, where the first words are "When they, my elders, . . ." So Wittgenstein is already talking about intergenerational moments.

TWO

SKEPTICISM AND LANGUAGE

FOUR

SKEPTICISM, ACKNOWLEDGMENT, AND THE OWNERSHIP OF LEARNING
Paul Standish

I

Questions concerning the ownership of learning have been prominent for a number of years. Sometimes they relate to the control of the curriculum, sometimes to matters of choice, and sometimes to more psychological dimensions of learning and enquiry. They emerge in various contexts and take different forms. Consider the following examples.

(a) Concern with the ownership of control over what is learned is to the fore in various aspects of adult education—especially where this is inspired by the emancipatory pedagogy of Paulo Freire or by Malcolm Knowles's concept of andragogy.

(b) These types of learner-centeredness have their counterparts, and in certain respects their precursors, in the progressivism of various forms of child-centeredness.

(c) In recent decades, learner-centeredness has come to be found more generally in higher education, as well as in community college provision, where the student is seen as a consumer and the emphasis is on a choice of educational products to suit the individual's needs or preferences.

(d) Certain forms of constructivism have encouraged a conception of knowledge as the learner's own construction.

(e) The redefinition of what is learned in terms of competences and the idea that these can be collected in an individual portfolio have reinforced the notion of objects of learning as things that the student comes to possess.

(f) The multifaceted and much vaunted idea of the "knowledge economy" has dovetailed with the commodification of knowledge.

(g) Theories of learning have thematized "personal learning styles," promoting a self-conscious reflexiveness on the part of students.

(h) The possession of research evidence as a basis for policy and practice, a commitment that characterizes the prevailing empiricist language of educational research methods, reinforces assumptions regarding the separation of theory or research from practice, where the research evidence is reified in terms of "data."[1]

There are obvious political dimensions to these questions and important challenges to the power interests that have, sometimes with harmful effects, shaped curricula in the past. There is also resistance to the mindlessness of a curriculum characterized exclusively by transmission. Such recognition is crucial to social inclusion and the overcoming of barriers to widening participation, and it may be also a pragmatic recognition of the market-dominated, customer-oriented contemporary world, the world of the discriminating consumer, and of the need for institutions of learning to compete on its terms.

While not doubting the seriousness of the problems to which these developments have been responses, I want to take issue with the sometimes strained idea of "ownership" that is found here. This seems to bring with it three kinds of degeneration or pathological forms to which the above practices are prone: in the various forms of learner-centeredness, there is the danger of a *sentimentalization*; in the reductiveness of the commodification of learning, there is a kind of *neutralization* of content; and in the theorization of learning styles and the self-consciousness of research methods, there is a kind of *mystification.* Diverse though the examples listed above may be and different though these forms of degeneration are, my suspicion is that there are connections between them. I do not wish to suggest that the sense of ownership in education is always and necessarily bad but rather to show something else: that while it opens some possibilities, it forecloses others, with implications for the nature of knowledge and the nature of the learner alike. I am interested in dispossessing learning of its possessiveness. I shall try to do this in the present discussion by way of the idea of disowning knowledge found in the work of Stanley Cavell. What is sought here is the possibility of a nonconsumptive relation to knowledge.

II

The abiding theme in Cavell's work is the nature of skepticism. Skepticism is the tendency to doubt or to submit things to doubt, and it extends from some of the most well-known passages of philosophy to aspects of our personal and professional lives: How do I know that I am not dreaming? How do I know that I exist? How do I know that you are telling the truth? How do I know that learning is taking place? The basis for Cavell's response to skepticism is laid in his reading of the ordinary language philosophy of J. L. Austin and the later writings of Ludwig Wittgenstein. The nature of the problem of skepticism to which these philosophies are addressed can be understood in terms of the following axis:

certainty$<<<<<<<<<<<<>>>>>>>>>>>>$doubt

The typical concern of epistemology has been with grounding or securing knowledge claims, where knowledge is understood in terms of this axis. It exposes putative knowledge claims to doubt, ostensibly to move them toward the pole of certainty. But, as Wittgenstein shows—repeatedly, for example, in *On Certainty*—there are pathologies attached to thinking this way.[2] Thus, in response to the question, "How do I know that the world exists (that there are other minds/ that I exist/etc.)?" his strategy will be not to provide evidence but to show the ways in which the existence of the thing in question is pre-supposed by, or built into the very terms of, or necessarily constitu-tive of the background to the question that is asked. That he shows this successfully is abundantly clear, but the discussion that follows will take us beyond the terms of epistemology.

It is sometimes supposed that the cogency of the strategy here is sufficient to *refute* the skeptic and that this was the burden of Witt-genstein's later achievement. But Cavell takes this to be a mistaken view, believing that it both mischaracterizes Wittgenstein's purpose and seriously underestimates that achievement. If the concern were refutation, this would scarcely explain the almost obsessive recur-rence of this theme in Wittgenstein's work, its personification in the interlocutor who continually disturbs his text. Why is it, if the prob-lem is solved, that Wittgenstein will not leave it alone? The question-ing is stilled and reasoning finds peace, it seems, but only for a while, only until it all starts up again. To see skepticism as refuted, Cavell claims, is to miss its driving force. It is to miss the *existential* motive to skepticism, our compulsion to doubt, and so, it is to lose sight of the truth *in* skepticism, the way it speaks to or expresses something deep in the human condition. This is to be understood in terms of what Cavell calls "our disappointment with criteria," our persistent urge to extract something further to secure our knowledge and our sense of deflation at the Wittgensteinian response to the demand that our practices be grounded: "This is what I do."

But let us pause at this point over a reformulation of the skeptic's question that signals toward the various ways in which Cavell has pursued these matters in many aspects of his work. Imagine, if you will, the following. Being consumed by doubt, I ask you: "How do I know that you love me?" When at your ready reassurance I am not satisfied, you point, of course, to the wonderful times we have, the candlelit dinners, the way you always call me, the flowers you send . . . But how do I really know? There is, it seems, something elusive about your love, something I cannot get hold of, and I can never quite rest content with this.

We shall shortly see something of the way that things are going wrong here, but first let us turn back to the nature of knowledge and the axis of skepticism. What of expressions of knowledge where the point does not to seem to be a matter of *claiming* knowledge? Consider, for example, the following cases. I arrive late for our appointment, fully aware both that this is the case and that you must know this too, and I say: "I'm sorry. I know that I am late." Excessively anxious about arriving at the airport in time, I make my family, much to their irritation, take me there three hours in advance, and again I say: "I know that I am a nuisance." Or, to take a less negative case, feeling honored to be giving the keynote address, you begin: "I should like to express my thanks for the invitation. I realize that this is an important occasion." It is not that a claim is being made in these cases, for it is clear that those involved are already party to the knowledge in question: the point of the remarks is *acknowledgment*.

It is important to see that an expression of acknowledgment is unlike a claim of knowledge in that it does not relate to any question of doubt. In other words, it cannot be positioned on the above axis that extends from certainty to doubt. If the failure of knowledge involves doubt, what might a failure of acknowledgment be like? What would it be like to refuse to acknowledge that I am late, I am a nuisance, and so on? Consider the following axis:

acknowledgment<<<<<<<<<<>>>>>>>>>>>denial

Passing you in the street and for some reason not wanting to see you, I willfully avoid greeting you: this is a kind of denial. Deep down, I know I am a coward, but I cover this over in various forms of bluster: denial once again. Or perhaps knowing I have cancer, I refuse to face up to my condition. And finally, seeking proof that the world exists, I pare down my thoughts to what I cannot doubt, I make my exacting demands in rigorous observance of an axis stretching from certainty to doubt, yet, as you point out, my question presupposes language, and language presupposes other beings and social practices: I pare down my thoughts but the world sneaks back in. This, then, is the epistemologist's denial. We deny facts, people, aspects of ourselves, the world itself—here, in the anxious grasping for security or grounding, with its complementary suppressions and repressions, is an amplification of skepticism's existential truth.

Recalling for a moment the shift from "How do I know that the world exists?" to "How do I know that you love me?" let us turn to the broader range of Cavell's writing, in which he traces themes of skepticism and denial not only through epistemology but through film and literature, through Hollywood "weepies," through Beckett, Ibsen, Coleridge, Shakespeare. Consider the following remarks that bring together symptomatic features of Shakespearean tragedy:

> To overcome knowing is a task that Lear shares with Othello and Macbeth and Hamlet, one crazed by knowledge he can neither test nor reject, one haunted by knowledge whose authority he cannot impeach, one cursed by knowledge that he cannot share. . . . Lear abdicates sanity for the usual reason: It is a way not to know what he knows, or to know only what he knows.[3]

Lear more or less begins the crucial opening court scene by asking his daughters, "How do I know that you love me?" Now very old and ready to divide his kingdom between his three daughters, matching benefit to evidence of desert, he asks:

> Tell me, my daughters
> (Since now we will divest us both of rule,
> Interest of territory, cares of state),
> Which of you shall we say doth love us most,
> That we our largest bounty may extend
> Where nature doth with merit challenge.[4]

When Goneril rises to the occasion, rendering herself available to these demands of accountability, it is only to find that her statement is at once emulated and exceeded by the still more inflated declaration of her sister, Regan. Cordelia, deflated, unable or unwilling to speak, refuses to recognize or accept the terms of the performance by which she is to be judged. Ultimately, in response to her father's

> what have you to say to draw
> A third more opulent than your sisters? Speak.[5]

her "Nothing, my lord" *is* in a sense an account of her genuine love, precisely the love that is no-thing, that cannot be reified or reckoned against the opulence that her sisters seek.

Indicators of performance and economies of exchange can take a still more excessive, exorbitant form, however, where the exaction of evidence or proof inflames close scrutiny into a kind of voyeurism. Othello, crazed by doubt and clutching at a handkerchief, demands evidence of his wife's unfaithfulness: "Give me," he says, "the ocular proof." Othello ends up suffocating Desdemona with a pillow, taking away her breath and closing off the possibility of further words, further action, further uncertainty. For both men, the love they receive is a love they are inclined to deny, for all the evidence they in fact have to the contrary. The possessiveness and voraciousness of their own conceptions of love, revealed in an imagery of material acquisition and exchange, on the one hand, and of fixation and containment, on the other, is shown to lead in the end to a kind of self-consumption or consumptiveness ("Humanity must perforce prey on itself,/Like monsters of the deep").[6]

The Hollywood melodramas Cavell examines are strewn with examples of the desire of the man to contain the woman, typically by in one way or another denying her voice and motivated typically by various anxieties over control or security or possession. The man is drawn or provoked by the otherness of the woman but with a view to converting it into a further means of his own recognition.[7] Cavell ponders the question that these films seem to prompt: of how far these pathological forms of doubt or anxieties for security may in fact be a "man thing." This is a question whose edge acquires a particular keenness in his reading of *The Winter's Tale.* When Leontes says to his young son, "Art thou my boy?"—a remark that under other circumstances might have passed as affectionate and playful but that is burdened here with Leontes' doubts about his paternity—the thought arises that this is not a doubt that a woman could entertain, at least not in the same way. A woman may, under certain circumstances, wonder as to who is the father of the child she is carrying, but she cannot doubt that it is her child. Is it easier for a man to imagine himself as a disembodied mind and harder for him to accept the physical terms of existence?

Cavell speaks of a "stratum of symmetry in which what corresponds to *acknowledgment* in relation to others is *acceptance* in relation to objects," suggesting that failure in these respects has to do with an "inability to acknowledge, I mean accept, the human condition."[8] Failure to accept the conditions of knowledge—or, more broadly, the conditions of our relation to objects—is manifested in a grasping or clutching relationship to those things, as if we were never satisfied with the kind of security that these relations ordinarily afford. A further symmetry here would be with a failure to accept the ordinary conditions of learning, and the substitution for these of various systems of "quality control," with its inflated demands for accountability and its voyeuristic scrutiny of performance indicators. (The approach to teaching and learning that is based on the idea of the High Reliability Organization, as developed by Sam Stringfield and David Reynolds, would be a salient example of this, though in reality this should be evident in the performativity that currently pervades so much educational practice.)[9]

The grasping relation to objects of knowledge and understanding, the acquisitive and accumulative, perhaps totalizing assumptions of empiricism, tend also toward a kind of reification of those objects. Cavell's exploration of these matters shows the closeness of these tendencies of thought and practice to two myths. The prospect of gaining knowledge without reserve—that is, ideally of gaining unlimited knowledge—is tantamount to a pact with the Devil, the damnation of Faust. And the fact that knowledge, in the "knowledge economy," is commodified invites the thought that everything that one comes to know may somehow turn to gold, that learning has become tainted, as it were, with the Midas touch. Corollaries of this would be that commodification—with its visibility and commensurability—becomes the gold standard for what is studied and that learning itself is fetishized.

What, though, would a nonconsumptive relation to knowledge be like? Perhaps no one has done more than Heidegger to reveal the acquisitive, grasping, containing tendencies built into the very terms we use—in "concept" and *Begriff*. Heidegger traces the pattern of a grand fall from Greek to Latin and thereafter, hoping for some kind of latter-day salvation in the recovery of resources from deep within German thought and language. His account of the need for a shift from "calculative thinking" to "meditative thinking" and toward a relation of *Gelassenheit*—a receptiveness to things, a letting things be in order that they should shine forth—is indeed powerful and a resistance to such an acquisitive knowing.[10]

But Heidegger is also part of the problem, it turns out. For Heidegger, the notion of "mineness" (*Jemeinigkeit*) is central to the idea of authenticity in *Being and Time* as well as to the celebration, in the later essays, of the relation to the land. The fact that "Dasein is in each case mine"[11] and the proximity in German of the word for "authentic" (*eigentlich*) to "own" (*eigen*) underline the theme of ownership that pervades *Being and Time*.[12] Later, Heidegger laments that it is a characteristic of the modern age that "the *rootedness*, or autochthony, of man is today threatened at its core!"[13] The loss of a homeland is not so much a matter of local political concern as indicative of the metaphysical condition of the age, a condition that must be resisted or overcome, in Heidegger's view, through a kind of ecology in which the plundering effects of technologization are contained in favor of a more harmonious relation to the earth. But the relation to the hearth and the home in the later writings is, in the original sense, a *nostalgia* (literally, a home-sickness), and, in this context, the ways that notions of belonging and possession can degenerate do not need elaboration.[14] In short, the emphasis is on a kind of permanence in building, dwelling, and thinking—the title words of his celebrated essay[15]—that is, for all its receptiveness, ultimately vulnerable to vices of possessiveness.

When he wrote "Building Dwelling Thinking," Heidegger could hardly not have been aware of Thoreau's attempts about a century earlier, in the course of his sojourn at Walden Pond, to find a right way to live, though this is not acknowledged. Those, let it be remembered, were attempts in the living and the writing, rolling together living and language in an economy of thought that more than a little anticipates aspects of Heidegger's later ruminations. In "Thoreau Thinks of Ponds, Heidegger of Rivers," Cavell compares Heidegger's relation to the land (and to the waters of the River Ister in Hölderlin's poem of that name) to the experiment of *Walden*—Thoreau's experimental book about his experiment of two years of living beside the waters of Walden Pond, just away from the town and about a mile from his neighbors, and close enough, that is, for his experiment to stand as a kind of example.[16] Crucially for Thoreau, the "ownership," if that is what it is, of the land and the hut that he builds and lives in is provisional: Walden is also a place that he will leave. This opens the possibility of a relation that, in contrast to the possessiveness of belonging, is ready to let go and sometimes to lose; after all, as we are reminded through the countless Biblical allusions in the text, "What does it profit a man, if he gain the whole world but lose his own soul?" *Without* setting down roots, then, in its readiness for departure, where each day brings a new dawn, this suggests a modified kind of nomadism. It shows the possibility of dwelling lightly on the earth in a parable of acceptance of the human condition, including the conditions of our knowing and learning. Given the frequency of *Walden*'s reference to questions of teaching and learning, it becomes all the more plausible to see the text as belonging to a line of perfectionist writings about education that extends back through Rousseau's *Emile* to Plato's *Republic*.

III

It will perhaps be objected that I have run together two different senses of "own" and of the possessive terms that go with it. Thus, on the one hand, we have "the car that I own," "my own computer," etc., and, on the other, "my own daughter," "my husband," "my obligations," "my own fault," etc. We might think of the former as relating to material possession and the latter to matters of belonging. Language is curiously resistant to tidiness here, however. We can try to legislate over these meanings, but even the categories offered here are unsteady—witness the ways that "my belongings" slips back into and that the multiple nuances of "possession" exceed the former category, material possession. (Consider "possessing a right" as against "he was possessed.") Our distinction is likely to hide rather than remove the seepage that occurs and hence be less true to the way things are.

But a further factor demands to be considered. "Disown" should function as a negation of "own" as a result of its prefix, but this is plainly not the case—at least, not on the face of it. To sell your car is not to disown it. The opposite of disowning is acknowledgment. As a result of her refusal to spell out her love for him, Lear disowns Cordelia, no longer recognizes her as his daughter. Hence disowning falls at the negative end of the axis of acknowledgment and denial. But there is a sense of "own" that is more or less unrelated to questions of material possession, as is captured in the colloquial expression "own up," meaning confess. And this in turn relates to a more archaic usage, where "I own" equates more or less with "I claim" or "I assent."

In *The Claim of Reason*, a major burden of Cavell's account is to reaffirm the importance in ordinary language philosophy of assent.[17] This may seem like a minor matter, but it should be clear that a whole metaphysics is at stake in these terms. In contrast to the impersonal metaphysical voice of modern philosophy, which states or questions what is the case, ordinary language philosophy characteristically proceeds with expressions of the form "When we say . . . we mean. . . ." (For example, "When we say 'education,' as opposed to 'training,' we mean that what is learned is not relevant only to a particular task, that it is of value in itself, that it is for the good of the learner.") The verbal form here is in the first person, which authorizes the judgment, and plural, which binds the speaker to the community. And this statement is made not as some kind of empirical generalization; a survey of usage, for example, would be beside the point. It is made rather as something closer to a commitment or an expression of assent, depending both upon the sincerity of the speaker (how it seems *to her*) and on her affirming her alignment or community with others (her faith that she shares this judgment *with them*, can speak for them). In sincerity, she shows where she stands, "owns up" to her allegiance, and, in this archaic sense (and perhaps tautologically), "owns" what she voices.

Cavell mitigates any tendency toward the "subliming" of rules by throwing emphasis on the location of rule-following practices in the hurly-burly of the form of life, the cohesion of which depends upon agreement in judgments. Moreover, there is something projective about such assent, because the rule following of language does not finally determine future usage but is always open to new development. Assent here is not only obedience to a rule but connects with something like membership in a *polis*, a common world in which judgments are shared, in which (together) we find things the same, in which we project things (together). Bridging epistemology and politics, this implies a kind of political equality. In making such judgments, the speaker exercises a kind of responsibility: she speaks for herself and for others, her morality at stake in all her judgments. Of course, she only comes to this position through her inculcation into the practices of her community, but to the extent that this is how she finds things herself, her obedience is an obedience to her own laws: "citizenship in that case is the same as my autonomy; the polis is the field within which I work out my personal identity and it is the creation of (political) *freedom*."[18] In recognizing the proximity of agreement in judgments to our political community and to our citizenship, the sense in which our city is a city of words requiring our assent becomes all the more apparent. Something of this is buried in the archaic sense of owning. It needs to be understood as other than the prevailing senses of ownership in my opening examples.

Criteria then come to be seen not just as something into which the potential speaker is inculcated but ultimately as something that depends upon her for their sustenance. Criteria are not the cause of her judgment so much as the result. The maintaining of criteria requires this continual giving of assent by the members of a culture, and this can be done in creative and in moribund ways. Suppression of voice would be a form of the latter, and skepticism is one of its forms. Ordinary language philosophy is committed to the recovery of the voice of the ordinary from its suppression or denial by the impersonal metaphysical voice of philosophy. Good education is committed to the recovery of an ordinary understanding of teaching and learning from its denial by the metaphysical voices of performativity and quality control and from the empiricism of educational research.

It will be recalled that the possibility that there may be a "stratum of symmetry" linking *acknowledgment* in relation to others with *acceptance* in relation to objects, as Cavell suggests, means that failure in these respects is significantly connected with an inability to acknowledge or accept the human condition.[19] (Think of the better possibility here as a relation to alterity.) Failure to accept the ordinary conditions of learning has, on the present account, led to various excesses, and these deny education at its heart; this denial includes the failure to acknowledge, accept, or properly give attention to objects of study—to forget that to study is originally to love (*studere*). In this context, the vocabulary of ownership is found in diverse practices, but the ideas it connotes are subject to a common degeneration. It is not that this vocabulary should simply be outlawed, for in subtle ways it unavoidably permeates what we do. But there is reason for resisting its unquestioned adoption and for looking again at the values it surreptitiously reinforces.

The nature of the relation to alterity sketched briefly as an alternative here—the symmetry between relations to other people and relations to the objects of our understanding (and hence the modes of our teaching and learning)—is, I have tried to show, an antidote to the sentimentalization, neutralization, and mystification of learning implicit in my opening examples. I have tried also to provide insight into the possibilities of a deeper and more subtle relation to what is learned—to content in its otherness, nonconsumed, nonpossessed—and to the possibilities for personal growth that such a relation might sustain.

REMARKS FROM DISCUSSION

CAVELL: An interesting question for me is why, for almost the entire history of philosophy, the issue of skepticism has concerned external-world skepticism and not skepticism towards others. When I have asked philosophers when they think this discovery of the other begins in Western philosophy, the answer is generally that it was with Hegel, which seems already very stretched. When I have asked scholars of ancient philosophy if this discovery is there, they all seem to say no.

CAVELL: Does one know how one writes? If you ask me how I write, I simply draw a blank. I don't know what to say about it. In part, this is a way of understanding what Emerson means by partiality. And it's also a way of understanding what Wittgenstein means by philosophy coming to an end. I say, for example, that philosophy comes to an end in part 1 of the *Investigations* 693 times, which means that it starts 693 times. But what I wanted from it, what I learned from it, was a precision in exactly those things that other people complain about being vague. When that comes up, I think of Wittgenstein's use of the duck-rabbit, and what's so beautiful about it is that everything is different. Each thing is different yet all accounted for.

CAVELL: While I try to let language be as conscious of itself as I have it in me to do, as if there is a constant commentary or caution about what is being said, there is another level of writing where you have to stop every word; there are ways of having language be aware of itself that I am not fond of and that I distrust.

FIVE

SENSUAL SCHOOLING

On the Aesthetic Education of Grownups
Gordon C. F. Bearn

Not a single one of his myriad sensations ever submitted itself to the deformity of words.

Virginia Woolf, *Flush*

A Public Danger: Higher Education

Let's start with a problem that higher education has been fumbling with for some time. Here is Whitehead at the end of his 1925 Lowell Lectures, speaking on the Victorian topic of "Requisites for Social Progress":

> the rate of progress is [now] such that an individual human being, of ordinary length of life, will be called upon to face novel situations which find no parallel in his past. The fixed person for the fixed duties, who in older societies was such a godsend, in the future will be a public danger.[1]

This is hardly news, but still, the dramatic rhetoric Whitehead uses ("a public danger") makes us realize that the platitude according to which things are changing faster and faster presents an urgent educational situation. Some years later, Whitehead identified another public danger, one also related to education. Here he is addressing the

Harvard Divinity School in April 1941: "Learning preserves the errors of the past, as well as its wisdom. For this reason, dictionaries are public dangers, although they are necessities."[2] As we shall see, these two public dangers are almost identical.

The danger caused by a population of fixed persons with fixed duties is being made worse by the vocational or professional turn that higher education in the United States, to go no further, has taken. Whitehead is concerned that professional training not only doesn't *address* the public danger posed by a narrow professional training but actually *contributes* to that danger. Whitehead again:

> The modern chemist is likely to be weak in zoölogy, weaker still in his general knowledge of the Elizabethan drama, and completely ignorant of the principles of rhythm in English versification. It is probably safe to ignore his knowledge of ancient history. Of course I am speaking of general tendencies; for chemists are no worse than engineers, or mathematicians, or classical scholars.[3]

It may be surprising to hear Whitehead criticizing classicists in the same terms he uses for mathematicians, engineers, and chemists. But this is a good thing, and corrects one illusion of many defenses of liberal education, namely that professors of philosophy are innocent. There is no field of study that cannot be ruined by its professors. And what ruins most is success.

Yes. Success is the problem. Success in working with the abstractions relevant to one's own practice almost inevitably leads practitioners to think that their favorite abstractions are the keys to reality in general. "The pleasurable satisfaction that 'Now we know.' "[4] But there is no practice whose presupposed abstractions are adequate to an understanding of the whole of reality. Remembering one of my own teachers, I am happy to cite:

> From the demands of practical business life, for example, no adequate ethics can be derived. From a devotion to religious literature—no matter if that be one of the most practical things we can pursue—no suitable account of the material world can be derived. . . . And from the powerful conception of justice in political society there can be no image made which will satisfy the family needs

of the developing child, even if Plato thought so, as he apparently did.[5]

And the same applies down the line to all the fields taught at all the universities. There is no intellectual practice whose presupposed abstractions are adequate to reality in general. Yet success in our narrow fields makes us think we are doing our colleagues a favor by forcing our favorite abstractions down their throats.

It is bad enough that the man with only a hammer treats everything as a nail. What if there were a group of people trying to work together while restricted to different tools? This one only has a hammer and everything's a nail; this one only a screwdriver, everything's screws; that one only a calculator, everything's numbers. As we approach the faculty meeting, someone is hammering a screw into a calculator.

Whitehead's Solution: Habits of Aesthetic Appreciation

There are standard solutions to the problem identified by Whitehead, the problem that professional education exacerbates the dangers of rapid change by producing graduates overcommitted to their own favorite abstractions. The standard solutions are called by various names, sometimes "great books" or a "core curriculum," sometimes "distribution requirements" or "general education," sometimes "the minor," in rare cases "the double degree." Some form of one or the other of these solutions is what most people suppose a commitment to liberal education will amount to. Whitehead disagrees. He thinks that these so-called solutions, as valuable as individually they might be, do *not* address the *fundamental* problem, at all. Whitehead:

> I do not think the secret of the solution lies in terms of the antithesis between thoroughness in special knowledge and general knowledge of a slighter character. The make-weight which balances the thoroughness of the specialist intellectual training should be of a radically different sort from purely intellectual analytical knowledge. At present our education combines a thorough

study of a few abstractions, with a slighter study of a larger number of abstractions. We are too exclusively bookish in our scholas-
tic routine.[6]

The problem is that no single abstraction, indeed no set of abstractions, is adequate to concrete reality. What must balance a specialist
intellectual training is not different intellectual analytical knowledge
but something else altogether. Neither intellectual nor abstract, what
must balance professional training will be intuitive and concrete. But
what are we talking about? Whitehead risks this formulation: "What
I mean is art and aesthetic education."[7]

It's risky because, as you can imagine, the professionalized study
of the history of art employs its own set of abstractions, and so it
would succumb to the same criticisms that Whitehead offers of classics and chemistry. There is no privileged set of abstractions. What is
privileged is the concrete reality that always exceeds whatever abstractions we use, however successfully, to understand and control it. So
his advice is "to strengthen habits of concrete appreciation of the individual facts in their full interplay of emergent values."[8] Or again:
"What is wanted is an appreciation of the infinite variety of vivid values achieved by an organism in its proper environment."[9] These habits of concrete appreciation are perfectly general and apply not only,
or even mostly, to art works. Whitehead singles out factories as examples of the complex organisms that we should habitually appreciate
in all their sensual dimensions.[10]

In this context, Whitehead suggests that the success of the revolu-
tion in political economy sparked by Adam Smith is more than a little
to blame for the dehumanized face of nineteenth-century industrial-
ization.[11] The very real success of these abstractions in their own do-
main made the factory in its completeness invisible and thus did little
to stop its dehumanized development. The British Empire and its
Commonwealth no longer count for much, but this problem, in ever
changing forms, is with us still.

When Whitehead risks "art and aesthetic education," he is using
art in what he calls "a general sense," which he characterizes in this

way: "any selection by which the concrete facts are so arranged as to elicit attention to particular values which are realizable by them. For example the mere disposition of the human body and the eyesight so as to get a good view of a sunset is a simple form of artistic selection. The habit of art is the habit of enjoying vivid values."[12] So artistic skill in this general sense is not only, or even necessarily, such things as the ability to make a fair two-dimensional representation of a house plant. It is, rather, the ability to enjoy the singular sensual power of each singular thing. Not, in Whitehead's scheme, a singular thing existing independently. The notion of independent existence is one of two misconceptions that, on his account, have "haunted" European philosophy and theology.[13] In the Lowell lectures, the notion of aesthetic value is introduced by a discussion of the romantic reaction to the scientific successes of the previous centuries: "Both Shelley and Wordsworth emphatically bear witness that nature cannot be divorced from its aesthetic values; and that these values arise from the culmination, in some sense, of the brooding presence of the whole on to its various parts."[14] Habits of aesthetic appreciation are habits of attending to our experience of the singular way that any thing receives and reveals its seamless surroundings. The creek flowing liquid green under leafy trees.

The reason that Whitehead considers art and aesthetic appreciation to be a corrective to the public danger posed by professional education makes it a corrective also to the other public danger, the one posed by dictionaries. This is the space where Whitehead's thought meets that of Bergson and James, at least James the defender of the nonconceptual.[15]

Whitehead's thinking was always inspired by a commitment to the democracy of experience, here manifest in a quite striking sentence that I quote just to enjoy its abundance:

> Nothing can be omitted, experience drunk and experience sober, experience sleeping and experience waking, experience drowsy and experience wide-awake, experience self-conscious and experience self-forgetful, experience intellectual and experience physical, experience religious and experience sceptical,

experience anxious and experience care-free, experience anticipa-
tory and experience retrospective, experience happy and experi-
ence grieving, experience dominated by emotion and experience
under self-constraint, experience in the light and experience in the
dark, experience normal and experience abnormal.[16]

Whitehead believed that sensations, as, for example, of a color characterizing a particular region, originate in the "brooding presence" of
the surrounding world on one singular event. "Our developed consciousness fastens on the sensum as datum: our basic animal experience entertains it as a type of subjective feeling. The experience starts
as that smelly feeling, and is developed by mentality into the feeling
of that smell."[17] Thus the raw experience of any actual thing will de-
feat any attempt to grasp it conceptually, or in Whitehead's lingo: "it
is impossible to complete the description of an actual occasion by
means of concepts."[18] So while he wants to resist what he calls Bergson's anti-intellectualism, because there is a place for logical precision, he also insists that "the success of language in conveying
information is vastly over-rated, especially in learned circles."[19] Typically, as Bergson puts it, "we do not see the actual things themselves;
in most cases we confine ourselves to reading the labels affixed to
them."[20] That blindness is what sensual schooling would correct.

The public danger posed by dictionaries and the public danger
posed by professional education are thus both offspring of the comfortable attitude that the surrounding world is conceptually charac-
terizable without remainder in more or less the terms currently on
offer at our best professional schools. "Now we know." I have called
Whitehead's corrective "sensual schooling" because I think of the
sensual as the liquid experience that can precipitate into the conceptualized sensations of philosophers. Habits of aesthetic appreciation
are habits of attending to those sensual singularities that overflow any
linguistic characterization of them. Someone who has acquired habits
of aesthetic appreciation, therefore, need not be a museum hound at
all, but they will have become vividly aware, by their own experience,
that the success of any set of abstractions, ethical, economical, or historical, rides oceans of repressed sensual energy, energy that, from the

other side, might provide an intense joy that is inaccessible to those seeking satisfaction merely from the purchase of expensive products. Intense joy. Floating sensual in liquid corporeality.

At one and the same time, a university refigured to draw out *habits of sensual appreciation* will help both to avert the public danger posed by our professionalized system of higher education and stand a good chance of educating students whose lives will be touched by a joy beyond the mere satisfaction of any specific desire. Perhaps this is an aspect of that sensual beauty Whitehead invokes as "a beauty beyond the power of speech to express."[21] Sensual schooling would be a corrective to the traditional educational indoctrination in the practice of labeling. If this is philosophy as the education of grownups, it is not about what we normally think of as growing up at all. It is not about growing up; it is about becoming children. Growing green. Although this rhymes with Cavell's imagining philosophy becoming the education of grownups, I think Whitehead has almost the opposite inclination. Where Whitehead inclines to becoming children again, Cavell's education is to bring us up, a second time, to adulthood. Let's look and see.

Cavell and the Education of Grownups

What is the force of Cavell's sentence: "In this light, philosophy becomes the education of grownups"?[22] In particular, what light is he talking about? Our sentence follows immediately on this one: "In the face of questions posed in Augustine, Luther, Rousseau, Thoreau . . . we are children; we do not know how to go on with them, what ground we may occupy."[23] Some questions find us, in a particular way, unable to answer. If someone asked me what city is the capital of Cameroon, I would not know the answer, but I would know how to go about finding the answer. I would know how to go on. Although I was not, just then, thinking about the question and do not, just now, know the answer, I am, nevertheless, prepared for the question in the sense that the question had a recognizable spot.

During a discussion of ostensive definition, Wittgenstein remarks: "One has already to know (or be able to do) something in order to be capable of asking a thing's name."[24] In the succeeding paragraph, a series of examples is presented, each describing various situations in which it would be possible to explain to someone the name of the chess piece we call the king.[25] During his consideration of one of these examples, Wittgenstein remarks that when the name of a chess piece can be successfully explained, it is because a "place for it was already prepared."[26] A little later, the series of examples is suddenly broken off when a voice reminds us that "we can imagine the person who is asked replying: 'settle the name yourself'—and now the one who asked would have to manage everything for himself."[27] It is one of my favorite moments, a moment Cavell might now call aphoristic.[28] The deep and troubling difficulty of how you can, ever, teach someone what a thing is called, the great question of how language attaches to the world, suddenly seems no trouble at all. What were we thinking?

We may not know what city is the capital of Cameroon, but a place for it is already prepared, and that is why the question is one that we know how to go on with. And that is why it is not the kind of question that calls for philosophy; it calls for an encyclopedia. What kind of question calls for philosophy? Wittgenstein seems to think that Augustine's question about time was a paradigm of that kind of question: "What then is time? If nobody asks me, I know, if I am asked to explain what it is, I don't know."[29] I don't know how to go on with the question. It is characteristic of this kind of question, as opposed to those Wittgenstein calls questions of "natural science," that they leave us lost, not knowing where to turn for an answer, and so, in some way, not even understanding the question.[30] Brought up short like this, it is as if we have become children. Children not in the sense of children naïvely enjoying their toes, but children in the sense of: why do grownups take everything so seriously?[31] Children looking in on grownup life from the outside.

In what light does philosophy become the education of grownups? Cavell is well known for his "having responded to Wittgenstein's *Investigations* as written, however else, in recurrent response to skepticism," and so it would be natural to interpret the light in which philosophy becomes the education of grownups as the light of skepticism.[32] If this is, finally, true, it is not how Wittgenstein's texts, first of all, present themselves. That is, they do not present themselves as being concerned with typical epistemological questions such as "How do I (you) know that X?" but rather with questions such as *The Blue Book's* "What is the meaning of a word?" or the *Investigations'* opening discussion of a "particular picture of the essence of human language."[33] In other words, Wittgenstein's investigations are first of all stimulated not by epistemological but by metaphysical questions: What is X? The relevance and deep truth of Cavell's interpretation of the *Investigations* comes as a result of Wittgenstein's response to these metaphysical questions. It is in response to these metaphysical questions that Wittgenstein appeals to criteria, and it is also in response to these questions that philosophy becomes the education of grownups. Let's see how this happens.

The Blue Book famously describes the immediate effect of questions that call for philosophy as being a kind of mental cramp:

> The questions "What is length?", "What is meaning?", "What is the number one?" etc., produce in us a mental cramp. We feel that we can't point to anything in reply to them and yet ought to point to something. (We are up against one of the great sources of philosophical bewilderment: a substantive makes us look for a thing that corresponds to it.)[34]

Most of the usual philosophical solutions to this cramp do not address the fundamental problem at all. "(It is as if one had a hair on one's tongue; one feels it, but cannot grasp it, and therefore cannot get rid of it.)"[35] I will point to two responses to that cramp, responses that, in Wittgenstein's view, do not get to the bottom of our bewilderment, and then I will turn to his own favored grammatical response.

Sometimes, giving in to the feeling that we must point to some thing corresponding to the word "meaning," and sure that nothing material will do the trick, we invent an "aethereal object" in a fruitless attempt to give our cares some peace.[36] This, for example, is how the

idea of the proposition as a "queer thing [*merkwürdiges Ding*]" surfaces.[37] But these aethereal objects, with all sorts of powers, only have
those powers because they are aethereal. We have no explanation for
how they manage to do what they do, for example, how aethereal
objects manage to accomplish what merely material objects cannot.[38]
The aethereal object, therefore, only serves to remind us that we have
not yet solved this problem. In the mythology of today, aethereal objects sometimes become neurological, but the frustrations are the
same: yesterday's aethereal is today's neurological. Problems and
methods, once more, pass each other by.[39]

Sometimes we respond to a question such as "What then is time?"
with a definition of time. "The question makes it appear that what
we want is a definition. We mistakenly think that a definition is what
will remove the trouble (as in certain states of indigestion we feel a
kind of hunger which cannot be removed by eating)."[40] In 1937,
thinking back over his early work with Russell, Wittgenstein wrote:

> In the course of our conversations Russell would often exclaim:
> "Logic's hell!"—And this *perfectly* expresses the feeling we had
> when we were thinking about the problems of logic; that is to say,
> their immense difficulty, their hard and *slippery* texture. . . . But
> that is the difficulty Socrates gets into in trying to give the defini-
> tion of a concept. Again and again a use of the word emerges that
> seems not to be compatible with the concept that other uses have
> led us to form. We say: but that *isn't* how it is!—it *is* like that
> though!—and all we can do is keep repeating these antitheses.[41]

Neither ethereal metaphysical objects nor carefully subclaused definitions give us peace. Logic's hell. And it is precisely here that criteria
begin to play a role. Let's see.

Wittgenstein's approach is direct. Unbelievably direct. We know
how to use the word "time," we know how to say that people are late
or on time or taking too long, and we can measure how long the
banana cake has been in the oven, all with very little difficulty. But
when, suddenly, we find ourselves confronted by simple children's
questions such as "What is time?" then we don't know what to say.
Rather than trying to answer the question with aethereal objects and

rather than trying to answer the question with a definition, Wittgenstein simply reminds us of the features of our use of "time" that we were comfortable with before the question showed up and ruined the party. Those unsystematic features of the use of the word "time" are articulated by criteria, and grammatical investigations are the investigations that turn them up, again. Still on the first page of *The Blue Book*, and so in direct response to the mental cramp produced by metaphysical questions, Wittgenstein writes: "Asking first 'What's an explanation of meaning?' has two advantages. . . . Studying the grammar of the expression 'explanation of meaning' will teach you something about the grammar of the word 'meaning' and will cure you of the temptation to look about you for some object which you might call 'the meaning.' "[42] In the face of metaphysical questions of the form "What is X?" we forget everything we ever knew about how to use the expression X. The relevant grammar slips our mind. Wittgenstein's idea is that if we didn't forget, if we remembered our ordinary use of that expression, we would be able to stand up to the metaphysical question without collapsing into aethereal metaphysics. "A main source of our failure to understand is that we do not *command a clear view* [nicht übersehen] of the use of our words.—Our grammar is lacking that kind of perspicuity [*Übersichtlichkeit*]."[43] Grammatical investigations are investigations undertaken with the hope of using perspicuous representations of our uses of words to silence the metaphysical voices in our head, but only for a spell, not once and for all. To put a (momentary) end to our restlessness: this isn't how it is . . . yet that is how it must be!

Excepting Rorty, who would like to read Wittgenstein as putting an end to philosophy once and for all, there is widespread agreement about this rather formal characterization of Wittgenstein's method. But there is some controversy about how precisely to give content to the notion of a perspicuous representation. On one widespread view, defended by Baker and Hacker in their first commentaries on the *Investigations*, a perspicuous representation is an arrangement of the various uses of the words in a patch of language that permits that patch to be taken in at a glance.[44] In his final writings, Baker distanced himself from his earlier conception of a perspicuous representation, defending instead a functional conception according to which a perspicuous representation is whatever in a person's restless philosophizing helps them, at that point, find their way to seeing their restlessness in a new way, a new way that will permit them, for a moment, to breathe easily, once again free from metaphysical cramp.[45] Cavell is clearly closer to the later Baker than to the more familiar line defended by Baker and Hacker, but I am not now ready to measure the distance that remains between Cavell and the later Baker.

Cavell discriminates three ways that the concept of a perspicuous representation is invited by the procedures of the *Investigations*:

> So here's the surprising premise in my argument for taking Wittgenstein's writing as essential to his philosophizing, the manner to the method: the concept of the perspicuous, governed by the criteria of completeness, pleasure, and breaking off, is as surely invited by contexts of aphorism as it is by those of proof and of grammatical investigation.[46]

Cavell doesn't slight proof, but it is the other two contexts, grammatical investigation and aphorism, that are more relevant to the concluding educational paragraphs of part 1 of *The Claim of Reason*. Let's return to those paragraphs.

Here is Cavell characterizing the kinds of questions that call for philosophy, for grammatical investigations, and finally for aphorism, too. I will break this paragraph in two and pick it up again later. The first half reads:

> When my reasons come to an end and I am thrown back upon myself upon my nature as it has so far shown itself, I can, supposing I cannot shift the ground of discussion, either put the pupil out of my sight—as though his intellectual reactions are disgusting to me—or I can use the occasion to go over the ground I had thought foregone. If the topic is that of continuing a series, it may be learning enough to find that I *just do*; to rest upon myself as my foundation.[47]

I had thought some ground was foregone. "Foregone" is Cavell's inflection of *selbstverständlich*, which Anscombe translates as "matter of course," for example, in this passage: "The rule can only seem to me to produce all its consequences in advance if I draw them as *a matter of course*. As much as it is a matter of course for me to call this color 'blue.' "[48] I tell people I will be early or late or very late without wondering what time is. My mastery of the grammar of "time" raises no problems or anxieties for me. I use it as a matter of course, without a second thought. But then a child, or Augustine, asks me what time is, and I don't know what to say. Nothing about the grammar of "time" goes any longer without saying; the use of this word suddenly seems completely unimportant, even irrelevant, so in response, we may try to launch an actual metaphysics of time. Don't. "Drop it."[49]

What we need for "time," as for every word we use, is a grammatical investigation uncovering the criteria for its use. Cavell distinguishes two kinds of criteria, (1) Austinian and (2) Wittgensteinian or grammatical. Austinian criteria help one distinguish specialized objects: bitterns, goldfinches, Stella's Indian bird paintings. They relate a name to an object of a specific sort.[50] And when I am not a master of Austinian criteria, I am simply unable to identify objects of that specific sort. As Cavell observes, failure to know Austinian criteria won't generalize to the skeptical denial of knowledge as a whole.[51] Wittgensteinian or grammatical criteria strike deeper. Cavell puts it this way. Wittgensteinian or grammatical

> criteria do not relate a name to an object, but, we might say, various concepts to the concept of that object. Here the test of your possession of a concept (e.g., of a chair, or a bird; of the meaning of a word; of what it is to know something) would be your ability to use the concept in conjunction with other concepts, your knowledge of which concepts are relevant to the one in question and which are not; your knowledge of how various relevant concepts, used in conjunction with the concepts of different kinds of objects, require different kinds of contexts for their competent employment.[52]

To know the grammatical criteria for a word is to have mastered what Cavell called its grammatical schematism: "the set of criteria on the basis of which the word is applied in all the grammatical contexts into which it fits and will be found to fit (in investigating which we are investigating part of its grammar)."[53]

Cavell composed the first part of *The Claim of Reason* in response not only to the *Investigations* itself but also in response to those of its first readers who saw in Wittgenstein's appeal to criteria an answer to skepticism. But the central lesson of Cavell's interpretation is that this cannot be true. There are two very different dimensions to any attempt to resolve a philosophical question with a grammatical investigation, and assembling criteria is only one of them. In addition to the (intellectual) dimension along which we are reminded of the grammar of the relevant words, there is the very different (volitional) dimension along which we are led to or shocked into accepting the grammar we have been reminded of. (Cavell identifies these two not as two dimensions of one activity but as two different activities.)[54] These two dimensions resonate with the two conceptions of a perspicuous representation that were mentioned above, and, as the later Baker points out, the relatively little space that Wittgenstein gives to the first of these dimensions indicates that when Wittgenstein tells us that "the concept of a perspicuous representation is of fundamental significance" for him, he is mostly referring to its volitional significance.[55] This is the dimension along which we can be helped to overcome what Cavell calls the disappointment of criteria. Let's see.

Cavell not only writes about ordinary language philosophy; he also, sometimes, practices the art itself, exquisitely. One of those times is when he begins a grammatical investigation of the word "pain" that sketches its differences from "pleasure" and "joy," for example, and charts the way "pain" meets verbs such as "giving," "taking," "causing," and so forth.[56] He remarks that attending to all these differences, many of which are, however forgotten, still surprisingly familiar, "rather dampens the mood of worry about whether I ever know another is in pain."[57] And this is just as Wittgenstein predicted. Shaken by the metaphysical question "What is pain?" grammatical investigations cure the temptation either to look for an object that is pain or to construct a perfect little definition of the word "pain." And if grammatical criteria were superstrong conceptual connections, then we could use them to answer skepticism about our ever knowing another was in pain. But it is not to be. What Cavell aims to show is that "the fate of criteria, or their limitation, reveals ... the truth of skepticism—though of course this may require a reinterpretation of what skepticism is, or threatens."[58]

Cavell worked out his interpretation of the truth of skepticism in contrast to an amalgamated interpretation of criteria that he attributed to Malcolm and Albritton, but the more recent interpretation of Baker and Hacker is almost equidistant from Cavell's interpretation, for they use criteria to make room for defeasible knowledge immune, nevertheless, from skepticism.[59] Cavell concedes that the restless worry about whether another is in pain is rather quieted by the grammatical study of "pain," yet, after a healthy dash, he wonders:

> —But maybe that is because we haven't finished yet. We haven't arrived at the specific criteria by which we are to exit from the schematism into the world. (Exiting from the schematism is perhaps a dangerous picture. The schematism is the frame of the world, and to exit from it should mean to exit from our mutual attunement. The picture came up here because I wanted to note that the order of a grammatical investigation is an academic one; you might call it reconstructed.)[60]

These second thoughts, in the wake of enjoying grammatical investigations, reveal what Cavell refers to as the fact that criteria are disappointing. As much as we may enjoy discovering the way our use of the concept of pain laces itself with other concepts and actions, as much as we know that *this* is wincing in pain, those very grammatical connections are the tools of every masquerader and confidence man. Betrayal by a kiss, if it is to be successful, must respect or exhibit the very same criteria for being a kiss as an authentic kiss. Criteria, after all, answer the metaphysical question "What is X?" and not a question about knowledge: "How can I know that this is really a kiss?" Grammatical investigations and the criteria they elicit tell us what it is to be a kiss or a pain, not whether or not Fred's is an authentic kiss or a real pain. Nor could they: every proposed criterion of real authenticity could equally be used to *simulate* real authenticity. And that is why criteria are disappointing. "There is something they do not do; it can seem the essential. I have to know what they are for; I have to accept them, use them. This itself makes my use of them seem arbitrary, or private—as though they were never shared, or as if our sharing of them is either a fantastic accident or a kind of mass folly."⁶¹ Grammatical investigations can leave us with anxious second thoughts, and no further appeal to criteria will help. When the issue is another's pain, all that remains is in my hands. "I (have to) respond to it, or refuse to respond. It calls upon me; it calls me out. I have to acknowledge it. I am as fated to that as I am to my body; it is natural to me."⁶²

It is this idea of naturalness that Cavell reads as being a matter of course, a forgone conclusion. And, at long last, this takes us back to the first half of a paragraph here recited:

> When my reasons come to an end and I am thrown back upon myself, upon my nature as it has so far shown itself, I can, supposing I cannot shift the ground of discussion, either put the pupil out of my sight—as though his intellectual reactions are disgusting to me—or I can use the occasion to go over the ground I had thought foregone. If the topic is that of continuing a series, it may be learning enough to find that I *just do*; to rest upon myself as my foundation.⁶³

Using the occasion of the question to go over the ground we had thought forgone is using the occasion of the question to begin a grammatical investigation. And at the end of that investigation, we are told, briefly enough, that it may be enough to find that I *just do*. Cavell is citing a passage in the *Investigations* that he has since come to call Wittgenstein's "scene of instruction."⁶⁴ The motivating question in that passage concerns my justification for following a rule as I do, and a voice comments: "If I have exhausted the justifications I have reached bedrock, and my spade is turned. Then I am inclined to say: 'This is simply what I do.' "⁶⁵ We have seen that grammatical investigations sometimes leave behind a wake of disappointment. Cavell's idea here seems to be that when, in response to a crisis of interrogation, grammatical investigations unearth the grammatical schematism of a word, there are *sometimes* no second thoughts, no wake of disappointment. In those cases, Cavell seems to believe that our linguistic life returns to being forgone, a matter of course, simply as a result of the grammatical investigations themselves. And perhaps when the topic is continuing a series according to a simple arithmetical rule (+1 or +2, for example), this is enough. This is naturalness as a discovery, a discovery that lasts until the next interrogation that brings the next crisis.

In *The Claim of Reason*, this discovery of what I *just do* is the discovery of which conclusions are forgone, a matter of course, *selbstverständlich*. However, this "just do" is not rock solid. It can feel that way, as if all our anxieties were overcome in a fit of unilateral (or collective) decision. But for Cavell, this is at least an open question:

> I find it at least as plausible to take what Wittgenstein actually writes, namely "Then I am inclined to say: 'This is simply what I do,'" in which perhaps nothing [further] is imagined to be said, to be a *weak* gesture, even passive, implying something like "I cannot see here where or how to make myself plainer, but here I am, doing what I do, whenever you find yourselves interested again."[66]

What we return to when we return to the ordinary is not fixed firm and final. It is delicate. It is a wonder. At best, it achieves what Cavell calls "moments of intellectual peace."[67] For Cavell, peace (*die Ruhe*) is not stable, once and for all. Philosophical restlessness (*die Unruhe*) is never fully and finally overcome.[68] The answers to the metaphysical questions that motivate Wittgenstein's philosophizing are never direct, but they can, for a spell, be put to rest. "What is time?" makes us think perhaps we never knew what time is, and by clutching at definitions and fantastic objects we only increase our anxiety. But turning quietly back to the language we speak and the life we lead, our anxieties can, for a while, recede. What may be stable or, rather, metastable, is how our footing on the earth swings back and forth from restlessness to rest. But I am getting ahead of myself—we still haven't finished reading the paragraph that prepares Cavell's remark about the education of grownups.

Our long ago interrupted paragraph continues with questions that are mostly unlike those that Wittgenstein himself uses to raise trouble for himself.[69]

> If the topic is that of continuing a series, it may be learning enough to find that I *just do*; to rest upon myself as my foundation. But if the child, little or big, asks me: Why do we eat animals? or Why are some people poor and others rich? or What is god? or Why do I have to go to school? or Do you love black people as much as white people? or Who owns the land? or Why is there anything at all? or How did God get here?, I may find my answers thin, I may feel run out of reasons without being willing to say "This is what I do" (what I say, what I sense, what I know), and honor that.[70]

These are questions, like those about continuing a series, to which we don't normally address ourselves. But unlike "How do you continue the series {2, 4, 6, 8, . . . }?" they are questions that, in some sense, we don't have to be taught to ask; we can reach them right from where we are: our daily lives. These overlooked philosophical questions are different from continuing the +2 series because our prior stake in them makes the volitional dimension of grammatical investigations more complicated.

In addition to the (intellectual) dimension along which we are reminded of the grammar of the words in our troubling patch of language, there is the very different (volitional) dimension, along which we can be brought, in various ways, to accept the grammar thus returned to awareness. Apart from such an acceptance, our instability will not, not even momentarily, be quieted. When the topic is continuing the +2 series, it might (sometimes) be enough just to be reminded of how we learned to do this and of what therefore we do when asked to continue the series. It might be enough in the sense that, here, the second dimension of grammatical investigations might take care of itself, without the need for an aphoristic release. Sometimes, there is no more to settling our recurrent philosophical anxieties than being reminded of our "common mastery of language," identifying the thirteenth member of the +2 series here coming into view as akin to identifying a goldfinch of a different color.[71] Where there is no more at stake, criteria will not be found to be disappointing. But often there is more at stake, because we have more at stake. And where criteria are disappointing, different procedures will be necessary. Cavell speaks of them as literary or aphoristic, seeking perspicuousness of a nonformal kind.[72]

These aphoristic procedures can restore peace, even in the face of our disappointment with criteria. How? In various ways. Often by releasing the drive to answer metaphysical questions metaphysically, by definition or with aethereal objects, and then revealing, all of a sudden, that these procedures are not helping or are irrelevant. I have already mentioned one of my favorite of these moments, which comes during a stretch where Wittgenstein is considering how it is possible to learn the name of a chess piece, or anything else, at all: "And we can imagine the person who is asked replying: 'Settle the name yourself'—and now the one who asked would have to mange everything for himself."[73] At such moments, realizing that our philosophical torture is self-inflicted, we can *break off* our restless thinking *completely* and with *pleasure* (if only for a moment), which is how Cavell characterizes the aphoristic.[74] What were we thinking?

The questions in the light of which philosophy becomes the education of grownups are more difficult still. We have something at stake in "Do you love black people as much as white people?" and "Who owns the land?"—something more at stake than simply the philosophical drive for the icy smooth and unconditioned. And that makes the anxieties prompted by these questions even more difficult to settle. Not only have we been surprised into forgetting or resisting what we would ordinarily say, not only are we freighted with the philosophical eagerness for the unconditioned, but we are not even sure how we, ourselves, feel about what our culture says we *should* feel. Here is Cavell describing what, in these kinds of cases, the activity of philosophy becomes:

> In philosophizing, I have to bring my own language and life into imagination. What I require is a convening of my culture's criteria, in order to confront them with my words and life as I pursue them and as I may imagine them; and at the same time to

confront my words and life as I pursue them with the life my culture's words may imagine for me: to confront the culture with
itself, along the lines in which it meets in me.[75]

This is philosophy become the education of grownups. Children, having gained a common mastery of language, head off to
school, where they learn more and increasingly more specific ways
of talking: about languages and literatures, about flowers and pro-
jectiles, about historical change and economic, and more. It is
later when all of this is more or less settled in place that we can be
knocked down by the questions of Augustine, Luther, Rousseau,
Thoreau . . . and then we are all children again, looking in our
lives, as it were from the outside. The education of grownups is
their re-education, re-entering the grownup world. It may change.
It may involve conversion.[76]

There is much to be said on behalf of the value of philosophy become the education of grownups. Most of our lives are conducted without thinking. Most of our judgments are made in conformity with the
judgments of others. Philosophy become the education of grownups
may chagrin us and incite us to listen to ourselves, *ourselves*, against the
appeal of conformism. But this is not sensual education. Quite the re-
verse. When in the face of Augustine's questions we become children,
this is not an experience to be enjoyed. It is to be overcome. Not once
and for all, for there is no escape from our swinging between *die Unruhe* and *die Ruhe*, but it is to be overcome. The point, the goal, the
hope of Wittgenstein's philosophical investigations is to achieve (however briefly) peace. That is why he writes. And that is why he can't
stop.[77] Our becoming children again is a figure, on this page of Cavell's,
for our not knowing our way about. A figure for philosophical anxiety,
not, as Whitehead would have it, a figure for sensual enjoyment. It is
the little child looking in on the grownup world from the outside, not
as I would prefer, the little child mouthing toes burbling joy.

Wittgenstein's Metastability

I have no objection to Cavell's reading of Wittgenstein, as a reading
of Wittgenstein. In particular, I have no objection to his interpretation of the peace that Wittgenstein seeks as never achieving more

than "moments of intellectual peace."[78] Although Wittgenstein's peace is not stable, there is something else that is stable: the metastability of our swinging between restlessness and peace. This metastability has been rather underinterrogated by Wittgenstein's many readers. The suggestion that I want to make, all too telegraphically I am afraid, is that it is Wittgenstein's flight from the sensual that is both the source of this metastability and the reason why philosophy as the education of grownups must ignore the sensual schooling encouraged by Whitehead. The thought is, first, that it is the looseness of fit between our experience and its ordinary linguistic characterization that destabilizes Wittgenstein's momentary peace, and, second, that attending to this experience is precisely the aesthetic attention that Whitehead advocates in thoughts about education.

One mark of the tentativeness of these suggestions is that I am not even sure where to turn to find Wittgenstein discussing sensual experience. When I started looking around for places in *Philosophical Investigations* where experience is under discussion, the whole book began to fall disappointingly into place as something like a limiting case of the early twentieth-century effort to escape metaphysics on the wings of formalism. In this case, formalism taking the shape of Wittgenstein's robust conception of grammar, which was to make philosophical problems "*completely* [vollkommene] disappear," for a moment.[79] Like Cavell's "successfully, if momentarily," this is not strictly speaking a contradiction, but it is in some tension with itself.[80] G. E. Moore reports hearing Wittgenstein in the 1930s describe his new way of philosophizing as being like housekeeping, in that every object has to be touched more than once, and in no special sequence, if we are ever to get the house really tidy.[81] Nevertheless, the problems of housekeeping may, in some sense, completely disappear: the stovetop can be cleaned, the floor mopped, the counters wiped, and then the kitchen will be completely clean, until the next moment. But the larger the space we are cleaning, the harder this will be. When the house is as large as a cow barn, or the job is painting the Brooklyn Bridge—or making the problems of philosophy disappear—then ever to say we are completely done is less true than always to say we are never done. If we are done at all, we will only be done in the sense that our current cares are here and now put to rest, not in the sense that the source of these cares has been drained. So philosophy and housekeeping will only ever be finished, as we might say, practically speaking. Maybe, after all, Cavell was not wholly mistaken to have been reminded, by the *Investigations*, of pragmatism.[82]

Early in the *Investigations*, Wittgenstein remarks that although it is difficult to say just what a clarinet sounds like, many people nevertheless do know what a clarinet sounds like.[83] I do not think this is a sign that he is interested in attending to the sensual experience of a clarinet; rather, he is reminding us that careful attention to the special sound of the clarinet is irrelevant to this particular recognitional capacity. But the recognitional capacity may only be good enough to pick out clarinets from distantly related instruments, as if you could tell a bittern by its booming call but only when the only other birds around are ducks. Being able to recognize a clarinet is consistent with not having given much attention to the particular way clarinets sound. Why is Wittgenstein so sure it would be a waste of time, or worse, to attend to the sound of the clarinet?

The moment that we start attending to the sensual experience of the clarinet, we are on the road to discovering that there is something unique about the sound of this clarinet now in this room, and then we will have overshot our mark. We were trying to attend to the sound just enough to pick out the clarinet-sound but not so carefully that we are left with the this-clarinet-hereandnow-sound. Yet once you start attending to sensual experience, there is no natural stopping place. "'Where is this going to end?'"[84] That is why, when tempted to describe the different way it feels to see this aspect or that in a face, Wittgenstein remarks, "here we are in enormous danger of wanting to make fine distinctions."[85] The enormous danger of attending to fine distinctions is that once we start we will not be able to stop at the right level, at grammatical distinctions; rather, we will slip all the way down to the singular sensual experience itself. It is an ancient metaphysical problem.

What is it that makes apples apples? What is it that makes understanding understanding? Plato knew that there was nothing empirical that could be that in which being an apple consisted, and so he turned away, buying forms at the price of participation. Wittgenstein too knows that there is nothing psychological common to all that we call expecting or understanding, so he turned away, not to the aethereal but to the volitional: acceding to our natural reactions. Apart from this maneuver, apart from turning away from the experiential, there is no hope of finding clean lines separating kinds, kinds of apples, kinds of tastes, kinds of psychological phenomena. And when it comes to grammar, Wittgenstein will not permit blurred distinctions. "(There are no subtle distinctions between logical forms as there are between the tastes of different kinds of apples.)"[86] Often, when doing philosophy we may feel that "the difficulty of the task consists in our having to describe phenomena that are hard to get hold of, the present experience that slips quickly by, or something of the kind."[87] But if we gave in to this temptation, then there would be no end to our investigations. We would only discover that every singular thing was a unique coming together of everything. But isn't it? Practically speaking we can, of course, classify and count, but only practically speaking.

In recent writings, Cavell has used the attraction of the sensual or the experiential to help explain the disappointment of criteria, for instance, when we spurn the generous detail of Wittgenstein's grammatical investigation of "expectation" because we're so sure that "expecting" is

> really a particular feeling (say the one developed in waiting in the dark with others for the birthday person to open the door upon her surprise party), so that either the concept expressed in the ordinary word "expecting" is basically vague or grossly conventional in its reference to a variety of behaviors, or else there really is no such thing as expecting, but at best a collection of unnamed and perhaps unnamable inclinations.[88]

Roughly speaking, I am agreeing with this voice: the ordinary word "expectation" is a cutting from the sensual life of expectation. Call this cutting the grammar or the use of the word "expectation." For all their glorious detail and practicality, uncovering the grammatical criteria for "expecting" depends on our turning away from the sensual detail of our experiences. This would be justifiable if that sensual detail were irrelevant to the sense of "expectation." And this is just what Wittgenstein says: these experiential details that can (as Cavell notes) seem the essential thing about expecting are, according to Wittgenstein, in fact merely "characteristic accompaniments or manifestations" of the concept under investigation.[89] But are they only that? Is there no more to the sense of expectation than its grammar, its use?

Grammatical investigations are robust. They attend to the role of material samples of color and of the corporeal fact that *this* is what we call sitting in chair. That is why grammatical investigations are a *limiting case* of the last century's love affair with form. An investigation of the grammar, the use, of a word must leave to one side the affect of our life with words on our skins, our hearts, our mouths. The sensual dimension of sense is repressed for the simple reason that were it permitted to enter, there would be no stopping it in time to save the notion of cleanly separated kinds of things. Before we knew it, all differences would count, and the differences between any two things would be like the subtle differences between the tastes of apples. The metaphysical question "What is X" would, in that case, not be able to be answered grammatically any more than it could be answered by appeal to aethereal objects or definitions (or neuroscience).

Wittgenstein's opposition to taking sensual experience seriously comes out in the otherwise surprising attention he gives to the idea of the atmosphere of a word. "Suppose someone said: every familiar word, in a book for example, actually carries an atmosphere with it in our minds, a 'corona' of lightly indicated uses."[90] He encourages us to take this idea seriously and then promises we will see that such an atmosphere is "not adequate to explain *intention*."[91] The idea of a corona of lightly indicated *uses* is a rather thin characterization of this atmosphere, one already prejudiced toward grammatical investigations. It leaves out of the atmosphere of a word any of the emotional or sensual aspects of that atmosphere. As it happens, this notion of a word's atmosphere brings us, at long last, back to Whitehead, who resists what he calls philosophy's "excessive trust in linguistic phrases."[92] He insists that it is "quite untrue" to suppose that language can enunciate well-defined propositions: "language is thoroughly indeterminate, by reason of the fact that every occurrence presupposes some systematic type of environment."[93] Or again: "every proposition proposing a fact, must, in its complete analysis, propose the general character of the universe required for that fact. There are no self-sustained facts, floating in nonentity."[94] And, in general, "the determinateness and self-identity of one entity cannot be abstracted from the community of diverse functionings of all entities."[95] All entities. So perhaps it is not so surprising that Gertrude Stein held Whitehead in such high esteem. Whitehead insisted that words never simply indicated their meanings; rather, there was always some backwash from the meaning to the symbol and back again. From the various uses of the word "expectation" to the various experiences of expecting, and back again. Here he is at the University of Virginia in 1927:

> In every effective symbolism there are certain aesthetic features shared in common [between the meaning and the symbol]. The meaning acquires emotion and feeling directly excited by the symbol. This is the whole basis of the art of literature, namely that emotions and feelings directly excited by the words should fitly intensify our emotions and feelings arising from contemplation of the meaning. Further in language there is a certain vagueness of symbolism. A word has a symbolical association with its own history, its other meanings, and with its general status in current literature. Thus a word gathers emotional signification from its emotional history in the past; and this is transferred symbolically to the meaning in its in present use.[96]

Each word's atmosphere is, finally, inseparable from each singular occurrence of the word. No wonder this is no way to define the sense of "intention."

Wittgenstein reaches the same conclusion, that "the atmosphere is inseparable from its object," and so he concludes that it is not an atmosphere after all but rather the beginning of an entire metaphysics where everything belongs to everything else.[97] And so, naturally, the atmosphere of a word will not be that in which intention consists. Intention will consist, like understanding, in the "particular circumstances" that justify one in asserting that one intends this or that.[98] These particular circumstances are precisely the grammatical criteria that were Cavell's concern. So we know already that they are going to be disappointing. They will only do their job if we let them do their job. Intending something consists in the particular circumstances that we *accept* as justifying the claim to intend. But, of course, those particular circumstances are in each case just as singular as the putative intention itself, so that for those circumstances to be those circumstances is, once again, not something that can be decided apart from *acceding* to our natural reactions.[99] That is why Wittgenstein says that the difficulty of philosophy is a difficulty not of the intellect but of the will.[100] And I think this is what makes Wittgenstein's writings—and Cavell's—deep; they reach deeper than conceptual machinery, and that is one lesson of Wittgenstein's discussion of rules: rules are not enough. Deeper than conceptual machinery is the will to accept or acknowledge our life with language and with others. Perhaps deeper still is a labyrinthine metaphysics no longer committed to protecting familiar conceptual distinctions.

I want to suggest that the metastability of restlessness and peace in Wittgenstein's later work is made inevitable by his resting grammar on volition, although, as I have said, this is a very special kind of volition, acceding to our natural reactions. But the grammatical schematism of our concepts fits loosely over our experience and is only held in place by our gritting our teeth. Turning away from sensual experience so that we can preserve familiar conceptual distinctions: this is a perfectly practical thing to do, but it is a matter of will, not philosophy. None of this should be surprising to readers of Whitehead or James. Not the James of *Pragmatism*, but the posthumous James of *Some Problems of Philosophy*:

> Conceptual knowledge is forever inadequate to the fullness of the
> reality to be known. Reality consists of existential particulars as

well as of essences and universals and class-names, and of existential particulars we become aware of only in the *perceptual flux*. The flux can never be superceded, we must carry it with us to the bitter end of our cognitive business, keeping it in the midst of the translation even when the latter proves illuminating, and falling back on it alone when the translation gives out. "The insuperability of sensation" would be a short expression of my thesis.[101]

James as much as says that if one tried to live wholly without the perceptual (as do Wittgenstein's grammatical investigations), then any peace that could be achieved would only be momentary. Moreover, an educational system that spurned the sensual would have tethered itself to conceptual knowledge forever inadequate to the fullness of the reality to be known. It is in this sense that Wittgenstein's flight from the sensual is both the source of the metastability of grammatical investigations and the reason why philosophy as the education of grownups must ignore the sensual schooling encouraged by Whitehead.

Sensual Schooling

Squint as we will, something always exceeds our conceptual descriptions, and if Wittgenstein is unconcerned to attend to that excess, Whitehead certainly is. But how can we follow Whitehead's advice? How can we begin to attend to the sensual dimensions of what we study?

In two familiar phases. Drop and draw. They might be familiar from Debord's discussion of the *dérive*: "In a dérive one or more persons during a certain period *drop* their usual motives for movement and action, their relations, their work and leisure activities, and let themselves be *drawn* by the attractions of the terrain and the encounters they find there."[102] First, drop your commitment to classification and conceptual representation. Second, allow yourself to be drawn into the sensual plane of the object, subject and object dissolving in delight. The trick is not to judge but to *enjoy*, to let the sensual power of the singular thing draw you away into a plane beyond subject and object, alert to the irregularity of every commonplace. First break the spell: turn the chair upside down. Then caress the sensual singularity with all your senses. Not just with your eyes. Touch it. Slap it. Taste it with your tongue. Open your mouth. We know that our mouths are amazing organs of sensation, yet we restrict them to food and to sex. When we were children, we put everything in our mouths, and we should continue to do so. And the more senses we loose on the singular object, the more we will enjoy beauty beyond representation.

Whitehead already prepared a place for this kind of enjoyment in his characterization of the rhythm of education. The rhythmic is, he asserts, "essentially the conveyance of difference within a framework of repetition."[103] The framework of repetition is his three-stage model of the educational process: the repeating stages of romance, precision, and generalization. Whitehead introduced these stages in broad chronological order but insists that with differences of emphasis, each stage or, better, each *dimension* of the process of education is present at every chronological stage. The middle stage of precision is described in terms of grammar: "In this stage, width of relationship is subordinated to exactness of formulation. It is the stage of grammar, the grammar of language and the grammar of science. It proceeds by forcing on the students' acceptance of a given way of analyzing the facts, bit by bit. New facts are added, but they are facts which fit into the analysis."[104] This characterization of the stage of precision in terms of forcing reality into the framework of analysis provided by the current scientific categories is a fine example of the kind of educational process for which sensual schooling would be a corrective. Moreover, by characterizing this stage in terms of grammar, we can see that there would be Whiteheadian reasons for supplementing grammatical investigations, even those as tangled as those described as the education of grownups, with a more sensual dimension.

The sensual corrective is characterized by Whitehead as romance. It is the first stage of the educational process, the stage of ferment: "education must essentially be a setting in order of ferment already stirring in the mind."[105] Here is Whitehead's characterization of that fermentation:

The stage of romance is the stage of first apprehension. The sub-
ject-matter has the vividness of novelty; it holds within itself unexplored connections with possibilities half-disclosed by glimpses
and half-concealed by the wealth of material. In this stage knowledge is not dominated by systematic procedure. . . . Romantic
emotion is essentially the excitement consequent on the transition
from the bare facts to the first realizations of the import of their
unexplored relationships.[106]

It is characteristic of this dimension of the process of education that
objects are not approached with a typology ready to hand, a circumstance that, when the students are young enough, can be taken for
granted. But when the students are older, perhaps even grownups,
there we might appeal to drop and draw.

Habits of aesthetic attention can be cultivated by dropping our
usual motives for action and reflection and letting our senses be
drawn by the objects or situations at hand. I sketched how this might
work with a chair, but there is no reason it couldn't also be accomplished in more formal educational circumstances. The main point is
to approach the problematic or the text, as much as possible, without
the tool kit of familiar grammar, linguistics, science, and history. This
may mean many things. Remembering Donald Campbell's crack that
you can't teach language over the phone, we should remember that
sensual schooling requires that we get off the phone. When the text
is very old, perhaps it will be helpful to wander through books and
museums in an effort to see what the author of your texts might have
seen, to feel the difference between shoes at the mall and shoes that
your author was wearing. Again, it will be important not to have texts
predigested, in the manner, say, of those who translate Locke, Berkeley, and Hume into modern English while preserving, they assure us,
all the valid philosophical arguments.[107] Reading anything in the language in which it was written is a well-known way of feeling the drag
of other ways of thinking. Another way might be to stand on the ancient site itself: noticing the mountains in the distance and the power
of the hot sun. Maybe the spell of the present will be broken by a
fragment of pottery from the university museum, or a coin, or a gad-
get from a past time.[108] Engineers have perhaps the easiest task here,

but also the most difficult. There is no engineering problem that doesn't reach through the whole of human space. Building a bridge is not just a technical project. It is an aesthetic project, and a social project, and a cultural project. Language itself can be changed by populations crossing bridges. Yet the mastery of precise detail makes us slight the habits of aesthetic appreciation that would permit us to see the world in the abundance of its sensual flux. And we are back again to the problem first lifted from Whitehead: "The fixed person for the fixed duties, who in older societies was such a godsend, in the future will be a public danger."[109]

Whitehead's solution to this public danger is the aesthetic education of grownups, which I have been calling sensual schooling.

> When you understand all about the sun and all about the atmosphere and all about the rotation of the earth, you may still miss the radiance of the earth. There is no substitute for the direct perception of the concrete achievement of the thing in its actuality. We want concrete fact with a high light thrown on what is relevant to its preciousness.[110]

At one and the same time, a university refigured to draw out *habits of sensual appreciation* will both help to avert the public danger posed by our professionalized system of higher education and stand a good chance of educating students whose lives will be touched by a joy beyond the mere satisfaction of any specific desire.[111]

REMARKS FROM DISCUSSION

CAVELL: The two sentences I am going to gloss (and this is what glossing often means for me) are: "Who should say what prospect life offers to another?" and "Could there be a greater miracle than to look through each other's eyes for an instant?" To gloss for me often means to toy around with words, in the way that Thoreau does. So I am trying to elicit, to extend the thought. And the extension begins in my mind from what I take these lines to be a parable of—perhaps not quite a parable, but what the lines point to. And that just is reading. It's a moment that it points to. Could there be a greater miracle?

I was an adolescent when I was given Thoreau to read, and I was probably too impatient. If it wasn't *War and Peace* or *Crime and Punishment* or *The Red and the Black*, then I couldn't sit still long enough to peel the onion. In my experience, seeing what something meant involved the tenderest moment of insight, anything but a thunderclap, the extended moment in which I had the thought that every sentence, every word in *Walden* meant something. It was a thought that didn't come to me, that didn't occur, until I was fifty years old. I take that as what Thoreau means by looking through another's eyes. It could be the merest thing: "Oh, I see," that is, "I see what you see." Or it could be extended. And then the miracle seems to mean our not saying too much about it, that this is all of it, that it all makes sense. How can that be the case? It all makes sense, and none of it at any depth. And now I am living underwater with sense.

CAVELL: What interests me also is the role of the teacher's own interest. It's easy to say that the teacher has to be willing to feel himself to be getting an education as well as teaching, but how it is you show or fake—is it, is that what it is? How do you make the thing you are talking about already surprising to yourself? Now that is something.

CAVELL: For the ideal of a classroom in philosophy, or of any kind of classroom, the teacher should not be guided always simply by the superego, where you are always looking over your shoulder about whether this is ok to say or not ok to say.

THREE

MORAL PERFECTIONISM
AND EDUCATION

SIX

VOICE AND THE INTERROGATION
OF PHILOSOPHY

Inheritance, Abandonment, and Jazz
Vincent Colapietro

Introduction: Attending to the Child's Voice

We are trained to dissociate our philosophical voices from their uniquely autobiographical inflections. Initiation into philosophical discourse demands, at the very least, working hard to erase merely idiosyncratic inflections. But the literary achievement of an author such as Stanley Cavell—his philosophical accomplishment being inseparable from his literary practice—invites reflection upon the personal and even intimate narratives of a philosopher's lives (including autobiographical accounts) as valuable sources of philosophical illumination. Such reflection enables us to appreciate that identity, persona, and voice are, in particular, bound up in our names and acts of naming, just as they are in youthful experiences but also subsequent ones. It also assists us in probing the deeper meaning of the most commonplace terms, not least of all such terms as home, inheritance, and exile.

In "Philosophy and the Arrogation of Voice," Stanley Cavell suggests that "philosophy and autobiography are to be told in terms of each other."[1] In this and the other two essays in A Pitch of Philosophy, tellingly subtitled Autobiographical Exercises, he does nothing less than this. Of the three, however, "Philosophy and the Arrogation of Voice" is the most personal and autobiographical, arguably also the most probing, precisely as an autobiographical exercise. In it, Cavell confesses, "I might summarize my life in philosophy as directed to discovering the child's voice."[2] Indeed, he concludes this piece by recalling that, along the way, he "*identified with* the perhaps absent, silenced child of Wittgenstein's parable of the turned spade."[3] The allusion here is to a famous passage in Wittgenstein's *Philosophical Investigations*, one to which Cavell has often returned: "If I have exhausted the justifications. . . . I have reached bedrock, and my spade is turned. Then I am inclined to say: 'This is simply what I do.'"[4] In one of his characteristically startling readings of this passage, Cavell is suggesting that this justification might be imagined as Wittgenstein's *response to* the query of a child, one *whose question*, as clearly as any utterance possible, makes imperative the exigency to maintain an authoritative voice but also makes inescapable questions about the exemplars of authority (in the first and possibly also the last analysis, parents or their surrogates). The absent, silenced voice of the child is, thus, imagined as the one calling forth the utterance "This is simply what I do." The discovery, by way of recovery, of the child *before whom* we as adults, hence as in some respects authorities, stand adds a dimension to Wittgenstein's text hardly ever considered, even as a possibility. The scene of initiation into language with which the *Investigations* opens is one we never entirely leave: on countless occasions, we are not only speaking in the presence of children but also *in response to* their queries about *why* this is to be done rather than that, about what justifies this manner of proceeding, this mode of acting. To recover the questioning voice of the child involves hearing the quivering voice of authority—or the irritable voice, or the impatient one, or, all too rarely, the patient and humane one of the adult who desires to be at once instructive yet not authoritarian.

The reach of Cavell's identification, however, does not stop with the imagined child who prompts a person to acknowledge, "This is simply what I do," or, more likely and less satisfactorily, "This is how it is properly done" (an utterance in which the "I" is absent, the human presence effaced). For he identifies "no less with its [this Wittgensteinian parable's] present, silenced grown-up, who keeps himself or herself visible, waiting with hovering attention."[5] If philosophy is education for grownups, as Cavell has argued so persuasively, it is because it continues to live in the unresolved tensions, conflicts, and affiliations between this child and this adult. That is, if philosophy is education for grownups, it is so because the recovery of our silenced questions, our blocked queries, our disquieting dissatisfaction with the inevitable frustration resulting from being told when we were children, "This is simply how it is done," is integral to the modes of interrogation and reflection we, at least some of us both within and without the professionalized discourses of academic philosophers, are disposed to identify as philosophy.

Section 217 of Wittgenstein's *Investigations* is hence, conceivably, imaginably, the fragment of a dialogue involving a child and an adult. To imagine it as such is to pull into the *center* of the drama a figure critical for an understanding of such works as *Philosophical Investigations* and *On Certainty*.[6] In *A Pitch of Philosophy*, Cavell sets the context for the recollection of this figure in the most poignant terms imaginable, for it is in unblinkingly autobiographical terms. In recalling his own childhood, he recalls the contrasts between his parents growing

> frighteningly polarized between his [father's] continuing rages
> . . . and her periodic silences . . . between his contempt for the
> world and self-contempt for failures in it, and her disdain for the
> world and for its ineffectual praise of her local successes in it;
> between the inexpressiveness of his wild love of the eloquence he
> would never have, and the glad unsayability of her knowledge of
> the utter expressiveness of music.[7]

It is understandable why such a child would withdraw into himself and also why he would try "to escape quarrels that were meant to have no ending."[8] Cavell arguably sees himself in the child imaginable in the folds of the *Investigations*, caught between his parents making impossible demands upon each other, their son, and indeed the world.[9] In any event, the figure of a child being addressed by, perhaps receiving a response to a question from, an adult is integral to Cavell's refiguration of Wittgenstein's *Investigations*.

> A comparable isolation, and absence of voice, cloaks the teacher and the student to whom the teacher of the *Investigations* is inclined to say, yet refrains from saying, "This is simply what I do." It is such an experience that has led me to the child in the quotation from Augustine's *Confessions* that opens Wittgenstein's *Investigations*—hence the child that recurs throughout the *Investigations*—as invisible to the elders among whom it moves, attempting to divine speech for itself, and as in a position of isolation and unintelligibility so complete as to reveal childhood as such a state akin to madness.[10]

In a pattern familiar to parents and teachers alike, justification is sought and one is given, and then, what is given itself elicits a question regarding what justifies *it*. But justification comes to an end somewhere—reasons give out and, most likely, our patience gives out even before our reasons do. The appeal to *what is done*, to our practices, is here sounded not in the confident voice of the pragmatist, especially the Deweyan, but in the uncertain voice of an exemplar all too conscious of limitations, doubts, and inadequacy. The impertinence of the child is, in effect, to call the adult into question, to render maturity, at least in this form or this instance, questionable. Here is an invincible form of skepticism, a recurrent pattern of doubt.

Our initiation into language[11] is a complex affair in which desire as much as doubt and affirmation, affection and aggression, seize linguistic media for their pressing articulation. Not infrequently, both parties are *at a loss*—a loss of words and much else. How abiding is this loss, how deeply marring, personally stultifying? How difficult is it to gauge the measure of this loss, of what has not been said, what has not been accomplished—or secured or rescued?

Whatever may be the answers to these questions in the actual circumstances where they inevitably arise and often *erupt*, the two figures remain in the presence of each other, not utterly despairing, not completely exhausted. Moreover, Cavell is able, in reference to the relationship between just these figures, to articulate in a telling and indeed moving voice his "idea of philosophical tragedy": "the child *returning* with a question and I unresponsive, unable so much (it is very much) as to provide the assurance of my listening."[12] Such a tragedy recalls that on which Cavell has written so insightfully: for the impulse to avoid such tragedy is, as much as anything else, "the fear to be seen in old Lear, unable to bear his children's silence, unable equally to bear what she has, and has not, to say."[13] The failure of adults to provide even the assurance that they are listening amounts to nothing less than the failure of indicating their presence. In other words, the child in the absence of such assurance is almost certain to feel abandoned and alone.

"There Is No Place Like Home"/There Is No Such Place as *Home*

Cavell's insights on Wittgenstein and Lear connect us with a memorable yet unsettling claim made by Salman Rushdie about the *Wizard of Oz*. The relevance of Rushdie's reflections to the foregoing is uncannily direct and, indeed, intimate. This relevance is nowhere more evident than in the guiding insight of one of Rushdie's autobiographical reflections ("Out of Kansas"): "*The Wizard of Oz* is a film whose driving force is the inadequacy of adults, even of good adults; a film that shows us how the weakness of grownups forces children to take control of their own destinies . . . and so, ironically, [to] grow up themselves."[14] Most children learn very early that many adults are untrustworthy and that even the most admirable, often especially the most admirable and lovable, are unreliable, at least regarding what matters most (such as saving one's dog from the clutches of a witch). That is, children learn *as children* that they are on their own. When they cry for their mothers or fathers, they do so *as agents* suffering from their improvisational exertions, animated as much by un-bounded longing and disordered desires as anything else. In any event, Rushdie seems to have accurately identified "the driving force" of the *Wizard of Oz*: the childhood realization that adults—not only Auntie Em and Uncle Henry but, more importantly, the Wizard him-self—are *inadequate* as judged by all the available measures, those of the adults themselves as much as those by which childhood is effec-tively defined (measures bound up with unbounded longing and im-possible requests).

Rushdie concludes this wonderful essay by stressing:

> Now, as I look at the movie again, I have become a fallible adult. Now I am a member of the tribe of *imperfect parents who cannot listen to their children's voices*. I, who no longer have a father, have become a father instead. Now it is my fate to be unable to satisfy the longings of a child. And this is the last and most terrible lesson of the film: that there is one final, unexpected rite of passage. In the end, ceasing to be children, we all become magicians without magic, exposed conjurers, with only our simple humanity to get us through.[15]

In Rushdie's judgment (though in Cavell's terms), we see here "the human effort to escape our humanness" and also the necessity to re-sist this effort insofar as it drives us to posit a transcendental ground for human practices and, indeed, human existence.[16] As it is discern-ible in Rushdie's autobiographical reflections, resisting the drive to escape our humanness[17] demands a humbling acknowledgment: in becoming magicians without magic, exposed conjurers, with only our uncertain humanity to get us through, "We [the adults] are the hum-bugs now."[18]

In the essay from which I have been quoting, Rushdie notes that the series of books concerning Oz concludes with one in which Doro-thy not only returns to Oz, but Auntie Em and Uncle Henry join her there. Moreover, Dorothy becomes a princess. The recollection of this outcome prompts him to assert:

> So Oz finally *becomes* home. The imagined world becomes the ac-tual world, as it does for all of us, because the truth is that, once

we leave our childhood places and start to make up our lives, armed only with what we know and who we are, we come to understand that the real secret of the ruby slippers is not that "there's no place like home" but, rather, that there is no longer any such place as home—except, of course, for the homes we make, or the homes that are made for us, in Oz. Which is anywhere—and everywhere—except the place from which we began.[19]

Home can but designate our place(s) of origin, but these are the places from which—like Dorothy from Kansas—we are inevitably exiled.

It is telling and pertinent that the place from which Rushdie began, according to his recollection, is one in which he as a child was silenced and also one in which his fears regarding this movie were not acknowledged, his perspective not glimpsed.

In the place from which I began, after all, I watched the film from the child's—Dorothy's—point of view. I experienced, with her, the frustration of being brushed aside by Uncle Henry and Auntie Em, busy with their grownup counting. Like all adults, they couldn't focus on what was really important: namely, the threat to Toto. I ran away with her and then ran back. Even the shock of discovering that the Wizard was a humbug was a shock I felt as a child. . . . Perhaps, too, I felt something deeper, something I couldn't then articulate; perhaps some half-formed suspicion (one likely to grow into a deep-rooted skepticism) about grownups was being confirmed.[20]

As we are reminded by Rushdie and Cavell, even the silenced child cannot be erased. But, however much philosophy the day after tomorrow may be successful in refusing to cede to our culture the having of our experience, that is, however successful it might be in the recovery of everyday experience in its surprisingly subtle and expansive significance, philosophy the day *before* this one, and the day before that, and (again) the day before *that*, running indefinitely into our personal pasts, is a day in which children have been silenced as well as hurt in large and small, horrific and seemingly trivial ways. It is a day in which each one of us might have inadvertently, even unknowingly, brushed aside a question or observation, a suggestion or even a gift—put before us by a child. It is assuredly a day in which a child has been brushed aside or nullified in some other way, hence, one in which he or she has been silenced, at least momentarily and, more likely, much longer than that. For instance, the threat of having one's dog seized (or arrogated) by a powerful, malevolent force or individual, coupled with the inability of good people (say, Aunt Em and Uncle Henry) to have the resources to stand up effectively for what the child desires with all her heart, is the kind of experience responsible for engendering the longing to travel far from home. There *must* be a place where the child's deepest longings and even wildest desires (not least of all those for efficacy and importance) can come true, a place where the child as such and as an imaginable adult can be the effective, ingenious actor or hero. The child at such moments, caught in such dramas, is availed the opportunity to become what she is.

Cavell reveals a very different tornado and fantastic realm in his youth in the form of a recollection, in "Philosophy and the Arrogation of Voice." This recollection is all too likely to be overlooked by professional philosophers, yet it bears in a complex yet illuminating way upon some of the themes just sounded. After learning in February of his senior year in high school that he had accumulated the necessary credits for graduation, he spent his nights working as a musician. While most nights he played in a commercial band, "on incomparably the more significant, rarer, of them," he "played lead alto in an otherwise black swing band, the biggest and best swing band anywhere near Sacramento, playing music so advanced, in addition to its advanced racial mixture, that it was unhireable."[21] The world of jazz can seem as foreign to an outsider as the Land of Oz. Even so, this focus on jazz provides us with an invaluable perspective from which to explore the imaginably intergenerational exchange in which one of the elders is forced to acknowledge, in justification of a performance, "This is simply how *I* play." As it actually took place, especially during the middle decades of the twentieth century, such musical exchanges exhibit as forcefully as any other phenomenon "the wild intelligence of American popular culture."[22] They also provide us with the kind of encounter in which the elders cannot help but feel the fear of old Lear, also one in which the young cannot escape the always proximate possibility of being silenced for life in some crucial respect. For the purpose of probing the ongoing struggle to compose oneself, to acquire one's own voice, is it possible to conjure a more arresting image than a young Jewish adolescent in Sacramento in the 1940s playing lead alto sax in a black swing band? Is it possible to identify a more telling experience to interrogate?

The young Stanley Goldstein was the outsider[23] who might have felt more at home in this swing band than anywhere else (it is, at least, hard for me to resist drawing this inference from what he says about the other settings of his early life), the precocious youth animated by complex longings (not least of all joining the army despite a readily detectable physical disability—"a scarred tympanum"[24] disqualifying him from military service), a youth who indeed might have had in his *experience* of playing with these musicians one of the most memorable experiences of human community as an ongoing negotiation and, therein, fulfilling undertaking.

As a youth, in any event, Cavell experienced the necessity of making a home in a new place, since his family moved from Atlanta to Sacramento (spending the first decade of his life in Georgia and the second in California). And he was himself the son of Jewish immigrants from Central Europe who sought to make a home for themselves in America. What is true of this individual and his family is, in some measure and manner, true of all of us. For human consciousness is virtually by definition *exilic* consciousness. Such familial and personal experience seems to have enabled Cavell to make himself at home in the black swing band. Regarding such matters as home and dislocation, exile and return, again the words of both Rushdie and Cavell invite deeper consideration.

In a review of Cavell's *Philosophy the Day After Tomorrow*, Michael Wood integrates these themes. He concludes, "Why praise Astaire?" by quoting Cavell himself.[25] Wood is struck especially by questions guiding Cavell's reflections in the book and no less by Cavell's answers to his own questions. Do we, Wood recalls in his review, " 'recognize what we are capable of in the undramatic, repetitive, daily confrontations' " to which the more dramatic renderings of Hollywood movies and Shakespearean plays call our attention? If we are candid enough to acknowledge what so often goes on in such confrontations, we shall

> see that in our slights of one another, in an expressed or disguised meanness of thought, in a hardness of glance, a willful misconstrual, a shading of loyalty, a dismissal of intention, a casual indiscriminateness of praise or blame in any one of the countless signs of skepticism with respect to reality, the separateness of another—we run the risk of suffering, or dealing, little deaths every day.[26]

The little ones, the children, run the greater risk of suffering such little deaths, though such slights are for them experientially far from slight or little.

At the conclusion of his review, then, Wood observes that "What philosophy has to do, says Cavell, and what he has been doing in his relative isolation, is pay attention to language not only as the place of meaning and of words as forms of action, but [also] as the place of desire, the articulated realm where our wishes get expressed or get lost"—where our longings get enacted and then, all too likely, brushed aside, the site where "little deaths" are endured or perpetrated. Though not intended, the link with jazz could not be more salient (and its salience is brought home by Cavell's own words, the ones quoted by Wood at the conclusion of his review): " 'The one uttering the passion must have the passion' and the one 'singled out' to receive this declaration 'must respond here and now . . . and respond in kind." But the passionate utterance of passion is quite distinct from the distinctive class of utterances to which Austin so memorably called our attention (one of the contributions by Austin on which Cavell has written so insightfully). And Cavell himself memorably marks just this difference: "A performative utterance is an offer of participation in the order of law. And perhaps we can say: a passionate utterance is an invitation to improvisation in the disorders of desire." Do we actually hear such invitations to improvisation anywhere more clearly and vibrantly than in the voicings of jazz musicians, in that still vital form of the wild intelligence of American popular culture? Indeed, in the ensemble improvisations of, especially, the accomplished elders, the actual grownups. Do we not witness an activity, at once "cooperative and competitive," a communal celebration of the irreducibility of the individual voice?

In the *Investigations*, Wittgenstein famously advised his readers: "Don't think. Look and see." In a conversation with a younger musician, Charlie Parker himself advised: "Don't think. Quit thinking." Parker might have added: Listen—and then listen again, only this time even more carefully. (Parker was himself a tornado, not one cutting across but coming out of Kansas.) Here the performance is itself "an offer of participation," because it is first and foremost "an invitation to the improvisation in the disorders of desire."

The performer who may serve here as a foil for the youthful Stanley Goldstein (aka Stanley Cavell)[27] is Stan Getz. From various accounts, Getz appears also to have been much like Anis Ahmed Rushdie, who, in the words of his son, "was a magical parent of young children, but he was prone to explosions, thunderous rages, bolts of emotional lightning, puffs of dragon smoke, and other menaces of the type also practiced by [the Wizard of] Oz."[28] Salman Rushdie acknowledges that, and although for years he thought "my Wizard was a very bad man indeed," he came halfway through his life to realize "he, too, was a good man but a very bad Wizard." His life was full of "fits and fights." This makes the portrait of Stan Getz with his son, on the cover of one of his albums, all the more poignant.

The Refusal to Cede One's Own Experience to Culture or Anything Else

I have already mentioned Wood's review entitled "Why Praise Astaire?" Allow me an autobiographical recollection: In typing on an index card the title of this piece "Why Praise Astaire?" I actually typed "Why Praise Cavell?"! When I went to file this card, I noted my Freudian slip. But, then and now, it seems fortunate, for it formulates a worthwhile question: "Indeed, why praise Cavell?" The beginning of an answer to this question might be this: Because his is a life given to life, thus to recovery and reparation, to recollection but also to forgetting (not least of all, letting go and going on, remaining attentive but also wandering off)—to natality and thus to mortality. In writing about William Wordsworth, Cavell stresses, "our powers of being drawn from elsewhere ('we come from afar'), of being interested, in heaven or in earth, are deadened. Otherwise we would not require birth, or poetry, or philosophy."[29] Our powers of being drawn into the world are recovered, our interest renewed, our passions improvised, above all, by the disorder of our desires (more accurately, the disorder*ing* of our desires.)

Philosophy the day after tomorrow is, at once, a continuation of and a rupture with philosophy the day before this one and the day before that. It is an ongoing attempt to come to terms with the impossible self who we were and still are, the one making not only unreasonable but also impossible demands upon the world, most of all upon those whom we love (and, in this instance, most of all in dictating the terms in which their love for us must be defined, the form in which it must be given). If anyone is in danger of being unable to deal with "the fear to be seen in old Lear," it is most likely the *very* young child. If anyone is in danger of falling silent before the impossible demands of the infinite longings and unbounded desires of children, especially our own—that is, if anyone is most likely in danger of inhabiting the entombing silence of Cordelia—*or* uttering the false words of her sisters, it is almost certainly an adult, especially one off to the studio to cut an album or to a conference to give a paper or to the café to revise a novel. Philosophy is education for adults, in part, because it is a recollection—and reenactment—of childhood. Cavell is explicit on this point:

> The child is a philosopher because we are to learn from the fact of childhood [and this means, at bottom, learning from the *fate*

of our natality] that we are the bearers of our childhood [and, here again, by virtue of our natality we are the subjects of our inheritances and indeed dependencies], Participation and Recollection; and initially by recollecting and participating in our own childhood.[30]

But these will be specifically philosophical, not merely psychological, modes of *experience* and recovery, participation and recollection. "These will be [in particular] *philosophical* ways of letting childhood go, of bearing childhood as gone, as having become what we are, sharing our fate."[31] While philosophical, they are also experiential. What is at stake in Cavell's writing is nothing less than philosophy as itself a distinctive mode of human experience, certainly not only a theory of experience. This is perhaps the deepest reason why considerations of jazz as the *experience* of contesting inheritances, transforming traditions, acquiring a singular voice in contrast to and with support from rival voices, playing with the textures of temporality, and an expansive array of other factors are relevant to an appreciation of Cavell's achievement.

Such recollection and reenactment, especially as they are distinctively *philosophical* processes (or activities), are in the service of recovering the ordinary. If human life is a series of inevitable disillusionments, there is always, within our everyday engagements, the possibility of (and this is Cavell's own expression) "a happier disillusionment."[32] We live in the uncertainty of not being loved, worse, of never having been loved, truly and absolutely.[33] Here is the most inhuman—and all too human, too inescapably human—face of skepticism. Here is part of the reason why all of our losses and disappointments, our frustrations and failures, can so quickly become momentous and devastating. But we also live by such realizations that, say, this man, so tender yet volatile, so attentive yet (in a flash) so unavailable, "too, was a good man but a very bad Wizard"—or this woman was truly a witch and, nonetheless, a very good woman and, given the cunning of history, an unimaginably good mother. Nothing less is required here than (to recall Cavell's own words) "to replace the ordinary in the light in which we live it, with its shades of the prison-house closing upon us young, and its custom lying upon us deep almost as life, a world of death, to which we are dead— replace it accordingly with freedom . . . and with lively origination, or say birth; with interest [or say passion]."[34]

Our homes become, for most of us at fateful moments in our contested lives, alien places from which exile and self-exile are difficult (if not truly impossible) to distinguish, just as our parents become strange creatures, mostly by coming into sharp focus as *human* beings (men and women rather than wizards or witches).[35] The ordinary, the commonplace, the everyday (*home* in its variable yet invariant significance) are the places from which we are exiled or self-exiled (for example, when the aggrieved parent says to child, "You left," and the aggrieved child hurls into the face of that parent, "No, you threw me out!"). In their broadly human and also pointedly philosophical significance, the ordinary, the commonplace, the everyday are *experienced*, first and foremost, as loss. This makes home what we have so fatefully made it, the site of lost familiarity, abandoned intimacy,[36] the place wherein I am most skeptical regarding my place (the one where the question of belonging here—and hence longing to be here—are more deeply perplexing and troubling than this question regarding any other site or locus). There is no question that the everyday is also that keeping us afloat, even holding us aloft, that by which we are sustained and nourished, enveloped and enlivened. Moreover, the little and not so little deaths woven into the fabric of the quotidian are roughly matched by the epiphanies and graciousness not infrequently marking our transient days.[37] Even so, the presence, possibilities, and significance of everyday revelations and aids are brought home to us most acutely upon their eclipse or loss.

The everyday is, hence, the scene of loss but also that holding within itself the only possibilities and resources of the recovery of the everyday. Philosophy arises in this very place, in the everyday precisely as a scene of loss.[38] These points bear directly, albeit complexly, on the ethos of home, as interrogated by Stanley Cavell, Naomi Scheman, and others in the wake of Wittgenstein, also by Salman Rushdie,

David Rieff, and still others with no reference to Wittgenstein.[39] Scheman's reflections are informed by an explicit acknowledgment of her subject position, just as Cavell's are informed by his autobiographical exercises. One question is whether we are at home in our own experience. Another is whether experience as lived through and by us is intelligible in the world we understand, or imagine, or indeed experience (in other words, whether our experience is at home in our world). Such questions obviously bear upon the topics of home, inheritance, and intelligibility (thus, always at least by implication upon the topic of self-understanding)—hence, exile, disinheritance, unintelligibility, and self-opacity. For the moment, however, I want to reflect on the home of jazz itself, though as a way of sounding just these themes.

All That Jazz

Jazz is, in a straightforward sense, today *more at home* in Europe and Asia than it is in America. But we have in no small measure disinherited the music arguably most critical to questions of inheritance, hence to the question—or problem—of America. When asked about professional philosophy in the United States, in particular, about the then (1994) emerging currents, Cavell began his response by stressing: "The problem is always, ultimately, America itself."[40] America is, after all, the home of immigrants in which questions of immigration are hotly debated, indeed, in which the influx of immigrants is righteously condemned. It is as much as anything a tradition of antitraditionalism concealing itself, mostly from itself, *as a tradition* by proclaiming the myth that here we can perpetually begin anew *without models.*[41] In response to another question in another interview, one concerning what he finds "philosophically interesting in opera," moreover, how this interest in music might relate to his fascination with films, Cavell notes: American musical comedy "is not just popular art. It's not high art. But it is a popular high art of a sort of high popularity that America is known for being able to create." Then he immediately adds: "These matters that were for years dismissible, like musical comedy and *like jazz*, dismissible as film used to be, are becoming less dismissible."[42] What he *then* goes on to say is also critical for our topic: "To ask me, therefore, what my interests in such things as jazz and musical comedy are is to ask me what my interest in America is, and that question is really all over my work now [the interview was published in 1999], and I want to be able to say something more about it." Insofar as *his* autobiography and philosophy "are to be told in terms of each other," then the question of America is bound up with that of jazz no less than that of film. But he turns from this family of musical genres to the one on which he has focused more intensely, recalling that he opened his course on opera by asking "how an American could hope to claim *the depth of experience* of opera, to write about it usefully, given the fact that America is not a culture that has produced opera until very recently."[43]

The issue for Cavell is, at bottom, always one concerning "the depth of experience," the quality, texture, and integrity of our engagement with, say, a text or practice, ritual or trauma, loss or discovery. This focus of concern *is* experience, though experience understood broadly enough to encompass the activities of writing and reading, especially when these activities are interwoven with such processes as mourning and recollection. I know of no more illuminating articulation of this central feature (of what is arguably the "driving force") of Cavell's philosophical authorship than a text responding to the question, "Why praise Astaire?" We might paraphrase this question: Why, *as philosophers*, should we spill ink on Fred Astaire or *Stella Dallas*, or (for that matter) Charlie Parker or *Now's the Time*—"Why not chalk up the experience of pleasure and value [derived from seeing Astaire dance or hearing Parker play] to an idiosyncrasy of my own, and of whomever happens to share it?"[44] To begin with, such experiences do not feel to be utterly idiosyncratic. "*If I am to possess my own experience*," Cavell adds, including such experiences as listening to opera and jazz, musical comedies and Hollywood melodramas (I might add), "*I cannot afford to cede it to my culture as that culture stands. I must find ways to insist upon it, if I* find it unheard, ways to let the culture confront itself in me, driving me some distance to distraction."[45]

How are we to come into possession of our own experience? This is a peculiar yet perfectly intelligible question concerning the complex fate of human inheritance. It bears as much on the very *having* of experience as the *significance* of our engagements, involvements, and entanglements. We might regret, with T. S. Eliot, that

> We had the experience but missed the meaning;
> And approach to the meaning restores the experience
> In a different form.[46]

But the deeper regret would have been to miss the experience itself, often by being preoccupied with its significance, especially as expressible in established modes of utterance, everyday forms of articulation.[47]

Jazz is not so much *about* the having of experience as it is the very having of experience in which what this means is interrogated. It is, in some sense, skepticism *par excellence*. It is uniquely the music of this country, even if (to repeat) jazz so rarely finds a home here. Accordingly, interest in jazz cannot be severed from interest in America, from what this ever new yet ever unapproachable place and culture means for us here and now. In turn, these interests cannot be severed from questions concerning home and inheritance, thus ones regarding exile and dispossession, diaspora and disinheritance.

Human Habitation from a Diasporic Perspective

Allow me to turn to an author who has written insightfully about this topic but who complains about *not* being at home in Cavell's discussion of home.[48] In "Forms of Life: Mapping the Rough Ground," Naomi Scheman not only takes up the topic of home in much the manner as does Rushdie but also takes it up in reference to *The Wizard of Oz*.[49] She does so without mentioning Rushdie, though she does engage Cavell in this context. Indeed, her endeavor to recover the meaning of home is here one indebted to but critical of Cavell's reflections on this topic.

Scheman implies that what we need, philosophically and personally, is "that the world is my world, that it makes sense to me, [also] that I make sense in it, that I inhabit it with others who are intelligible to me and to whom I am intelligible."[50] But this very demand "leads words away from our uses of them not capriciously, but because those uses [themselves] are seen as misleading, as not giving what we think we need of our words, be that definiteness of sense or assurance of reference." Somehow she imagines this is a criticism of Cavell. Like him, she is interested in foregrounding a distinctive preoccupation of the philosophical genius on whom both write so insightfully: "Wittgenstein was concerned, throughout his work, with questions of where and how the self stands to the world."[51] In losing my knowledge of my way around a world I share with others, I inevitably also lose my sense of how to identify my concerns, to express my questions, and to understand myself.[52] I become unintelligible to myself in no small measure because I am unintelligible to others, because I cannot make myself understood on my terms in their ears. Our shared language not only exacerbates but also (in a way) partly generates these difficulties and impasses, not because what I am so desperately trying to articulate is inherently private but because it is insistently communicable (what I am struggling to articulate demands of me articulation, imposes upon me a task). The words at my disposal work to frustrate my efforts; of greater moment, the *world* as my habitat does not allow for the forms of expression I am driven to craft, along with the modes of experience themselves I suppose myself *to have* (more specifically, to enjoy, to suffer, to bear, and in countless other ways to live through [*Erlebnis*]). In brief, my world *as I experience* it nullifies me and my experiences (think here of Scheman's own example, the young gay man in Harvey Fierstein's 1988 film *Torch Song Trilogy* who attempts, while in the cemetery with his mother, to recite Kaddish over the grave of a lover who has died of AIDS and, as a result, is accused by her of blaspheming her marriage and their religion). The grief he feels is inexpressible in the world of *his* experience, but it demands expression; it insists upon an adequate and, thus, a public articulation.

The link between intelligibility and communicability can become attenuated but never severed. Given the undeniability and (for most of us) inescapability of such an experience of the world, Scheman invokes a diasporic understanding of human identity and also of human habitation. In direct opposition to Cavell's invocation of Kierkegaard in this context,[53] she recalls "the task of Diasporic Jews"—that of finding "oneself properly in the world precisely not 'at home.'"[54] This prompts her to suggest that "we can think about our words as diasporically linked to home, building on a diasporic identity . . . in which home is neither any presently existing location nor some place of transcendence."[55] Such a home is never antecedently *given*, not even readily available. So it is that Scheman reminds us, at the end of her essay, that: "At the end of *The Wizard of Oz* Dorothy and the others appear before the Wizard to ask for what they take themselves to lack: a heart, a brain, courage, and the way home." Dorothy had landed in Oz because of her "yearning for some place both obscurely grander and more in keeping with a dimly perceived sense of a 'true self' inexpressible in Kansas," not because of the tornado (the inner forces of longing are, in their usually more subtle ways, as propulsive as the outer fury of nature).[56] All Dorothy has to do in order to return home is acknowledge her desire to do so: the ticket home is simply the public acknowledgment of one's personal desire. But Scheman tellingly notes, just in the face of such advice: "All very well and good, but what about those of us who cannot quite bring ourselves to click our ruby slippers and intone 'there's no place like home'? We may see through the illusions of Oz, give up on wizards, and still not be able to return to Kansas."[57] Indeed, if we see through Oz and give up on all other wizards as well, it is almost certainly the case that we are exiled from the home of our childhood forever. There is no more childish thing than home in the nostalgic sense.[58] In contrast, there is, at least for Scheman (and I would concur with her on this point), no more experientially compelling understanding of home than that forged in the diasporic experiences of various peoples. But Cavell is hardly saying that we can be safely returned home (transported back to Kansas) by simply acknowledging the place of the everyday as the only site of human striving, desire, and passion. Rather, he is acknowledging, in the enactment of a form of skepticism, the theoretically undecidable meanings of home. At the same time, he is bearing witness to the inescapability of practical decisions in the face of theoretical undecidability. Given his subtle involvement in, and "skeptical" appropriations of, the traditions by which he is partly borne, also variously nullified, his position does not reduce to a form of decisionism in which the blind fiats of an arbitrary will make up the actual shape of human decisions (or human decisiveness). His is so much a world of loss and longing that the illusion of a world in which one's "true self" in all of its facets might find a supportive habitat is exposed as such. But it is also a world in which a "happier disillusionment" is nearly a ubiquitous possibility. Whatever Dorothy's return to Kansas might signify, then, it does not signify anything approximate to Cavell's recovery of the everyday.

However unfair might Scheman's criticisms of Cavell's position be, important insights are offered in the course of formulating this particular critique. Above all, we must *acknowledge*: The world *as we experience* it is a place in which the self is called into question in such a way that the self and its experience become themselves questionable—and they become questionable, above all, to the self. This form of skepticism is not to be refuted: it is to be lived. This partly accounts for the slippage in Cavell's use of this protean word. On the one hand, he identifies skepticism as "the denial of the need to listen. It's the refusal of the ear. Skepticism denies that perfection is available through the human ear, through the human sensibility."[59] On the other hand, it is easy to imagine (from Cavell's own perspective) a form of skepticism, like that exemplified in Shakespeare's plays, in which the rough-and-tumble of self-and-world is an engagement in which the identity of both self and world is continually threatened. Moreover, it is a fateful entanglement in which the identity of the one requires identifications, thus intelligibility, in the other. The self has an inevitable stake in the world (for without an arena of action there is no possibility of the self being an actor—and without this possibility there is no chance of the self becoming what it is). On the other hand, the world makes multifarious, insistent, and unavoidable claims on the self. Self and world are accordingly of a piece. Their disintegration is not perfectly synchronized, but the implosion of the one is inseparably linked to that of the other. "The recovery from loss [and, here, it is always ultimately the loss of self and world] is, in Emerson, as in Freud and in Wittgenstein, a finding of the world, a returning of it, to it." But, as Cavell goes on to say, the "price is necessarily to give something up, to let go of something, to suffer one's poverty."[60] Such is the cost of our inheritance: our inheritances exact their own abandonment, and only thus do we stand a chance of coming into possession of these inheritances. For example, Lester Young was appropriated by Charlie Parker only through the younger musician's painstaking *abandonment* of the elder player's incomparable voicings. And it is to their invitations to improvisation that I now turn, by way of conclusion.

Conclusion: The Refusal to Cede One's Own Experience (Reprise)

The aversive thinking and relentless skepticism exhibited in American transcendentalists such as Emerson and Thoreau is also evident in such distinctively American musicians as Thelonious Monk and Charlie Parker, Miles Davis and John Coltrane, Sonny Rollins and Jackie MacLean. No one helps us to understand the importance and intricacy of such thinking and skepticism as does Cavell. In this sense (to repeat), skepticism is to be not refuted but enacted, time and again. The living of this skepticism is integral to the writings of Cavell. Indeed, these writings are nothing less than the staging and enactment of such skepticism. But these doubts are lived for the sake of life, for the purpose of focusing and intensifying experience—for that of refusing to cede one's experience to a culture that makes the possession, the very having of this experience, such an arduous and precarious process—more exactly, such a demanding and uncertain *task*.

Here, then, is *an authorship and indeed life given to experience and life.* This means a life given to the reparation of the world, the recovery of the ordinary, and the recollection of childhood. Regarding the recollection of childhood in this connection, it must be "the discovery of the child's voice," especially where it is least suspected to be present. In conclusion, then, Stanley Cavell is a philosopher who gives every indication of knowing in his bones that there is no such place as home—but the name of that place is the *ordinary*. The invocation of this name most properly assumes a form analogous to that unique manifestation of "the wild intelligence of American popular culture"—in a word, jazz. For the invocation of this name, properly uttered (thus, passionately expressed),[61] is *an invitation to improvisation* in which the bounds of propriety and impropriety, also those in which attachment to and assault on the elders, are being imaginatively renegotiated and reenacted, *here and now*. Such invocation is not so much an act as a process, though a process in which acts of recognition and acknowledgment, of mourning and recollection, are needed in order *to go on*. While a process, it is as much as anything desirous to avoid "losing the name of action."[62]

The *experience* of playing or listening to jazz is just that—an experience. It is an experience in which the boundaries between performers and audiences are often blurred, in which the audience is drawn into the performance and the performers are drawn out of themselves. The accent must fall on process, action, extemporaneity, and (to repeat) experience. In "The Names of Action," Timothy Gould notes: "Almost anywhere you turn in the work of Stanley Cavell you will encounter some aspect of the problem of human action."[63] In America especially, human action as entangled in a creative appropriation of conflicting inheritances, made especially difficult by some of these inheritances being themselves established forms of *creative* endeavor, is nothing less than the problem of America itself, the animating drive of jazz performers, and an abiding focus of philosophical concern, especially for those of us who have learned by reading Cavell how to *hear* the nuances and dissonances so much a part of our discourses on action. In just this respect, the experience of jazz provides us with resources for the understanding of human action as such. Connected to this, the acquisition of a voice—including a distinctive style of acting, ultimately a unique manner of being in the world—

cannot avoid being, in some measure, an arrogation (a seizing of what is not one's own and, beginning with such an *act* of seizure, making it one's own and, in the process, making oneself someone other). But, just as Cavell in "Philosophy and the Arrogation of Voice" expressed the desire, some day, to describe what it meant for him to play lead alto in a black swing band, so all I can do here is express the desire to return to these points and develop them more fully on another occasion.

When we realize this, it seems not unimportant to *hear, in general,* how in Cavell's writings "philosophy and autobiography are to be told in terms of each other" and, *in particular,* how the figure of an intellectually and musically precocious adolescent, playing "lead alto saxophone in an otherwise black swing band" (indeed, "the biggest and best swing band anywhere near Sacramento"), sounds (better, resounds) when he puts down the sax but also the pen of the composer, taking up instead other texts and traditions, other modes of articulation and forms of sounding. In "Philosophy and the Arrogation of Voice," he tells us: "Certain questions of ear run through my life,"[64] and, I may add, *thus,* through his writings. He also expresses a desire I hope he will fulfill: "Some day I must describe what it meant to play lead alto saxophone with such a group; but privileged as I felt by their acceptance of my playing, I was at a different place in a different life" from the other members of that innovative group.[65]

If I have done anything to highlight facets of how questions of ear run through Stanley Cavell's writings, especially neglected facets (say, the ear attuned to hearing the voice of the child in every experience), and *if* I have done anything to make the work of jazz relevant to our interrogation—and arrogation—of experience, especially as the work of such interrogation is itself refashioned by Cavell, then the seemingly chaotic strains of my probings and affirmations might in their own way be an instance of music. If so, my claim on your time and attention will have been *justified.* And, like justification itself, even improvisations have to end somewhere.

REMARKS FROM DISCUSSION

CAVELL: I was surprised in my reading of Emerson to find myself speaking of him as an immigrant and wondered if this would be taken as fanciful. But then there is the emphasis in Thoreau on leaving—everywhere, incessant leaving, always. And here Heidegger is helpful, because Thoreau's leaving has both the Heideggerian leaving of *Gelassenheit* and the surface sense of leaving: leaving things as they are and leaving them behind. And this is again something that, I think, is in Wittgenstein: philosophy leaves everything as it is. Of course that sounds quietist, that sounds conformist, but how can one be just satisfied to say that, knowing how complex a figure and thinker Wittgenstein is? That that is all he wants to say? Philosophy leaves everything as it is, so don't touch it? To leave it as it is is a task for him. What he doesn't want is for philosophy to change things unnaturally, to change things mechanically, to change things destructively, and we know enough about ideology to know how it can change things destructively. Of course, in Thoreau this also means: keep the ploughs out of here and stop digging up the ground. But he doesn't expect everybody to live his life. He opens the book with this extraordinary sense of the strangeness of the world. The making of the world strange to us, that it has become uninhabitable—the combination of that calling with a willingness for immigrancy is deep in me. I feel that: Emerson, the Jew. But also the end of *Walden*, the very last sentences—"There is more day to dawn. The sun is but a morning star"— are an opening to allowing the world to be strange to you, not forcing it to be a home when it isn't. They are also a tip as to how you can allow there to be a tomorrow, how to allow a future to happen—a topic that was dear to Nietzsche's heart, dear to Emerson's heart, dear to every reformer's heart. How can we open the future to a better future? And in Thoreau it is through a process of mourning. It is painful. And in order to leave the future, to allow it to be inheritable, in order to give it to a future generation, you have to allow yourself to recognize that the way you have inhabited it is one that is going to be departed from.

CAVELL: I wouldn't be at ease with the idea that children are philosophers so you should sort of do philosophy problems with them. In my own limited experience with children, certainly they are having problems that eventually, we know, as they flower, will become philosophical issues. And they *can* be answered, but in the right kind of spirit—without trying to solve the problem but without denying them. It gives me the creeps when certain kinds of adults are very impatient with them, perhaps dismissing them as silly. There is real work to be done there. Where *does* light go when it's out? I just finished editing my autobiography, so I'm full of memories about these kinds of things, but when my four-year-old says to me, "I have sadness in my life," I don't want to pry, but I want to know what it is. So I ask my son a question, and he says, "I don't want people to kill animals." So you think "What animals are they killing?" and he replies, "They are killing whales." And he says, "You don't realize how hard a whale's life is." And so forth. That's one sort of question. Pretty soon it's going to be, "Why do we eat them?" And I think that those things can be addressed as though they are heartfelt problems, not just words. So what is the bargain you are establishing to be? A holding environment? That's what Winnicott calls it, and a classroom is also a kind of holding environment. I mean you are not going to settle everything here, but we're going to admit that we're in this mess together. Some things we can do, some things we can't do, but some things we're going to hold on to.

SEVEN

PERFECTIONISM'S EDUCATIONAL ADDRESS
René V. Arcilla

Like many professional school administrators, I have had to participate in my share of curricular debates about what constitutes the right balance between collegiate courses in the major and in the liberal arts. In my experience, such debates are not entirely reducible to clashes of material interests; they express reasonable differences of opinion concerning the respective values of these courses, values that must be responsibly reckoned next to soaring tuition costs. For the educator in a profession, the value of what he or she teaches depends instrumentally on the acquisition and mastery of a rewarding position. For the liberal educator, the noninstrumental quality of the teaching, the fact that it is supposed to foster "learning for learning's sake," makes estimating its value harder. Supporters often have recourse to claims that learning how to learn for its own sake will, in the end, produce more adaptive and creative workers and entrepreneurs and more critically engaged citizens. Yet in such arguments, the idea of learning for learning's sake threatens to lose any strict meaning. Defenders of liberal education, then, particularly in the face of competitors for their resources, can find themselves in a quandary. Either they must adopt some version of their opponent's instrumentalist reasoning, explaining how the consequential link between their teaching and general virtues like creativity or critical thinking is as strong and vital as that between professional training and professional success, or they must spell out more rigorously and persuasively the truly noninstrumental value of this education.

Let me try to do the latter. Why is learning for its own sake important for us? Because we are learning beings. My thesis is that unless we properly and constantly exercise our learning nature, much as we do our physical bodies, our development will stall and our lives more rapidly deteriorate. Of course, at issue in the curricular debate above would accordingly be what counts as proper care for this nature. Could taking professional education courses? Why not? Even if this thesis could be substantiated, it is not clear that it would preserve a role for a distinct liberal-education curriculum.

Here, then, is where I have gladly found a use for some of Stanley Cavell's thinking. Since I first encountered it in *Must We Mean What We Say?* as an undergraduate in the seventies, his thinking has profoundly marked my sense of what philosophical seriousness should sound like. Cavell's recent explorations in what he calls alternatively "moral perfectionism" or "perfectionism" articulate, I find, more of the basis of this seriousness. Following his lead, I shall try to explain how perfectionist texts illuminate our learning nature even as they stimulate it. However different from and contending with one another they are, these texts share certain features that compose a genre; many of these features serve the text's central rhetorical aim of attracting and provoking a particular kind of reader. I argue that the power of perfectionism to help establish the difference between liberal and other forms of education lies in its specific mode of address to those of us who can become existentially lost.

What is perfectionism? The term is not wholly unfamiliar; we know what it means to praise, or ironically denigrate, someone for being a perfectionist. But to employ the term philosophically rather than as a psychological characterization suggests that it amounts to a worldview based on a systematic set of beliefs. Departing in this fashion from ordinary usage, we would expect *Conditions Handsome and Unhandsome*, the text in which Cavell initially takes up the term, to proceed fairly directly to elucidating perfectionism's first principles.

Cavell demurs:

> A definition of what I mean by perfectionism, Emersonian or otherwise, is not in view in what follows. Not only have I no complete list of necessary and sufficient conditions for using the term, but I have no theory in which a definition would play a useful role. I emphasize accordingly that an open-ended thematics, let me call it, of perfectionism, which I shall adumbrate in a moment, is not to my mind a mere or poor substitute for some imaginary, essential definition of the idea that transcends the project of reading and thematization I am undertaking here. This project, in its possible continuations, itself expresses the interest I have in the idea.[1]

Unlike, say, utilitarianism or Lamarckism, perfectionism is not a theory of some part of life. It does not need to be fully formulated first in order to be tested subsequently against experience. Indeed, it claims little explanatory power. Rather, it is more descriptive in intent, like futurism or mannerism, but it surveys works of literature and philosophy rather than the visual arts and ranges over a wider swath of history. Based on a "project of reading and thematization," the term identifies a growing collection of general features, family resemblances, that group together a number of texts.

For Cavell, perfectionism refers less to a doctrine that these texts expound than to a topic, which can arise in a variety of historical circumstances and issue in very disparate beliefs, that places the texts in conversation with one another. They may agree or disagree about how to respond to this common topic. Because he wants to avoid restricting beforehand the set of works expressing it, because he is keen to discover and explore the perfectionist theme in as many diverse texts as possible, he emphasizes that even our recognitions and descriptions of this theme must remain provisional.

> That there is no closed list of features that constitute perfectionism follows from conceiving of perfectionism as an outlook or dimension of thought embodied and developed in a set of texts spanning the range of Western culture, a conception that is odd in linking texts that may otherwise not be thought of together and open in two directions: as to whether a text belongs in the set and what feature or features in the text constitute its belonging.[2]

A few sentences after this passage from *Conditions Handsome and Unhandsome*, Cavell begins to list some representative texts of perfectionism; a couple of pages later, he lists some perfectionist features of Plato's *Republic*. Although his focus on the *Republic* raises that work to originary status, and although he is avowedly partial to Emerson's revisions, he does not present any of these listed texts and features as more central to the substance of perfectionism than any other. Plato's concern for the soul imprisoned by ignorance, Emerson's aversion to conformity, *The Philadelphia Story*'s treatment of would-be goddesses: these are all on a par as variations on what perfectionism is interested in. To get clearer about this topic, we are encouraged not to strip away inessentials but to multiply associations so as to permit regularities to come messily into view.

This caution about foreclosing the meaning of perfectionism is surely salutary, as is the desire to keep the term open to surprising applications. These need not be incompatible, though, with trying to organize as many of the observed, contingent features of perfectionism as possible around a speculative center. Such a project would seek to maintain a reflective equilibrium between these features and an overarching or core interest that for now and to some degree explains them. I am suggesting that a soft theory of perfectionism, so long as it is not invoked to rule a text out—the latter should simply be a matter of the lack of any intriguing similarities with other perfectionist texts—can help us remain clear about why we want to gather these texts together at all, about what we find significant and valuable about this genre.

So let us start to think of perfectionism as an interest that, in running through a variety of texts, links them, and that, moreover, can be comprehended as linking them for a certain purpose. Until now, I have shied away from identifying the object of this interest. Here is a passage that I find eloquently nails its essence.

> Moral Perfectionism's contribution to thinking about the moral necessity of making oneself intelligible (one's actions, one's sufferings, one's position) is, I think it can be said, its emphasis before all on becoming intelligible to oneself, as if the threat to one's moral coherence comes most insistently from that quarter, from one's sense of obscurity to oneself, as if we are subject to demands we cannot formulate, leaving us unjustified, as if our lives condemn themselves. Perfectionism's emphasis on culture or cultivation is, to my mind, to be understood in connection with this search for intelligibility, or say this search for direction in what seems a scene of moral chaos, the scene of a dark place in which one has lost one's way.[3]

Self-intelligibility. This is what the authors of the texts that comprise perfectionism are evidently looking for. They are coming from self-obscurity troubled by a sense of what is intolerable about that state, of what is morally at stake in one's having lost one's way.

Why hold that one is supposed to know one's way in the world? Why not consider the darkness surrounding one an invitation to make up a way freely, or even, if one feels like it, to curl up and fall asleep? Why believe that one's perplexity about who one is violates a moral imperative? Cavell stresses the "threat to one's moral coherence" that such a condition of lostness would pose. Unless one is intelligible to oneself—which I take to mean not that one necessarily possesses complete knowledge of who one is but rather that one experiences no serious problem understanding for practical purposes one's identity—one cannot be in good conscience confident that one is responsive enough to all the responsibilities that belong to one, let alone presume that one is in a position to judge the intelligible status of others. One cannot deliberate morally without this minimal self-confidence; a commitment to self-understanding is part of the belief in and pursuit of the moral life. This is why we may distinguish perfectionism's moral significance, as well as its educational interest that Cavell notes (and to which I will return later), by its focus on "finding one's way rather than on getting oneself or another to take the way."[4]

Compare this account of perfectionism's interest to our commonplace notion of the perfectionist character. When we call someone a perfectionist, we are usually pointing to a tendency in that person to insist that his or her actions be performed to exact specifications so as to produce proper results and that there be no settling for good-enough approximations. If he or she were to require this only of others' actions, we would suspect that person of being a hypocrite. The term thus indicates a strict commitment to some ideal and a refusal of conventional compromises with imperfection. Depending on how meaningful we find the ideal, we will consider this character heroic or neurotic; generally speaking, though, the ideal should command some degree of shared respect if we are not to dismiss the character as a mere fanatic.

Now Cavell does not so much repudiate this notion of the perfectionist as he shifts its center of gravity. For him, the idea of perfection appears on the scene, if at all, as a kind of retrospective, explanatory afterthought. What initially inspires perfectionist behavior and constantly spurs it is rather the struggle with one's own unintelligibility. Things have to be just a certain way because one is trying to discover that one has a way. (The Emersonian inflection of this stresses that one has one's own unique way.) The insistence has a searching quality. The perfectionist sensibility is exacting not because of its dogmatism but because its quest casts doubt on the usual, socially acceptable measures. The attempt to discern how one should live motivates the refusal of conventional compromises with self-obscurity.

This shift entails a revision in what we find striking about perfectionism. It is not the presence of an ideal that is out of the ordinary but the crisis in self-understanding. That someone can lose his or her way, become a stranger to himself or herself, is a scandal exposing the very roots of society. How could the common socialization process produce such a misfit? And once produced, how could such a person be receptive at all to society? What disconcerts us about the perfectionist monster is the apparition of society reproducing itself in contradiction to itself.

Of course, this is nothing compared to the inward sense of disgrace suffered by the perfectionist. The very idea that I could have lost a firm grip on my identity seems impossibly wrong. How could I be so confused, compared to everyone else absorbed by their desires and projects, about such an elementary matter like why my life is worth living? Shame would seem to be a reasonable reaction to this manifest sickness. But this hardly puts me in a position to find help. If I have truly lost my bearings to such an extreme degree, it is unlikely I will know why I should even fight this condition, let alone how. Authorities and experts may rush to my rescue. But why would I listen to them if I cannot hear myself? Whose interests do they really represent? Alternating with guilt at being engulfed by this predicament can be a paralyzing helplessness and self-surrender as society recedes further into the distance.

Cavell flags the interest in self-intelligibility as central to perfectionism, then, because this interest boils down to anxiety about one's radical imperfection. Prior to any judgments about how one measures up to some standard, one's inability to know oneself prompts unhappiness, even disgust with oneself. Lacking self-understanding, ignorant about what direction to take in one's actions, about how to live, one is liable to experience the fact that one is nevertheless alive as a mistake. Kierkegaard captures this realization in a line that J. D. Salinger uses as an epigraph to his story "Seymour—An Introduction": "It is (to describe it figuratively) as if an author were to make a slip of the pen, and as if this clerical error became conscious of being such."[5] Perfectionist texts feature an engagement with this experience. They respond to fallenness.

Proceeding from Cavell's stress on the dark place at the origin of the perfectionist interest, I have been glossing what is extraordinary about this interest, linking it not to the height of its ideal but to the depth of its hopelessness. What separates us first of all from the perfectionist is the latter's perpetuating, if largely involuntary, skepticism (a longtime concern of Cavell's), skepticism about available ways of making sense of one's life.[6] They all appear unreliable. While such doubt may explain the perfectionist's fastidious dissatisfaction with what passes for adequate, it would seem at odds with our ordinary picture of the perfectionist insisting that things be a certain way. A purely skeptical perfectionist would be bound to be, if not self-destructive, then more withdrawn. Somehow, perfectionist assertiveness must grow out of an overcoming of this doubt, especially before it hardens into cynical assurance. But is this possible? If one is truly lost, lost too must be any confidence that one is capable of even recognizing a worthwhile, viable path for oneself; the skeptical reasoning is all-consuming. As Meno exclaims to Socrates in his moment of frustrating aporia, "But how will you look for something when you don't in the least know what it is?"[7]

The Platonic confidence that deep down the seeds of this knowledge are already inside one would have to come from the outside.

> Here also is the importance to perfectionism of the friend, the figure, let us say, whose conviction in one's moral intelligibility draws one to discover it, to find words and deeds in which to express it, in which to enter the conversation of justice.[8]

The drama of perfectionism, it turns out, involves at least two actors: one who is lost and the other, the friend, whose support enables the former to start to find his or her way. The lost person is preoccupied with his or her own unintelligibility; the perfectionist friend wants to help this person out of this condition. The friend's power to communicate, to reach and move the lost one, is thus essential. From here it is but a step to imagine the friend writing a text and the perfectionist interest emerging out of a scene of reading.

Before I elaborate on this, I should probably say a few words about why I do not envision the friend here writing a simple drug prescription, given our society's readiness to treat such dramas with pills. If one wants to aid someone who is so lost, why not directly attack the material causes of this deviation? The answer is that the friend expresses his or her friendship, in part, by taking seriously the lost one's discourse as a piece of reasoning, however flawed, rather than coding it as a collection of verbal symptoms. And why would it be essential for the friend do this? Well, suppose I were the one who was in these dire straits: how would I employ and understand my own inner and outer speech? Could I concentrate so detachedly solely on its causes, as if I were simply a talking machine? In the grip of a moral crisis of self-intelligibility, could I really let go of the idea that my speech has reasons for which I am responsible without feeling I was thereby running away from my conscience? Not me, and not, in sympathy, my friend.

So what kinds of texts do perfectionist friends produce? Or, by extension, what kinds of texts are perfectionist friends? This is the question out of which I would like to develop a theory of perfectionism. This concept, I am suggesting, designates a genre whose characteristics enable it to play the role of friend to a reader who is lost in self-obscurity.

The central characteristic of the perfectionist text on which I would like to focus is that text's mode of address. Perfectionism calls for the above kind of reader. It seeks to draw those so preoccupied with themselves to make an effort to understand its writing. This is its first challenge. And once it is holding their attention, it tries to communicate to them something that could help them become more intelligible to themselves; this is its second challenge. Such a mode of address distinguishes the perfectionist work from those that talk about such readers but do not talk *to* them. A study in treatments for depression, an investigation into emerging forms of anomie, a biography of an identity crisis: books like these may very well contain insights that can help us better understand the lost. But with few exceptions, the books do not take up the charge of helping these people understand themselves.

They do not respond enough to the difficulty of interesting such readers. Here is where the Emersonian emphasis on *self*-realization is especially convincing. Missing my own way, what use can I have for the ways of others? If I am haunted by ignorance of who I am, then suggesting that I become like someone else will seem beside the point, if not offensively manipulative. Such advice, far from communicating help, only reinforces the shame, helplessness, and incomprehension that separate me in this state from most texts.

Any authentic sense of who to be, of how to live, is inimitable. Although perfectionist texts may differ in how much they make of this, I would venture that they all feature some such acknowledgment. The only thing that can pull such a text and its reader together, the only thing that can serve as the basis for their communication, is a sense of what it is like to lack self-intelligibility. In order to attract the reader's attention, the text demonstrates above all a vivid understanding of this state. Not its objective properties and causes, but what it subjectively feels like. The text addresses to the reader an account of its author's *experience* of lostness. Sometimes, Cavell observes, the "sense of personal crisis [is] given a social projection," alluding to accounts of ills that affect society in general given by Nietzsche, Pascal, Hume, Rousseau, Kierkegaard, Marx, Heidegger, and Wittgenstein.[9] But for the text to be perfectionist, even the most impersonally worded of its diagnoses must express the unmistakable involvement of a first-person account. With this, the text appeals to the reader to recognize himself or herself in that experience. Are we not kin?

Suppose the text becomes the site of a recognition of what it is like to be unintelligible to oneself. The ensuing discovery that, contrary to the message one has received from others, one is not entirely alone, that there is at least a single person—and why not still more?—who resembles one, is bound to interest such a lost reader. This communication that starts to ease his or her isolation has the power to broach the possibility of other alleviations. Could this author, who has experienced what I have, also have found a way out? Could I have something to learn from him or her? Our kinship constitutes reason for these hopes and invests the perfectionist text with the stature of an encouraging figure.

The problem remains, though, that whatever this text may have to teach me, it cannot be who I am to myself. It would seem that all I have to learn from the text is that there is company for my misery. Such solace is better than none, but it still appears to leave a debilitating divide between us misfits and functioning, normal society.

Furthermore, as I read on, I am bound to realize that this picture of our relationship is too simple. True, the perfectionist is on my side, standing with me apart from those who live as if the point of the game were self-evident. But this person has evidently recovered enough from the fall into self-obscurity to want to communicate with others. His or her text palpably insists on meaningful exactitude, *le mot juste*. There is no denying that this investment in language testifies to a confidence that experience can truly be rendered intelligible. Like me, the perfectionist knows isolation. Unlike me, he or she claims to have overcome it. What am I to make of that claim?

"Truly speaking, it is not instruction, but provocation, that I can receive from another soul."[10] Let us imagine that, in the spirit of Emerson, I were to read the perfectionist's words with the hope only of being provoked. As Cavell notes earlier, there would be no question of looking for a text to get me to take the right way. Instead, I would be seeking simply to place myself in the way of the text's claims, challenging the text to back up its view of the world with reasons—and thus drawing the counterchallenge to account for why I see the world differently. Needless to say, if I am not sure how anything looks to me, I will probably feel inadequate to respond to such a demand by the text, at least at first. It will seem like more insult to injury by an unsympathetic outsider. But if I am able to stay reassured that our common experience of self-obscurity seals our friendship, I may discover myself being drawn into answering the text's reasoning with my own.

At this point a common objection may arise: could not the text's world in fact be incommensurably different from mine? What if the text were rooted in a wholly other set of historical circumstances? I believe we can acknowledge any such historical or cultural difference without having to accept that the work has therefore nothing to say to us, that it speaks only to its likeminded or likebodied. Yes, every text may be read as talking about the world it comes from. We may also read it speculatively, though, as addressing a world it never saw. Two hundred years from now, a reader may sensibly ask, "How would Cavell respond to a new line of thinking that appears to rule out the possibility of perfectionism?" And there will be better and worse answers, depending on how plausibly we discover in his texts a coherent and detailed set of explicit and implicit views that bear on this question, views that we assign to the author named Cavell. Every text houses some kind of understanding of our world, whoever we may be.

Thus my self-understanding could begin in criticism. The confident claim that the perfectionist text presents, to have discovered how to move from a state of being lost beyond the reach of conventional wisdom to a state where one understands oneself and one's world in one's own terms, may serve as a point of dialectical departure for an uncertain reader like myself. Struck by something off about this assertion, I may be moved, however haltingly, to articulate how its reasoning goes awry, implying some sense of how it ought to be improved. My criticism would start to turn me, convert me, urge me, to a better way, in my view, of making sense of life. Provoked by the text, I would have broached an understanding for which I may take responsibility and hence claim, embarking on the project of working out its implications for how I should live and how I should act on the demands immediately facing me. So awakens the perfectionist will. I may even find that this path intersects with opportunities to provoke others in turn to take the first steps of their own ways in their responses to mine.

The perfectionist text, then, asks to be read in a speculative and dialectical manner, in which writer and reader both subject their thinking on a particular question to the scrutiny of the other. The text advances a claim that invites criticism—this criticism implies a worldview that is in turn subject to question from the perspective of the text's claim. In this back and forth, it is natural for the reader at first to lack the text's assurance. He or she may even be pushed deeper into doubt by the force of the text's questions. But with this reader's very realization that he or she actually possesses a worldview, however inchoate and weak, and thus is not unintelligible all the way down, the proverbial spade is turned on any absolute skepticism about life. A way appears. Lostness is redeemed. The reader may not yet know how to support his or her views adequately, but the fundamentally cheering fact that he or she has such views is communicated by his or her reactions to the divergent and challenging claims of the text. From here, continued, serious engagement with the text's arguments can only help these views gradually develop and fuel self-confidence.

Indeed, because the reader finds his or her way by criticizing friends, we may say that this way represents a perfecting of the ways of others. Not only does the reader discover it is possible to go on, but he or she affirms that our lives are perfectible, that they can each be made yet more meaningful and fulfilling. However much we may disagree, judgments about higher and lower forms of life become possible on the basis of the shared experience of redemption.

Examining a perfectionist text is a process akin to, as Cavell puts it, "our thoughts returning to us, by way of a guide."[11] This echo of Plato's concept of recollection may now be appreciated as a potential guide's provocation for each of us to work out our own accounts of how we possess an understanding deeper than any doubt. We may still not, may never, be completely intelligible to ourselves, but we do have enough of an idea of what we are unclear about to seek to understand it better. And in a friendly way, we can be tricked into producing that idea.

This is how we may conceive of the perfectionist text addressing readers who are in a particular predicament. First, as a sympathetic equal, as someone who understands what it is like to be morally unintelligible to oneself. Second, it speaks to them as an encouraging prophet, as someone who testifies that he or she has found a way, which others may find as well, to move from self-obscurity to self-intelligibility. And third, far from pretending to speak for everyone, it invites readers as fellow individuals to respond critically to its way of understanding in the hope that they may start to find their own ways. Whatever airs are carried by the claim to prophecy are more than counterbalanced by the humbling acceptance that one's work is destined to be grist for critical departure. The text's attempt to win the trust of lost readers and to spur them to trust as well that they still possess critical, constructive intuitions constitutes, then, the expression of its friendship.

In sum, the interest that is perfectionism has two sides. On the one hand, it is an interest in self-intelligibility. It propels one on a quest, sometimes focused, sometimes wandering, that is bound to distance one from society, which carries on as if it were its own ground. This movement away can also be a movement toward a different kind of society, however, if one encounters fellow searchers—and their texts—that know self-obscurity. Out of such an encounter can grow probing conversations that make one's relative position more intelligible to oneself and to others. Accordingly, the other side of perfectionism is its interest in cultivating a community based on mutual learning. One plausible name for such a yet-to-be-realized community would be democracy. What may look like rigid self-discipline, then, represents a response both to the dubious lack of intelligibility in one's given conventions and to an opportunity to model whatever degree of intelligibility one can claim for the sake of provoking a friend and evoking a democracy. Such a modeling resembles the stereotypically perfectionist insistence that things be just so in its self-assertion. In this manner, the perfectionist commits himself or herself to stay engaged with the utopian potential released whenever we recollect what it is like to be most at a loss. "You cannot bring Utopia about. Nor can you hope for it. You can only enter it."[12]

Now it may appear that this perfectionist community is negligibly small. Most people act as if their place in established society is clear, even when they are unhappy with it. How many could be truly lost? Yet those who are often see no point in calling for help. Thoreau, among others, has observed that we are surrounded by masses living lives of "quiet desperation." To the possibility that some who are lost may be silently invisible, we should add the likelihood that some who are suffering may not yet realize they are lost. Persistently discontent and unable to direct their lives toward anything satisfying, such people may be only a step away from running into questions that cast into doubt their very intelligibility. All in all, our conventional understanding may be more fragile, less able to withstand searching scrutiny and the shocks of tragedy, than is conventional to admit. Anybody may find himself or herself receptive to perfectionism. Everybody is vulnerable to disorienting loss and disappointment.

We may now have enough of a theory of the perfectionist mode of address to open an examination, if only in the most introductory fashion, of how well it fits actual texts. Consider the list of candidates Cavell offers us in *Conditions Handsome and Unhandsome*.[13] Do these actually employ this mode of address? Most patently do, such as Augustine's *Confessions*, Kleist's *The Marquise of O——*, Arnold's "Dover Beach," Heidegger's *What Is Called Thinking*. Others are more ambiguous, such as the cited works by Kant, Mill, and Dewey, which raise the question of where to draw the line between talking about a state of confusion and talking to the confused. Furthermore, in mulling the list over, I could not help but wonder about three lines of work that appear to be underrepresented. One about which Cavell seems to be plainly ambivalent focuses on the critical theory of ideology. Although he includes a brief piece of Marx's on his list, he passes over without mention the legacy of Lukács, Gramsci, Benjamin, Adorno, and Althusser, as well as non-Marxists such as Foucault, that has so prominently shaped the humanities over the past half century. Perhaps it is because of this writing's hostility to individualism or its stress on dissent rather than consent. Nevertheless, can we deny that such studies in false consciousness often employ a perfectionist mode of address, in the process arguably refiguring individuality and solidarity? Is not ideology a rather more plausible figure for Descartes' skepticism-inducing evil genius? A related line of work that is largely absent, save for the example of Beckett, is modernism. Yet as Cavell himself has explained with an eye to painting, modernism may be understood as dramatizing the flight from fraudulence and the search for self-intelligibility with respect to the formal properties of the artistic medium.[14] Finally, there is existentialism, not only in philosophy and literature but in what has become known as the art film. Although the perfectionist struggle for authenticity is explored in some of the romantic literature Cavell cites, the existentialist movement plumbs a new range of experiences by moving the field of struggle from Nature to Being and from the pastoral to the metropolitan. Linking works in these three lines to the tradition of perfectionism, then, could be one way we could proceed from Cavell's insightful survey of this genre.

This brings me to my own modest departure from Cavell's argument. My reservations are provoked by the genre's name. I have been explaining how to interpret our ordinary notion of the perfectionist character as being based on the moral predicament of self-obscurity, one that broaches a redemptive role for a certain kind of text. In the end, though, I feel compelled to admit that this interpretation feels like a bit of a stretch. It does not seem to account enough for the impressive selflessness that characterizes perfectionist work or for the possibility that such work can pathologically negate itself and paralyze the worker. Moreover, anxiety about inauthenticity and the meaning of life is not the first thing that pops into mind when we hear the word "perfectionist," whereas I do find this is immediately associated with the term "existentialist." The struggle with the realization that one is alive without any reason to live may be more easily redescribed as one to acknowledge responsibly gratuitous existence. For these reasons, I am inclined to rename the textual genre that takes up this struggle "existentialism." This would make the nature of the genre more accessible to popular imagination. Conversely, our clichés about existentialism would be transfused and dispelled with works in Cavell's more Emersonian vein, such as William Carlos William's "The Red Wheelbarrow" or A. R. Ammons's "Corsons Inlet."

Furthermore, if we explicitly centered this genre on the confrontation with existence, we would open it up more to two useful currents of critical pressure. The first tempers the idealist emphasis on perfectibility with the materialist acknowledgment that the higher nevertheless depends on the lower. Instead of understanding our predicament as one of fallenness, where one has become separated from the normal, this current puts it in terms of humiliation, of seeing oneself and one's world as closely similar to and bound up with the most disposable piece of being. In concert with this, the second line of criticism tempers the emphasis on individuality and distinction. It appreciates the attaching, open-ended, ongoing process of what Cavell and I have been calling friendship, suggesting this may be a way of thinking of democratic *fraternité* or camaraderie. Criticism is considered a moment in a larger conversation, one that affirms and extends relationships, as Michael Oakeshott puts it, of "acknowledgment and accommodation."[15] In this spirit, let me make it clear that Cavell does register these critical interests in his work; I cannot forget his ruminations on what the "low" and the "common" mean to Emerson or his studies of the twists of conversation in remarriage comedies.[16] I am simply testifying to how he has inspired me to explore whether these currents can be coherently stressed even further, perhaps to a point where they transform the genre as a whole.

Let me stay for now with the term "perfectionism." From the list of texts Cavell finds that constitute this genre, we may turn to his list of features in the *Republic* that establish that that text belongs to the genre.[17] Here he is equally discerning; it is hard to quarrel with the pertinence of these characteristics to perfectionism. Yet what the focus on the text's mode of address helps us to consider is whether some of these characteristics may be more central and essential than others. In particular, features 13 to 28, which concern the nature of the good society and the practice of philosophy, now appear to be less definitive of the text's perfectionism than the previous twelve features, which bear more directly on the nature of the address, on how this particular text constitutes a communication between one person in one condition and another in another. As I acknowledged earlier, we should be careful about oversimplifying the criteria of what counts as a perfectionist text. Nevertheless, by highlighting the mode of address may we not bring out more clearly the common purpose running through the genre?

Which brings us finally back to education. By explicating perfectionism as an interest in helping one another recover from self-obscurity and affirm a personal way of understanding oneself and one's world, I am stressing its call for learning. The perfectionist text asks us to examine scrupulously our degree of self-understanding and to react to the self-understanding of others. Nothing is forced on us, but also nothing is done for us. We have to figure out for ourselves whether we are wanting and what to do about it. This learning, moreover, has no schedule and is never finally behind us. We cannot predict when we will feel its necessity again or when it will reach a provisional point of satisfaction. I think it is in this sense we may say that the call for this learning spans the whole of life. Although the need for perfectionist learning may ebb and flow, it is apt to rise up and throw us at any time. We should always be prepared.

Shortly, I will conclude with some preliminary suggestions about how a distinctively liberal-education curriculum could be organized around getting and keeping us so prepared. First, though, it might be helpful to distinguish this view of why learning is rooted in our nature from another such related view. Learning as a quest for self-understanding, Hans Blumenberg insightfully explains, has historically been in tension with learning as the gratification of curiosity.[18] Both of these are lifelong pursuits. Both may be appreciated as responding to an essential hunger in human beings. Alongside thinkers such as Cavell who stress the duty to know oneself are corresponding ones who argue that we possess a basic desire to know about the world, a desire that would be immoral to suppress. Why should I not be allowed to inquire into something that questions the Biblical account of Creation? But even if I agree it is important to guard against the dangers of unreasonable censorship, the significance of the two objects of learning is sharply different. Curiosity, its ancient and medieval critics contend, lends itself to evasions of the conscientious demand to make sense of one's life. Releasing and encouraging the desire to know about a starlet's secret marriage, for instance, may be the last thing that leads to self-understanding. This is not to deny that an overruling priority on self-examination may not be problematic in its own way: Blumenberg explains how it fed a theological absolutism that set the stage for the Cartesian and Copernican revolutions.[19] My point here is simply to differentiate the kind of learning that serves the quest for self-understanding from the exercise of curiosity.

It is the former that I propose to make central to liberal education. Earlier, I claimed that liberal education is concerned above all with fostering learning for learning's sake and that we require this learning because we are learning beings. What our exploration of Cavell's concept of perfectionism has illuminated is that we are such beings because we may always need to learn how to respond to our obscurity to ourselves. When our lives become opaque to us, they and their surroundings become ripe for destruction. We stand a better chance of dispelling this temptation if we have available friends to lean on and bounce off of in our efforts to see our way clear. We stand a better chance if we have developed the habit of being receptive to such friends, and of finding them in as unlikely a place as a text. Liberal education can cultivate in us this receptivity. This should be its distinctive mission.

According to this view, liberal education should not be principally about preparing us to enter society, let alone to enter it as a professional. Obviously, these are important goals, but no education restricted to them can possibly be complete. Obviously, too, liberal education can contribute to accomplishing them. But unlike professional or vocational education and K–12 or what Oakeshott calls "school" education in foundational forms of literacy, liberal education should focus on preparing us for the times we fall out of society.[20] It should be based on an appreciation that it is only in response to such falls that we may each form a valued individuality. At the same time, such an individuality can only grow alongside our cultivation of truly critical and encouraging, mutually questioning friendships. Learning how to acknowledge and turn from our self-obscurity is thus just as essential to us as these individual and friendly sides of our nature. I sketched above some reasons why liberal education is lifelong and is based on learning for its own sake. We now also have a way of understanding why this education is specially suited for free, democratic citizens. A democracy is precisely the kind of society that values our individual and friendly natures and so does not fear, but invites us to learn from, our periodic adventures in desocialization. Such learning calls for certain kinds of curriculum and pedagogy, ones that should support, I have been arguing, the study of texts distinguished by their perfectionist mode of address.

To what extent might our society be willing to acknowledge the reasonable questions that draw people outside it? To what degree could it be willing to take responsibility for attracting those people back into conversation? How might such a project revitalize and revise our programs of liberal education? Much more detailed inquiry into the educational power of particular perfectionist texts and the practical possibilities of our educational institutions needs to be carried out to answer these questions. By having gone so far in displaying the riches that perfectionism has to offer, Stanley Cavell has charted a promising course for liberal education's future.

REMARKS FROM DISCUSSION

CAVELL: To have perfectionist aspirations, to have them for your society, is not a matter of becoming a connoisseur of beautiful emotions. But it is a practice, because there is no perfectionism without a guide. Sometimes the guide is yourself. There is this spirit as early as there is a perfectionist aspiration. I mean whether it is in Plato or in Dante or in Nietzsche or Emerson, there is always this figure who is ahead of you. And the reason for emphasizing this is partly that democratic aspiration is utterly fundamental. But it is also democratic education that is fundamental.

PUTNAM: An important dimension of Cavell's perfectionism has to do with the possibility of democracy. The perfectionism that he is interested in is not addressed only to the reader who has experienced loss and disappointment; it is a perfectionism that is also preoccupied with the possibility of meaningful democracy and the hope for democracy. So looked at, the perfectionist task is as much to create the appetite for democracy, to make us aware of this need, as to speak to private existential concerns about being lost in the world. But it also seems to me that from the point of view of a religious writer, like Kierkegaard, there is also a concern for making us aware of a possibility and of a need, the possibility of and the need for what we might call a "life duty." We should not worry that there is no audience for perfectionism, that perhaps there may just be too few people around who are "lost and disappointed."

CAVELL: We are all cautious about saying that the teacher is a friend, though surely there is some sense in which that is true. I mean, I'm thinking of one of all the things that Aristotle calls revelations of friendship. It's not just the buyer and seller. There's also a relationship there. Any sort of relation where there is *this* possibility of risk is only so because of a certain kind of friendship.

Sometimes you don't know why this person is starting where they are and what steps they are going to take. So what gets you over this, what makes you subject to being addressed before you know how to be addressed? It's not that you take this rumpled teacher as a model for how you want to live, but that you think they have an interest that you are able to follow. I sometimes think it's a kind of tragedy in American education that philosophy is not generally taught in high school. There is a sense in which, if you don't have your head broken early, it's very hard to start. And the number of distinguished literary figures in American culture who have never had a philosophy course and who suffer from it! Every day you see them, avoiding it all the time. They make little odd remarks about philosophy, and grownups shouldn't talk that way: I mean serious intellectual grownups shouldn't talk as though somehow that part of Western culture is not necessary for them or as though they've never even bothered to find out about it. That's a tremendous absence.

But if I ask who's going to teach philosophy, are you going to put these things or those on the curriculum, how will it be and what will students do about it—in some way I don't care. What I care is that somebody does it. You don't know if you are going to respond to this or not, but if somebody feels they know why they've studied philosophy, let them try and teach it. And that would be a case in which, almost grown up, you don't know what you're doing. And that's ok by me.

CAVELL: Right at the beginning, my sense of what I was trying to point to was a sense that the problem with one's own "transparency" to oneself was not so much one of self-satisfaction but of a lack of curiosity about one's self. So the projection of that would be a lack of curiosity about others.

EIGHT

THE GLEAM OF LIGHT

Initiation, Prophesy, and Emersonian Moral Perfectionism
Naoko Saito

"Our Education Is Sadly Neglected"

The chapter [in Thoreau's *Walden*] on "Reading" identifies his readers as students—and himself, consequently, as teacher. Eventually, students will be anyone whose "education is sadly neglected" (III, 12); and one day we might all "become essentially students" (III, 1)—that is, one day we might find out what essential studying is.[1]

If these remarks of Stanley Cavell on Thoreau's *Walden* imply a questioning of the general culture of "reading," this must be all the more urgent in an age of globalization. What does it mean to read in philosophy, and what does this say about education? What can philosophy say about education? Certainly, the imperative that is sometimes imposed on philosophers of education to say something concrete about policy and practice has on occasion encouraged the assumption that theory is to be "applied," resulting in work that can disappoint through appearing contrived or forced or even vacuous and that ultimately, even at the practical level, is found by many to be unconvincing, and this quite misses the proximity of philosophy and education that one finds throughout Cavell. Moreover, the globalized network of technology, which intensifies the insistence on this imperative, brings with it changes to reading and understanding themselves, where knowledge becomes information and literacy a matter of its access and transmission. There is a general lack of interest in reading difficult texts and skepticism about language that falls outside the range of transaction. Reading is valuable to the extent that it is useful, and usefulness is optimized where reading and writing are reduced to the least complex and most accessible terms. The burden of thought is lessened to make it more efficiently transmittable in the global network of communication.

It is under these circumstances that the tide of language as transaction needs to be stemmed and the value of philosophical reading redeemed. In response to such a need, this chapter tries to elucidate a dimension of education that is "sadly neglected"—a value of philosophical reading that is obscured by the obsession with accountability and the instrumentalization of philosophy: we need to recover "what essential studying is." The task requires us first to be awakened to the sense of loss itself and then to present an alternative language and way of education. To accomplish this task, I shall examine Cavell's *Emersonian Moral Perfectionism* and his politics of interpretation. I shall try to shed light on a prophetic dimension of Cavell's idea of philosophy as the education of grownups—the reawakening of the "gleam of light" as the necessity for our continual perfection.

In what follows, I shall consider first the main features of Cavell's Emersonian moral perfectionism (via Emerson and Thoreau) and offer an account of the nature of his call for mutual education. This will reveal an apparent tension, however, between self-cultivation and the need for the other. In the light of this, I shall suggest, second, a possible means of releasing this tension with reference to Cavell's idea of the politics of interpretation, which emphasizes the intricate relationship between initiation into and departure from the language

community. I shall, third, highlight the prophetic nature of the gleam
of light as the educational implication of Emersonian moral perfectionism. The role of the other as a teacher attesting to the prophetic
moment is shown to be internal to this process. Finally, I shall conclude that a Cavellian approach to perfectionist education can show
us a way toward democratic participation—understood as the assidu-
ous commitment to a democracy always still to be achieved, from the
inmost to the outmost. It is this inseparable connection between democracy and education that is at the heart of his idea of philosophy
as the education of grownups.

Emersonian Moral Perfectionism and Mutual Education

> The doctrine of hatred must be preached as the counteraction of
> the doctrine of love when that pules and whines. I shun father
> and mother and wife and brother, when my genius calls me.[2]

> If one listens to the faintest but constant suggestions of his genius,
> which are certainly true, he sees not to what extremes, or even
> insanity, it may lead him.[3]

Although commonly identified as classic representatives of American individualism, Emerson and Thoreau make provocative remarks
about genius that raise questions in this respect: To what extent does
the self-reliant individual need the other? Does following one's own
genius have self-sufficiency as its goal? Cavell, in his idea of Emersonian (and implicitly Thoreauvian) moral perfectionism, gives a unique
response to the alleged paradox of Emerson's and Thoreau's ideas of
the relationship between the self and the other, and he does this in
such a way as to transcend the negativity of guilt, sacrifice, and defi-
ciency. A distinctive trait of *Emersonian* moral perfectionism (in contrast particularly to that of Plato or Aristotle) is that perfection is an
endless journey of self-overcoming and self-realization, whose central
focus is on the here and now: this is a process of attaining a further,
next self, not the highest self. Drawing on Emerson's idea of the "un-
attained but attainable self," Cavell writes: "The self is always attained, as well as *to be* attained."[4]

Emersonian perfectionism is characterized by "goallessness":[5] it refuses final perfectibility. This implies that, although Emerson uses the phrase "self-acquaintance," the perfection of the self is not geared toward the final grasp of the self as the object of knowledge. Cavell shifts our attention from the idea of the self-serving goal of self-reliance to Emerson's call upon the potential nobility of the self, which Emerson names "genius."[6] Genius is not the privilege of a few individuals but the "sound estate of everyman."[7] In the context of democracy as a way of living that involves the question of how we should live, each individual has a responsibility in contributing *her* response to *her* society. This Cavell calls the Emersonian (as opposed to the Rawlsian) version of the "conversation of justice."[8] In this sense, "the capacity for self-reliance . . . is universally distributed."[9] At the heart of Emersonian moral perfectionism is a call for, or invitation to, "social formation,"[10] in resistance to the cynicism of "shrinking participation in democracy."[11]

In this basic structure, one finds that there are dual aspects in Emersonian moral perfectionism, one with its focus on the self, the other on the other. On the one hand, following Emerson's idea of "the infinitude of the private man," Cavell highlights the notion of the absolute singularity of the self. It is, he says, "an announcement of the process of individuation (an interpretation of perfectionism) before which there are no individuals, hence no humanity, hence no society."[12] On the other, he reminds us that "we need not, we should not, take [Emerson] to imagine himself as achieving a further state of humanity in himself alone."[13] Seen through the lens of moral perfectionism, Emerson's *self*-reliance necessitates *the other* as the essential condition of the endless perfecting of the self and society. Echoing Emerson's idea of representativeness,[14] Cavell states: "This other of myself—returning my rejected, say repressed, thought—reminds me of something, as of where I am, as if I had become lost in thought, and stopped thinking."[15]

The key to untangling the apparent paradox of the self and the other is to be found in the theme of education. For Emerson, moral constraint is not given by the universal moral law of an "ought" but by the other as a friend, as an attraction: the friend reminds us of the state of our conformity, and it is thanks to the friend that we "*are* drawn beyond ourselves"; the "friend (discovered or constructed) represents the standpoint of perfection."[16] Encounter with another constitutes the moment of turning, a point of departure from the existing circle of the self, not only in joy and hope but also with a strong sense of "shame"—shame at the self in its conformity.[17] Cavell says that the role of friendship in moral perfectionism is both "recognition and negation": these are simultaneous movements of being, "toward and away."[18] The other of myself appears here, as it were, as a force of approval exercised through negation. Friendship is a reminder that we should "never fall into something usual and settled."[19] In Emersonian *moral* perfectionism, the moral task of a friend is not the full grasp of the other but is the remembrance of the other in the realm of the yet to be known. It is this endless, eternally unattainable nature of relationship that necessitates the process of its cultivation, that is, the process of education. As Cavell says: "we are educations for one another."[20]

With its strong focus on genius, the discourse of Emersonian moral perfectionism still may sound elitist. Its emphasis on language and participation into the "City of Words" may reinforce such an interpretation. Suppose Emerson's and Thoreau's "genius" is, as Cavell says, an antielitist, democratic concept. Then is its ultimate goal not that of *self*-cultivation? Perfection's obsession with education expresses its focus on finding one's way rather than on getting oneself or another to take the way.[21] But if this is so, how can the other be involved in this process of finding the self? Emersonian genius is something that only this "I" can be aware of, and if the "I" is unapproachable by the other, the role of the other, especially as a teacher, seems to be limited by nature. To put it in an extreme way, teaching may not be necessary for the cultivation of Emersonian genius. In search for an answer to this question, let us further explore the implication of mutual education suggested by Cavell.

The Politics of Interpretation: Initiation, Participation, and Community

Cavell's earlier work, *The Senses of Walden*, which in its 1981 expanded version includes two essays on Emerson, can, in conjunction with his "The Politics of Interpretation," help us here to develop retrospectively, as it were, the theme of mutual education in Emersonian perfectionism and in relation to the nature of language. It shows how such education exists in connection with language, reading, and writing. On the face of it, these works are not directly about education, at least not about what goes on in schools and universities. "The Politics of Interpretation" is an essay contained in his book *Themes out of School*. Cavell suggests the need to reconsider education *out of* school for the sake of redeeming an education that is otherwise sadly neglected.

Cavell says: "Emerson offers his writing as representing this other for his reader."[22] One of the central tasks of Emersonian moral perfectionism is the entering of "my" voice into the conversation of justice, in participation in the "city of words," which is the language community.[23] The *moral* force of perfection, Cavell says, hinges then not on judgment (as in conventional moral theories) but on "every word." Cavell's idea of the politics of interpretation, adumbrated in *The Senses of Walden* (1992), shows that the focus on language is not merely a literary matter or private activity. Cavell considers Emerson's and Thoreau's "interpretation of what you might call the politics of philosophical interpretation as a withdrawal or rejection of politics, even of society, as such." In this light, Thoreau's book *Walden*, Cavell claims, is "an act of civil disobedience," one that is effected or realized through "silence."[24] The foremost task in the politics of interpretation is to "free us and our language of one another, to discover the autonomy of each"[25] by returning ourselves and language to the ordinary, in order to let them rediscover their place in the world: to determine "whether the voice I lend in recognizing a society as mine, as speaking for me, is my voice, my own."[26] Finding "my voice" involves asking where this "I" stands in the world, and it is this question of standing that emerges as the essential condition for political participation.

Initiation, Participation, and the Language Community

The politics of interpretation is crucially related to one's participation and initiation into the language community. Cavell refers to what Thoreau calls the "father tongue"—"'a reserved and select expression, too significant to be heard by the ear, which we must be born again in order to speak' (III, 3)."[27] The father tongue is used here in contrast to the mother tongue, which is native, natural, and familiar, symbolized by the spoken word. The mother tongue is the essential starting point of one's being initiated into the language community, being characterized by immediate, intimate relationships. The father tongue, by contrast, is epitomized by the written word: it is the "maturity and experience" of the mother tongue, and our relation to it is indirect, symbolized by the bent arm that supports the book.[28] The relationship between the mother and the father, however, is not simply a matter of staged development in a kind of unitary trajectory from the immature to the mature. Rather, what is needed is to "keep faith at once with the mother and the father, to unite them, and to have the word born in us."[29] The union of the mother and the father is not a unification but a union that has issue. That is, we need both mother and father in order to experience the world in its full-blown form: we need always both initiation *into* and departure *from* the language community. The emphasis is on the dual elements of the "into" and of the "from" in movement and on the turning point from the familiar to the strange.

Cavell's notion of initiation already integrates the element of deviation. It is demonstrated in his treatment of the voice of the Emersonian child. In *The Claim of Reason*, the book in which he most fully interprets Wittgenstein's account of criteria, Cavell's words presage his later claims for Emersonian perfectionism and present the voice of Emerson's child. He discusses the relationship between adult and child as creating an "asymmetry between teaching and learning"—

where there is a discrepancy between the adult's and the child's per-spectives.[30] This asymmetry is most evident in the moment when an adult, in the face of the child's novel and unexpected questions about the facts of life, feels that his or her reason comes to an end.[31] The specific questions that Cavell asks with and for the voice of a child represent his view of perfection as filled with puzzles and uncertaint-ies. Faced with the natural reactions of the child, the adult, in the process of initiation, cannot simply rely on conventional criteria. This is the crucial moment when "attunement" between them becomes "dissonant."[32] Cavell speaks with the voice of the adult who submits the limitation of his reason to the novel, perhaps disturbing, perhaps threatening, impulse of the child. The child is described as "our famil-iar stranger."[33] Later in *Conditions Handsome and Unhandsome*, a book on Emersonian moral perfectionism, Cavell discusses the similar sense of deviation in connection with the exclusion of the newcomer from society: "If the child is separated out, treated as a lunatic, this shows at once society's power and its impotence—power to exclude, power to include."[34] If this is a condition of civilization, the process of initiation cannot simply be a matter of inclusion and assimilation: in-stead, it necessitates this element of the dissonant, the deviant, and even the abnormal. This is not a nostalgic romanticization of child-hood, whose purpose is to enable the adult to open her mind beyond his or her conventional views and cognitive understanding to the child's unexpected and unknowable horizon of life. Rather, it is the exacting obligation of remembering and confronting "the prospect of growth and the memory of childhood" within and without ourselves.[35]

Acknowledgment of the Other in Neighboring

Within this basic structure, the politics of interpretation suggests how the mode of this indirect relationship between reader and writer em-bodies one's relationship with others. This indicates a direction toward the other within the process of perfection. The relationship involves a relationship of intense confrontation, aversion, and provo-cation, which Cavell calls the "shock of recognition."[36] Words in-scribed in the text constitute a kind of juncture at which reader and

writer "conjecture"—"casting words together and deriving the conclusions of each."[37] This is a relationship of mutual "trials"[38]—testing
what counts, finding criteria of judgment through words. The reader
is "convicted" by the text in that she is caught in a position of responsibility, which is born of the necessity of her answering to the text
that she reads.[39] It is through this testing relationship with the writer
that the reader's power of words is tried—in a trial weighted with the
"power of life and death," through which the reader undergoes a kind
of rebirth.[40] This is the moment when "the word and the reader can
be awakened together."[41]

Cavell's call for an indirect relationship between the self and the
other, epitomized by the relationship between reader and writer, contrasts, for example, with the ethic of care—in which full receptivity
of the other (epitomized by the moment of complete absorption in
the state of "motivational displacement" and "engrossment") is a
condition for the fulfilling of the caring and educational relationship.[42] In contrast, this Cavellian approach is cautious about the illusions of "face-to-face," immediate relationships. As he says with
Thoreau, "Speaking together face to face can seem to deny that distance, to deny that facing one another requires acknowledging the
presence of the other, revealing our positions, betraying them if need
be."[43] Otherness in Cavell (found via Emerson and Thoreau) centers
on the idea of equality conditioned by the rift of distance, of encounter in mediation. You can never own the other, but still you owe responsibility to the other—responsibility neither in deficit nor with a
sense of guilt. In elucidating the unhandsome and perhaps avaricious
human condition, Emerson says: "I take this evanescence and lubric-
ity of all objects, which lets them slip through our fingers then when
we clutch hardest, to be the most unhandsome part of our condition."[44] At the heart of Emersonian perfectionism lies the awareness
of the illusion of this immediate grasping and the recognition of the
gap between the self and the world.

What alternative is there, then, to immediate, face-to-face relationships? Is his call for distance, indirectness, and separation merely a

return to the privacy of the self, a self eternally unknown to the other? This is a question concerning skepticism over other minds. In response, Cavell neither denies nor accepts skepticism. His alternative answer can be found in his Thoreauvian idea of *neighboring* and *nextness* as modes of acknowledging the other. Cavell says that Thoreau's reencounter with the world is directed toward the achievement of "outsideness" or "outwardness."[45] Thoreau articulates the "externality of the world as its nextness to me."[46] He finds in Thoreau a clue to the human being's imaginative power to reveal the reality of the world outside, starting from within one's consciousness. Cavell and Thoreau rebuild, even overturn, the relationship between inside and outside, not as two separate realms of experience but as the riven interaction of the two: there can be no perfect coincidence. This sense of a rift is experienced as the strange and the unfamiliar within oneself—an encounter with otherness not only without but also *within* the self and an acquisition of the standpoint of outsideness within the inside of the familiar. Cavell calls this "sense of distance from self" a relationship of "perpetual nextness."[47] "This other of myself" is manifested within the self in the way that outsideness is constructed within the same. Thoreau calls this a condition of "doubleness," the state of being "beside ourselves in a sane sense,"

> by which I can stand as remote from myself as from another. However intense my experience, I am conscious of the presence and criticism of a part of me, which, as it were, is not a part of me, but spectator, sharing no experience, but taking note of it; and that is no more I than it is you. (V, 11)[48]

In the light of Thoreau's ideas of the double and nextness, the Emersonian notion of representativeness can be reconceived as the presence of the other as a mirror. The mirror here is not the mere representation of the outside world in correspondence but more like the mirror whose surface clouds to show the breath of "my" life. "Thou art not my soul, but a picture and effigy of that."[49] This can be called an indirect relationship of *mutual reflection*, where the mirror's value is not just in the image's clarity but in the clouding that is a sign of life. Engaging this imagery, and echoing *Hamlet*, Cavell speaks of the responsibility of what Emerson and Thoreau call the life of our words as the burden of "holding, as it were, the mirror up to nature. . . . Then Hamlet's picture of the mirror held up to nature asks us to see if the mirror as it were clouds, to determine whether nature is breathing (still, again)—asks us to be things affected by the question."[50] Mutual reflection should be distinguished from mutual understanding and, for that matter, from the "politics of recognition." These are typically associated—for example in multiculturalism—with a direct "face-to-face" dialogue between the same and the different and oftentimes with the attitude of cognition of the other, as it were, as the object of knowledge. In Cavellian mutual reflection, the commitment of the other is more *indirect*—symbolized by a relationship through the father tongue, through the opacity of the written word. In observing the way that the other confronts his own self, language, and culture, the self is turned back upon her own self, now as a stranger. The other is next to my self—not only outside the self but also *within* my self—confronting me with the possibility of further perfection, as the sign of life, letting the self find its own breath.

The Gleam of Light, Prophesy, and the Gift of Teaching

The inseparable relationship between initiation and departure brings us back to Cavell's moral perfectionist stipulation: "the self is always attained, as well as *to be* attained."[51] These turning points are moments of "crisis" throughout one's life: "for the child to grow he requires family and familiarity, but for a grownup to grow he requires strangeness and transformation, i.e., birth."[52] How then can the moment of crisis, the crucial point of departure, be produced in the process of initiation? To find an answer to this question, I shall now move on to the role of the other as a *teacher* in Emersonian moral perfectionism—an orienter who, with more day to dawn, guides the prophetic moment in the self's perfection. This will reinforce its educational aspect and clarify further what Cavell means by saying "we are educations for one another." Simultaneously, it will amplify the Emersonian and Thoreauvian sense of "genius" beyond its elitist interpretation—opening horizons to the perspective of *the gleam of light.*

Cavell points out that, in the chapter on "Reading" in *Walden*, Thoreau identifies "his reader as students—and himself, consequently as teacher." He calls Thoreau and Emerson "philosophers of direction, orienters, tirelessly prompting us to be on our way, endlessly asking us where we stand, what it is we face."[53] As these remarks show, Emersonian perfectionism, combined with the politics of interpretation, suggests the necessity of the other as teacher, the other who contributes to the continuing perfection of my life—that is, *my* life where this life extends beyond the containment of its contained ego, that is, toward otherness, otherness both within and outside the self. A teacher, the actual other, is the outside other of myself who reflects the otherness within myself, the possibility of self-transcendence.[54] In the Cavellian mediated and indirect relationship of nextness, the teacher is never one who imposes or, in that sense, directly teaches, and influence is through neither imitation nor full acceptance of the other. Instead, the teacher is this other of myself who guides me by standing on the intersection between the inter- and intradimensions of my self. He becomes the occasion for crucial turning points in my perfection. The teacher does not face me directly but sees a direction to which I can orient myself, through my own eyes. In Thoreau's words: "If you would not stop to look at me, but look whither I am looking and further, then my education could not dispense with your company."[55]

In this respect, the politics of interpretation is replete with educational implications—with reading and writing a metonym for the teacher-student relationship. The goal of the reader's (student's) encounter with the writer (the teacher), Cavell says, is to "free us from our attachment to the person of the one who brings the message," namely, "freedom from the person of the author."[56] In the patient process of reading, and being read by, a difficult text (the very process of being tested by the father tongue), the reader, on trial in the relationship with the writer, learns to detach herself from her old self, from her old conception of the world, from her accustomed perception of others, both intimate and distant. Hence, one can see the "text as therapeutic," the means through which the self undergoes rebirth.[57] Cavell associates this with Freud's idea of "the work of mourning"—that is, of "undergoing severing" from "attachment."[58] "Nostalgia is an inability to open the past to the future."[59] This conjures us up the imagery of Emerson's expanding circles—circles that never negate or eliminate formations that are past but always move beyond.[60]

Teaching is an act that involves giving what cannot be given, grasping what cannot be grasped. It is Emerson's idea of *the gleam of light* that best captures the dual nature of teaching. The moment of departure is that of prophesy, a trust in and thrust into the unknown. In "Self-Reliance," Emerson says: "A man should learn to detect and watch that gleam of light which flashes across his mind from within. . . . In every work of genius we recognize our own rejected thoughts."[61] The gleam of light figures, in Emerson, with self-reliance and genius to suggest an inner being of the self but also, more strongly, the sense of who you are. It is, as the core of the self, however, anything but substantial. The gleam is like a Socratic daemon, the voice of conscience, one might say.[62] Yet the metaphor of light is not simply a sunny image. As is acknowledged by Emerson's original essays and by the sense of loss that permeates Cavell's Emersonian moral perfectionism, light faces the constant danger of being extinguished. Hence, in its evanescence and transitoriness, this light always awaits expression, and it is expressed through one's words. In this sense, the innerness of the light is anything but self-contained privacy. It is the embodiment of the life of the self, always holding the potential to transcend itself with a movement outward from within, from loss to awakening. But the light is rekindled only through mutual reflection with the other. Teaching is the process of learning to be with others as neighbors. It is not a matter of an epistemological task of knowing and identifying the source of the other's light. Instead, teaching is a gift. It is something that is unexpectedly given in mutual attunement when, in learning to let go and bequeath, a teacher encounters the moment of a student's conversion "from mourning to morning."

The Emersonian teacher embodies the paradox of the gift: she shoulders the task of influencing the other, but this without any kind of appropriation. The teacher cannot draw out my own light from inside. As Thoreau says: "you cannot receive a shock unless you have an electric affinity for that which shocks you."[63] This amplifies the Emersonian perfectionist sense that teaching is as much a matter of provocation: it involves inspiration in the processes of initiation and transmission but also an acknowledgment of the unknown and the unpredictable.

This renews the emphasis on leaving, abandonment, and departure in Emersonian moral perfectionism. The task of Thoreau as a teacher is, by implication, to leave the student alone, to let her recognize the singularity of her self. These authors thereby enact, through their writings, the role of the other of myself, as the " 'kindred from a distant land' " (I, 2). Their paradoxical teaching is that our kinship "is an endless realization of our separateness."[64] The teacher as the other of myself leaves the trace of his influence not through offering a permanent sense of home but through the act of leaving. The necessity of the teacher in the perfection of the self is, thus, a matter of offering not a place for security or settlement but rather the rough ground, the " '*point d'appui*' " (II, 22),[65] that can constitute the turning point for the student: "[The writer of *Walden*] is bequeathing it to us in his will, the place of the book and the book of the place. He leaves us in one another's keeping."[66] Bequeathing and mourning, loss and lack, however, are the conditions of remembering and reviving the intensity of light. The dual nature of loss and prophesy is at the heart of teaching as gift giving. Cavell restates this sense at the end of *The Senses of Walden*: "To say, 'Follow me and you will be saved,' you must be sure you are of God. But to say, 'Follow in yourself what I follow in mine and you will be saved,' you merely have to be sure you are following yourself. This frightens and cheers me."[67]

The Emersonian sense of the gift is pragmatic in that it acknowledges that the act of teaching receives its return—eventually, and perhaps, somewhere else. This better fits Emerson's idea of "the law of Compensation," in which the reward is an eventual intensifying of the gleam of light on the part of the student—a reward simultaneously for giver and receiver, though this may not be an immediate return.[68] This Emersonian sense of compensation saves us from puritan asceticism, from the guilt that is associated with desire. In Emersonian perfectionism, desire is affirmed (though never fully satisfied) as the precious source of the gift: the prophetic nature of the gleam of light is not ascetic but liberating. We cannot know beforehand, however, how such a prophetic moment is to be produced. As Cavell says, the power of "onward thinking" is demonstrated "only on the way, *by* the way."[69]

Philosophy as the Education of Grownups

The question was raised in the beginning of this chapter whether Emersonian moral perfectionism is a theory of self-cultivation and, if so, what Cavell means by mutual education. The discussion here has shown that in the politics of interpretation the self's relationship with language already and always necessitates the standpoint of otherness within and without the self. Assumptions about one's familiar, native culture are continually destabilized in processes of initiation. The politics of interpretation is, as Cavell says, a spiritual exercise for building and rebuilding a neighborhood from within.[70] It is then better to recast Emersonian moral perfectionism not as a matter of self-cultivation directed toward self-identification and self-knowledge but rather in terms of self-transcendence, or even, let us say, alterity.

In this reconfigured map, perfectionist education is surely education in service of genius. The prophetic nature of the gleam of light distinguishes it from elitism. Genius is not simply a matter of pre-given talent bestowed on particular individuals. Rather, it is a call to each and everyone to be awakened to the lost intensity of life—in resistance to the nihilistic crisis in democracy. It is demonstrated and practiced in our insatiable desire to express ourselves through language. The cultivation of genius through language, then, is a form of reeducation for democratic participation, starting with the inmost and eventually reaching the outmost—as Emerson says in "Self-Reliance."[71] Cavellian "education" is now reconfigured as a spiritual exercise of mourning and converting as a crucial condition for political, democratic participation. This is what Cavell means when he says, "to achieve the next step in democracy, not in a revolutionary way, but as a change through education."[72]

Cavell addresses the question: "I imagine that reading, so motivated, will not readily lend itself to classroom instruction. Would this be because of the nature of teaching or because of the nature of classrooms?"[73] The education that concerns Cavell cannot be translated immediately into classroom instruction—neither is this its intent. While it highlights the significance of reading and writing as linguistic practice, this is not something that can simply be applied in "new methods of teaching reading": neither is it a recipe for citizenship education. In resistance to the binary thinking of *applying* a theory *to* classroom practice, Cavell's approach to education for citizenship brings us back to a horizon of education that precedes political and moral education. It starts with the innermost origin of our being members of linguistic, political, and moral communities from which, gradually and eventually, through the eternal cycle of initiation and departure, the public and the common are achieved.[74] This dimension of education is sadly neglected, yet it necessarily continues lifelong. Cavell's thinking is not restricted to the education of adults—education for those who have already mastered the education of childhood in "common schools." "Education is sadly neglected," already in childhood, still in adulthood.

REMARKS FROM DISCUSSION

CAVELL: Whether the politics of interpretation can be brought into the classroom has to do with whether we can demand change from our students, because the politics that I am talking about is about allowing a text to assault you. How deep you are allowed to dig into these students' lives is something that is perplexing. To a certain extent, it has got to hurt or it is not education, but how can you dish this out, what is ok? I don't see rules about this, but how in the world can you talk about *King Lear* or *Othello* with a college classroom without, in *Othello*, talking about menstruation, the handkerchief spotted with strawberries? How far is it ok to press this subject? You can develop trust, but what must I do to develop that? You are saying it's ok if I talk this way, but you can easily talk that way seductively. That thing is pushing me just to raise that question and to ask what that has to do with the search for community. I am saying every sentence does, every utterance. Of course, empirically this is not so, it would be as dead as doornails. But this is a utopian moment.

PUTNAM: For much of one's childhood, one is childish, but there are moments, while one is a child, when one is more grown up, in the sense we're talking about, than one is in most of one's adult life. And school can, so to speak, encourage those grown-up moments, encourage what Naoko Saito has called the "gleam of light." I very often think about this in connection with our relations with our graduate students. One way to think about this might be to ask how one can encourage students to be one another's teachers.

CAVELL: Who have been the cosmopolitan figures in American culture? Or, in a clichéd way, who are among the American travelers? The greatest writer on this subject is Henry James. Take the concept of ambassadors. Is an ambassador a cosmopolitan figure? In a sense, of course, but then it turns out that they are never more American than when they get to Europe. I find it an interesting exercise to think of American writers in this way. Robert Frost, for example, Wallace Stevens, William Carlos Williams—they are among the major poets of the middle part of the twentieth century. You can't imagine them anywhere else but in America, Williams a country doctor and Frost having to live in this sparse landscape. Wallace Stevens never saw any of these places, he never went to the Florida Keys, but he has all kinds of descriptions and imaginations of these things: it's New Haven or Hartford really, that's where he was. But a figure like Hemingway, for example, couldn't live in the States. He came back to the States to blow his brains out. Otherwise he had to exist in Europe. So what is all that about? What is the welcoming of the stranger? Could anything be more cosmopolitan than that? That anybody from anywhere can find a place to live? That is a romantic thought about this place. It's an immigrant thought about this place. I think it is a fine subject too.

NINE

THE ORDINARY AS SUBLIME IN CAVELL, ZEN, AND NISHIDA

Cavell's Philosophy of Education in East-West Perspective
Steve Odin

Introductory Remarks

In this chapter, I elucidate "the ordinary" as the fundamental category in the Emersonian perfectionism underlying Stanley Cavell's philosophy of education in contemporary American philosophy and relate it to Zen/Chan Buddhism and Confucianism. Here I develop Cavell's notion of philosophy as "education for grownups" as an ongoing process of self-overcoming that moves from the actual ordinary to the next or transfigured ordinary, itself visualized through his Emersonian perfectionist image of ever-expanding circles. Moreover, I discuss how Cavell's Emersonian perfectionism as a transformative educational process is an ongoing task aimed at recovering the ordinary in response to the constant threat of skepticism understood as denial of the ordinary, including ordinary language and ordinary forms of life. This Emersonian perfectionist model of education for grownups views perfection not as an otherworldly transcendence of daily existence nor as realization of a fixed teleological goal but as instead a continuing dynamic process of returning to the ordinary. As will be seen, Cavell's return to everyday life and language involves a view of the ordinary as a paradox, whereupon it can be the locus of boredom, triviality, and the mundane, on the one side, as well as of the sublime, the fantastic, and the extraordinary, on the other. My particular emphasis will be on Cavell's Emersonian perfectionist vision of realizing the ordinary as extraordinary through a process of educative conversation.

The perfectionism of Cavell in American philosophy is a response to the problem of skepticism through the ongoing return to ordinary life and language. Cavell's perfectionism involves at least a sixfold synthesis of diverse Western traditions: (1) the ordinary language philosophy of J. L. Austin and the later Wittgenstein, which responds to the threat of skepticism by returning words from their metaphysical (transcendent) to their contextual use in ordinary life and language; (2) the American transcendentalism of Emerson and Thoreau, directed toward overcoming skepticism as the problem of "secret melancholy" or "quiet desperation" through a return to the ordinary, the common, and the everyday; (3) the literary-philosophical English romanticism of Wordsworth and Coleridge, with its resistance to skepticism through a poetic vision of the sublime in the ordinary; (4) the continental existentialism of Kierkegaard, Nietzsche, and Heidegger, which aims to overcome the anxiety of nihilism through an eternal return to and ecstatic repetition of the ordinary as sublime; (5) Freudian psychoanalysis of everyday life, wherein the therapeutic cure for anxiety as resistance to the ordinary lies in a return of the repressed familiar as uncanniness of the ordinary; and (6) a perfectionist reading of the arts, such as Shakespearean drama and American cinema, wherein the epistemic problem of "skepticism" is explored through responding to tragedy as avoidance of the ordinary by means of return to and acknowledgment of the poetry of the ordinary.

It is my intention in this chapter to examine various intercultural parallels discoverable between Cavell's American philosophy of the ordinary in the West and various East Asian modes of thought, focusing especially upon Sino-Japanese Zen/Chan Buddhism and its reformulation by Kitarō Nishida in modern Japanese philosophy, along with the related tradition of Confucianism.[1] Although both Cavell's American philosophy of education and Zen self-cultivation aim at creative transformation and perfection by means of dialectical alternation between conversation and silence, by "perfection" is not meant an escape from the ordinary but a moment-by-moment insight into the wonder of the ordinary. In Zen Buddhism, this has been thematized by the famous teaching that "ordinary mind is the Tao" (J. *heijō shin kore dō*). While for Cavell the response to the problem of skeptical doubt is recovering the ordinary, similarly, for *Rinzai* Zen Buddhism, the "great doubt" (J. *taigi*) of kōan practice is overcome by returning to "ordinary mind" (J. *heijō shin*). Yet another point of contact between Cavell and Zen is found in their response to skepticism in its aspect as nihilism by recovering the aesthetic, artistic, and poetic value of ordinary life in its beauty and sublimity. Moreover, I examine how the Confucian tradition, which itself had a deep influence on Zen/Chan Buddhism, aims at realizing the unity of Tao with ordinary life through a dynamic educational process described in terms similar to Cavell's Emersonian perfectionist image of ever-expanding concentric circles. Finally, I will emphasize how both Cavell and the Asian traditions underscore overcoming skepticism not only by reclaiming the ordinary but also by recovering the ordinary as extraordinary, wondrous and sublime.

The Ordinary as Tao in Sino-Japanese Philosophy

As indicated above, the Emersonian perfectionism of Cavell based on the American transcendentalism of Emerson and Thoreau is directed toward responding to the constant threat of skepticism by returning to the ordinary as extraordinary. However, one of the most remarkable aspects of American transcendentalism is the Eastern references to be found in Emerson and Thoreau. It is precisely these Eastern references that might prompt one to further seek out connections between Cavell's Emersonian perfectionism and various Asian modes of thought. Emerson and Thoreau were especially familiar with Indian philosophical traditions of Hinduism and Buddhism as well as Confucianism in China. Here I will examine some of these possible connections between Cavell's Emersonian perfectionism and the Asian philosophical traditions, including not only Hinduism, Buddhism, and Confucianism but also Daoism, Zen Buddhism, and their synthesis by Kitarō Nishida and the Kyoto school of modern Japanese philosophy. In particular, I will very briefly explain certain parallels between Cavell's Emersonian perfectionist vision of philosophy as education for grownups and the educational theories within various Asian philosophical modes of thought, including especially both the Confucian and Zen/Chan Buddhist pedagogical systems, analyzing how, for both, education is seen as an ongoing developmental process of self-overcoming that moves from the actual ordinary to the next or transfigured ordinary, visualized through the image of ever-expanding concentric circles, whereby around each perfect circle a still larger circle can be drawn.

The Ordinary as Tao in the Confucian Educational System

At key points in *Walden,* Thoreau cites various Confucian texts, using his own translations from then available French-language editions, including the *Chung-yung/Zhongyong,*[2] widely known by the 1960 translation of James Legge as *Doctrine of the Mean.* Wei-Ming Tu aptly retranslates *Chung-yung* as *Centrality and Commonality* (1989), this being one of the Four Books selected by the neo-Confucian philosopher Chu Hsi (1130–1200), which came to function as the basis of the civil service examinations in the Confucian educational system. Wei-Ming Tu explains that while *chung* can be rendered as "centrality," the term *yung* has been somewhat more problematic: "Chu Hsi, however, after systematically studying virtually all available interpretations, concluded that yung signifies that which is 'ordinary' and 'common.'"[3] Further clarifying the contextualized use of *yung* in the ordinary language of everyday Chinese discourse, Wei-Ming Tu adds: "In ordinary language, yung is often associated with notions such as 'common,' 'usual,' 'ordinary' . . . It is the Confucian belief that the ultimate meaning of life is rooted in the ordinary human existence."[4] This same Confucian text, *Zhongyong/Chung-yung*, was later retranslated as *Focusing on the Familiar* by Roger T. Ames and David Hall.[5] Explaining how positive habits of *li* or "ritual acts" cultivated through the everyday practice of *zhongyong/chung-yung* or "focusing on the familiar" in the Confucian educational system altogether function to transform familiar routines of common existence leading to an enchantment of ordinary, everyday life, they assert: "It is through the routine and ordinary that life becomes enchanted."[6]

Wei-Ming Tu's emphasis on "the inseparability of the Way and our ordinary experience" in *Chung-yung* as a primary source for the Confucianist educational program of self-cultivation echoes in many ways the return to the ordinary as extraordinary in Cavell's American concept of philosophy as education articulated through his Emersonian perfectionism, whereby education is explained as an ongoing process of self-transformation in a dynamic movement of ever-expanding concentric circles. Wei-Ming Tu writes:

> The true self, as an open system, is not only a center of relationships but also a dynamic process of spiritual and physical growth. Selfhood in creative transformation is the broadening and deepening "embodiment" (*t'i*) of an ever-expanding web of human relationships, which we can conceptualize as a series of concentric circles. As the process of "embodiment" never ends, we never reach the outer rim of these concentric circles.[7]

Indeed, this Confucian educational system would profoundly shape the pedagogical training curriculum of East Asian Sino-Japanese Zen/Chan Buddhism, underscoring *satori* or enlightenment by total attention to the familiar routines of everyday life as insight into Tao as the ordinary and the ordinary as Tao.

Overcoming Doubt Through Ordinary Mind in the Zen
Educational System

Both Sino-Japanese Zen/Chan Buddhist self-cultivation and the Emersonian perfectionism of Cavell can be understood as processes of
education and transformation arising through a communicative
process alternating between conversation and silence. Also, for both
Zen cultivation and the Emersonian perfectionism of Cavell's philosophy of education, the dialectical interplay of conversation and silence functions to illuminate the wonder of the ordinary. Moreover,
both self-cultivation through kōan practice in the Zen educational
program and Cavell's Emersonian perfectionism involve an ongoing
response to the standing threat of skeptical doubt by continual return
to the ordinary as extraordinary.

One of the deepest points of contact between the Emersonian perfectionism of Cavell's philosophy of education for grownups and Zen
cultivation is their common aim at recovering the wonder of the ordinary through an ongoing dialogical process of both conversation and
silence. As opposed to otherworldly religiophilosophical traditions
aiming to transcend daily life, the Zen/Chan-tradition Buddhist
thought is brought to consummation in a this-worldly, nondualistic
paradigm based on the realization of Tao as the ordinary, the common, the familiar, the everyday, and the natural. The Zen/Chan tradition represents a culmination of Buddhist nontheistic contemplation
of everyday life as the locus of dialectical interpenetration between
nirvana and *samsara*, thereby resulting in nonduality of enlightenment and the ordinary. In the words of Van Meter Ames: "Zen celebrates the wonder of the ordinary. It has too often seemed that to
become mature is to be disillusioned with what is common, as if
being wise had to mean turning to something higher. Man takes the
familiar for granted."[8]

Further comparing the standpoint of Zen to Ralph Waldo Emerson's American transcendentalist view, Van Meter Ames has written:
"In his [Emerson's] second essay on 'Nature' he spoke of conversation as the goal and test of life."[9] Then he goes on to relate the

function of "conversation" to silence in Emerson's thought, while at the same time showing a parallel to Zen Buddhism:

> At first, this may seem contrary to Zen, which is called the philosophy of silence, of meditation rather than of talk. Yet, the literature of Zen is mostly a record of conversations. If Zen arrived at silence it was by way of question and answer, leading up to a reply suggesting more than what could be said. And Emerson remarked: "Good as is discourse [conversation], silence is better, and shames it."[10]

With much insight, Ames discusses the importance of "conversation" not only in Emerson but in Zen. This is especially seen by the importance of conversation in the kōan tradition of *Rinzai* Zen, which is based on public records of intimate conversations in the spontaneous-encounter dialogues of the *dokusan* or ritual interviews between Zen masters and their disciples during *sesshin*, or intensive meditation retreats. Ames goes on to point out the dialectical relationship between conversation and silence in both Zen and Emerson. In his Emersonian perfectionist concept of philosophy as education, Cavell underscores the role of everyday conversation through ordinary language in the ongoing process of education, conversion, and transformation. However, in his chapter "Acknowledgment of Silence" from his first book about the ontology of film, titled *The World Viewed*, Cavell also underscores the function of silence in the background of ordinary language used in everyday conversation.[11] Thus, both Cavell's Emersonian perfectionism and Zen agree about the role of transformation through education by means of a dialectical alternation between conversation and silence aimed toward disclosure of the wonder of the ordinary.

For both Zen and Cavell, education through philosophical conversation results in a shift from the banality of common existence, with its dull routines of the actual ordinary, to the wonderment of common existence through a realization of the aesthetic, creative, artistic, and poetic dimensions of the transfigured ordinary. Alan Watts discusses this aesthetic dimension of the transfigured ordinary in *The*

Way of Zen: "When the Artist is feeling depressed or sad, and this peculiar emptiness of feeling catches a glimpse of something rather ordinary and unpretentious in its incredible 'suchness,' the mood is called *wabi*."[12] In the highly refined arts and crafts developed under the aegis of Zen in traditional Japanese culture, such as the tea ceremony and haiku poetry, the closely related aesthetic categories of *wabi* and *sabi* designate the simple, natural, rustic beauty of ordinary moments in the wonderment of their emptiness/suchness. The traditional sense of beauty as *wabi-sabi* has long since been cultivated by the aesthetic education of Zen meditation on the ordinary as sublime. Indeed, from the standpoint of a comparative view of aesthetic education, the Zen *wabi-sabi* aesthetic of traditional Japanese culture at once reminds us of Cavell's notion of art as openness to the beauty, sublimity, and poetry of the ordinary.

Here I will focus on the kōan educational curriculum in the Rinzai/Lin-chi kōan tradition of Zen/Chan Buddhism, showing how it continuously endeavors to overcome the skeptical attitude of Great Doubt by a return to ordinary life and language. But first it must be noted that the teaching of "ordinary mind as Tao," which was pervasive throughout the tradition of *Rinzai* Buddhism, also became central to the Sōtō Zen sect of Japanese Buddhism founded by Dōgen (1200–1253). It was Shunryu Suzuki Roshi who established the first Sōtō Zen monastic retreat center in America. In *Zen Mind, Beginner's Mind*, Shunryu Suzuki Roshi thematizes the ordinary and everyday in Sōtō Zen Buddhist thought and practice established by Zen master Dōgen: "Zazen practice and everyday activity are one thing. We call zazen everyday life, and everyday life zazen."[13] Again, "Zen is . . . concentration on our usual, everyday routine."[14] A chapter titled "Ordinary Mind, Buddha Mind" in *Not Always So: Practicing the True Spirit of Zen*, by Shunryu Suzuki Roshi, further thematizes the nonduality of Zen mind or Buddha-nature with ordinary mind (J. *heijōshin*): "Ordinary mind? Okay, I am ordinary mind. Buddha? Yes, I am Buddha. How do I come to be both Buddha and ordinary mind? I don't know, but actually, I am Buddha and ordinary mind."[15] He continues: "Buddha, in this sense, is not different from ordinary mind. And

ordinary mind is not something apart from what is holy. This is a
complete understanding of our self."[16]

The Rinzai/Lin-chi Zen/Chan teaching of Tao as "ordinary mind"
or "everyday-mindedness" (Ch. *p'ing ch'ang hsin*; J. *heijō shin*) is itself
a central and recurrent as well as distinctive and characteristic theme
of a most noble lineage, running through *Ma-tsu* (J. *Baso*, 709–788),
Nan-chuan (J. *Nansen*, 748–834), and *Chao-chou* (J. *Jōshu*, 788–897)
and through yet another branch tracing back to *Ma-tsu*, including
Huang-po (*Obaku*, d. 849) and his towering disciple *Lin-chi* (J. *Rinzai*,
d. 867), along with many other major and minor figures. Also, enlightenment through realization of Tao as ordinary mind is appropriated and thematized by the Japanese Sōtō Zen master Dōgen
(1200–1253) and the modern Japanese teachers who spread Zen to
America, including the *Rinzai* Zen of D. T. Suzuki and the Sōtō Zen
of Shunryu Suzuki Roshi. Furthermore, this Zen tradition of enlightenment through ordinary mind and religious celebration of everyday
life has been thematized by Kitarō Nishida (1870–1945). All of these
thinkers in the tradition of Zen aestheticism underscore the depiction
of the beauty of the ordinary in traditional Japanese literature and the
arts. It seems that the great attraction of Zen to Western culture involves its this-worldly direction, focusing on the multiple possibilities
for enlightenment through the ordinary activities of everyday life
with its familiar routines, thereby to see the extraordinary in the
ordinary.

As stated above, one of the most distinctive and characteristic notions of Zen/Chan Buddhism is the wisdom teaching that "ordinary
mind is Tao" or "Tao is ordinary mind" (Ch. *p'ing ch'ang hsin shih
tao*; J. *Heijō shin kore dō*). A primary source for this Zen/Chan teaching on the interpenetration of enlightenment and the ordinary is to
be found in the collection of forty-eight kōans titled *Mumonkan*,
"The Gateless Gate." The nineteenth kōan recorded in *Mumonkan*,
titled "The Ordinary Is Tao," is a conversation between the Zen/Chan
master Nan-ch'uan (J. Nansen, 748–834) and his student Chao-chou
(J. *Jōshu*, 778–897). I translate the key passage from this encounter

dialogue from the Japanese-language edition titled *Mumonkan* (Ch. *Wumen-kuan*) as follows:

> Jōshū asked Nansen, "What is Tao?"
> Nansen answered, "Ordinary mind is Tao. . . ."
> At these words, Jōshū realized sudden enlightenment.[17]

The above kōan crystallizes an underlying pattern of conversations recorded by the public-encounter dialogues between Zen teachers and their students used in the *Rinzai* Zen educational curriculum: the student asks for a clarification of Tao, Buddha, Zen, or Enlightenment, whereupon the answer is that Tao is the ordinary experience of common persons in their daily life with its familiar routines.

Nishida is regarded as the founder of the Kyoto school of modern Japanese philosophy, characterized by an East-West comparative philosophy and Buddhist-Christian interfaith dialogue rooted in the Japanese Buddhist concept of nothingness (*mu*) or emptiness (*kū*). In his maiden work, *An Inquiry Into the Good* (*Zen no kenkyū*, 1911), Nishida develops a Zen-like nondualistic concept of "pure experience" (J. *junsui keiken*) prior to subject-object division, influenced by the radical empiricism of William James in American philosophy.[18] In his later work, Nishida goes on to reformulate this idea of everyday existence as a stream of pure experience in terms of a Zen Buddhist notion of the *basho* (matrix) or field of "absolute nothingness" (J. *zettai mu*). Moreover, Nishida articulates the field of nothingness in terms of the Zen doctrine of enlightenment as ordinary mind in his penultimate work, *Bashoteki ronri to shūkyōteki sekaikan* (1945), first translated literally by Yusa Michiko as "The Logic of *Topos* and the Religious Worldview" (1986, 1987)[19] and later by David A. Dilworth in a book entitled *Last Writings: Nothingness and the Religious Worldview* (1987).[20]

Nishida's last work, titled *Bashōteki ronri to shūkyōteki sekaikan* (1945), "The Logic of the Field [of Nothingness] and the Religious Worldview," as found in *Kitarō Nishida Zenshū* (*The Collected Works of Kitarō Nishida*, vol. 11), argues that the field of nothingness or emptiness is ultimately disclosed in the familiar routines of ordinary, everyday life, invoking the classical Confucian and Zen/Chan teachings.

In this Japanese-language edition, Nishida can be literally translated as follows: "Nansen (Ch. Nan-chuan) said, 'Religion is not separate from ordinary mind.' 'Ordinary mind is Tao' said [Zen master] Nansen (Ch. Nan-chuan)."[21] After citing the Confucian educational text *Chung-yung* (translated by Wei-Ming Tu as *Centrality and Commonality*), Nishida again cites the reformulation of this idea in the kōan or conversation between Nansen and Jōshū: "It is said that 'Tao cannot be separated from us for even an instant. What can be separated from us is not Tao'. . . . Religion is not apart from ordinary mind. Nansen said, 'Ordinary mind is the Tao.'"[22]

As seen above, Nishida explicitly cites the famous nineteenth chapter of *Mumonkan*, or "The Gateless Gate," wherein Jōshū asks Nansen, "What is Tao?" Zen master Nansen responds, "Tao is ordinary mind" (J. *heijō shin kore dō*).[23] Nishida further explicates this teaching of classical Zen/Chan Buddhism when he relates the views of Zen master Nansen to those of Zen master Rinzai/Lin-chi, who instructs one to realize enlightenment by just being ordinary: "Nansen said, 'ordinary mind is Tao.' Zen master *Rinzai* (Ch. *Lin-chi*) likewise states: 'Buddhadharma does not have a special function, but is only "the ordinary and everyday."'"[24]

According to Cavell's notion of philosophy as education, return to the ordinary is an ongoing response to the constant threat of skeptical doubt, including skepticism of the external world, of other minds, and of oneself. Likewise, one can find response to the existential crisis of skeptical doubt through return to the ordinary in the kōan practice employed by the Rinzai/Lin-chi education curriculum of Zen/Chan Buddhism. In Mumon's own commentary on the very first kōan of *Mumonkan*, he states: "Then concentrate your whole self into this Mu, making your whole body with its 360 bones and joints and 84,000 pores into a solid lump of doubt."[25] According to Zen master Hakuin (1686–1769), kōan practice should begin with Chou-chou's "Mu!" meaning "No!" or "Nothing!" as recorded in the first public case record of *Mumonkan*, or, else, with the "Sound of the Single Hand" (J. *sekishu no onjō*), which he himself had devised.[26] Hakuin explains that one aims to achieve great enlightenment as kenshō or seeing into one's own nature through "great doubt" (J. *taigi*) when facing the kōan.[27] The "great doubt" of Hakuin might be viewed as a functional equivalent to the philosophical problem of skepticism in Cavell's thought, just as return to the ordinary is the therapeutic response to skeptical doubt in both the Rinzai Zen of Hakuin and the perfectionism of Cavell.

A further point of convergence shows an even deeper proximity between the Emersonian perfectionism of Cavell's philosophy of education and the kōans of the Rinzai Zen training curriculum. In the latter, the idea of "perfection" is represented by transformation of daily life through attainment of *satori* or sudden enlightenment. However, for Zen, as for Cavell's Emersonian perfectionism, the idea of perfection as *satori* or enlightenment does not mean transcendence of the ordinary in an otherworldly beyond or achievement of a static final goal in the future but instead an ongoing process of overcoming the bounds of the present moment, like ever-expanding concentric circles, within the flow of ordinary, everyday life itself. Thus, in the conclusion to his study of the educational dimension in the kōan training curriculum of the *Rinzai* Zen pedagogical system of Zen master Hakuin, Michel Mohr writes:

> A brief excursion into the field of education has . . . suggested that we might examine the function of kōans from the perspective of [cultivating] awareness. This concept furnishes a tool for envisioning the transformations of consciousness accompanying practice while avoiding the pitfalls associated with the inevitable discourse on "Zen experience." In that regard . . . the idea of "a *Rinzai* emphasis on satori as a once-and-for-all goal to be reached in the future," still heard, is a groundless misconception. Cultivation pursued in this tradition . . . intends precisely the opposite: constantly going beyond a first awareness of nonduality [*satori*] and aiming at integrating this insight into daily life until no trace of transient exalted states remains.[28]

Hence, in the educational system of Rinzai Zen, in its confrontation with Great Doubt, sudden enlightenment is not the realization of otherwordly transcendence nor a static goal in the future but is a dynamic process of constantly going beyond the actual ordinary into the next, transfigured ordinary, an insight into nondual *satori* as the interfusion of the ordinary and extraordinary.

Conclusion

The Emersonian perfectionism of Cavell in American philosophy and the Zen/Chan Buddhism of Eastern philosophy have converged upon the insight that the response to the standing threat of skeptical doubt is return to the ordinary—not the ordinary as the inauthentic banal, mundane life of everydayness but rather an ecstatic affirmation of authentic everyday life as the transfigured, redemptive everyday, through positive affirmation of the wonder of the ordinary as sublime. In this chapter, I have endeavored to show how the realization of the ordinary as sublime has been crystallized, from the Eastern side, in the Sino-Japanese Confucian and Zen/Chan teachings as well as their reformulation in the modern Japanese philosophy of Kitarō Nishida. If in Eastern philosophy the concept of the ordinary has been illuminated especially by Zen and its reformulation in the modern Japanese philosophy of Nishida, in Western philosophy in general and American philosophy in particular, it is Stanley Cavell who has done most to thematize, problematize, and analyze the concept of the ordinary, the common, the familiar, the everyday. Cavell and Zen both underscore the problem of skeptical doubt as inauthentic denial of, escape from, or resistance to the ordinary, along with the authentic response to the skeptical crisis as positive return to and affirmation of the ordinary. Whereas in traditional Japanese arts and crafts the Zen aesthetic value of *wabi* celebrates the beauty of the ordinary, the simple, the common, the rustic, and the natural, in the aesthetics of Cavell in American philosophy, the function of art, literature, cinema, theater, opera, television, and other art forms is likewise to open up the sublimity and poetry of the ordinary.

Concerning the pedagogical dimension of this essay, for both Zen cultivation in Japanese philosophy and the Emersonian perfectionism of Cavell in American philosophy, education is an ongoing communicative process alternating between conversation and silence, leading to transfiguration of the commonplace by illumination of the ordinary and everyday. Furthermore, both Zen cultivation and the Emersonian perfectionism of Cavell's philosophy of education regard perfection as not escape from or transcendence of ordinary life and language but a return to the ordinary as extraordinary and sublime. It is in such a manner, then, that Cavell's Emersonian perfectionist vision of philosophy as education for grownups might be seen as establishing clear parallels to the training curriculums of various Asian modes of thought, including especially the Confucian and Zen/Chan Buddhist pedagogical systems of cultivation, insofar as for both education is seen as a process of self-overcoming that moves from the actual ordinary to the next or transfigured ordinary, taking the form of an ongoing effort to overcome skeptical doubt by recovering the ordinary as extraordinary, visualized through the image of ever-expanding concentric circles, whereby around each perfect circle a larger circle can be drawn.

REMARKS FROM DISCUSSION

CAVELL: The closing image of Mizoguchi's *Ugetsu* is one of the greatest images known to me of the uncanny on film. The husband lies down on the floor, he sees the wife . . . What shall I say about it? I can't understand any of this. I have a very clear sense of my limits of understanding. Nothing could be more palpable. I feel it about Memphis as much as I feel it about Tokyo or Boston . . . But I had this reaction, and I believe in this reaction, and what I don't want is for somebody to tell me: "You don't understand what the depth of it is, and neither of us really understands what the depth of it is." I just put myself on the line, and I say: this is my response. Now that should be some opening of a conversation. That it could be wrong—God knows it could be wrong, but it's not wrong on the grounds that I am not in a position to say or that I was born in the wrong race. That is one thing that I like so much when it is said that Clinton is our first black president. I am proud of the culture for that becoming a commonplace. There is something deep about that.

CAVELL: I am myself so intent on rescuing the philosophical dimension and register in Thoreau that it is that feature that seems paramount to me. So if I ask whether he is American or cosmopolitan, I am asking whether the philosophy is American or cosmopolitan. Scholars of Thoreau tend to be shy, not to say somewhat guilty, not to say somewhat suspicious, about philosophy. It is as if they wish to say: "Do you want to make this philosophy?" What do they mean by that? Of course I want to make it philosophical. It's perfectly obvious that I am not taking it as a textbook in contemporary philosophy, but the very idea that it's not philosophical! The absence of the philosophical in that scholarly work seems to be so extreme and so insistent, it must be denial. I can understand a feeling of helplessness with respect to it, but that's where the interest would be for me.

As to whether Thoreau is American and cosmopolitan, I don't know actually what it means to say that Thoreau is cosmopolitan. Thoreau is famously used by Mahatma Gandhi. Is Mahatma Gandhi cosmopolitan? Or is he Indian? As for Emerson, Emerson is a figure very hard to assimilate anywhere. Of course, everybody *thinks* he is American, but then those of us who read him in a different way say that he hasn't been read. And in Europe he is always discovered by really marvelous European intellects. It is a superb roster of European writers. Nietzsche is the most glamorous and the most extreme of them but certainly not the only one. But then *he* gets it. *They* get it. You have to get it. And there is no standing way to get it. So I want it to be a bigger matter than whether he is American. The idea that Thoreau is not to the core American seems to me an impossible thought. The idea that he is not to the core a critic of American society also strikes me as inconceivable, and nothing could be, in some way, more in the American grain—not just a criticism of it but a disheartenment by it. This is the reason I think that Marxism never really became institutionalized in American society, because Americans were much more disappointed with America than Marxist criticism could register.

CODA

TEN

PHILOSOPHY AS EDUCATION
Stanley Cavell

I t is gratifying to me that the idea of conceiving philosophy as "the education of grownups" has recently been focused upon by readers of *The Claim of Reason* and has found some favor with them. And, of course, it is further gratifying to me that the point of the formulation seems quite well understood, namely as a sort of response that has in mind Wittgenstein's saying that "philosophical problems . . . are, of course, not empirical problems. . . . The problems are solved, not by giving new information, but by arranging [*durch Zusammenstellung*: by putting together] what we have always known."[1] The issues of philosophy are evidently ones requiring something like self-knowledge or, say, self-reflection. (The point of my unpacking the idea of putting together is its virtually interpreting the look of the English "re-membering." But *remembering* is also not quite right, since what is in question is not something we have *forgotten*.) But this quickly can become puzzling, not to say mysterious, because the issues are not seen as something peculiar to me personally but rather something common to persons as such. What is this knowledge? How is it arrived at?

I note that Wittgenstein's German does not strictly speak of "what we have always known" but just of what "we have long known [*bekannt*]." But the emphasis in the English is not wrong. The idea is that we *already* know what we need to know when philosophy comes into play, that what seems unknown is something in principle familiar to us. Moreover, the emphasis in "always known" is suggested in a further entry among the string of metaphilosophical remarks Wittgenstein offers in this region of the *Investigations* (§§89–133): "One might also give the name 'philosophy' to what is possible *before* [Wittgenstein's emphasis] all new discoveries and inventions."[2] I am prepared, I suppose even somewhat eager, to take this emphatic "before" with utmost seriousness, as suggesting something like what philosophers call the a priori. The suggestion is helped along by Wittgenstein's having just specified that the problems in question in philosophy are of course not "empirical"—empirical, or a posteriori knowledge forming the endlessly familiar contrast in modern philosophical discourse with a priori knowledge (the latter being the knowledge provided by formal logic and scandalously claimed by Kant for the basic categories of human understanding). I suggest this, with perhaps a trace of self-indulgence, to propose that for Wittgenstein human language plays the role of the a priori. What we have "always known" is the condition for our knowing anything whatever, namely human language. If one thinks that this is obviously false, as babies know things before they first have language and hence begin to address us and the world, one might think again what is meant by knowing and, especially, by (first) having language. So what we are to know, or put together, in philosophy is what it is we (always already) know.

But something more went into forming the thought of the education of grownups, prompted by Wittgenstein's further formulation about the (nonempirical) work of philosophical investigation, namely, that it does not, or cannot, give "new information."[3] I have, and had, in mind Prospero's reply to Miranda's remarking in wonder

(wonder naming the emotion in which philosophy was early said to begin), "Oh brave new world that has such people in it"; his reply, namely, "It is new to thee." Does Prospero here interpret Miranda's wonder to signify—because the humans in this new world are members of no different species than Miranda has always encountered—that before this new insight Miranda did not know that people existed? What is new to her? How is it arrived at? (It will not help to say that she has acquired an insight. We would thereupon have to ask, "What is an insight?") The idea to be grasped is that before this moment human others have not been real to her, which she expresses as the world itself having not been real. It is an access of knowledge that seems to exist only in its discovery.

It is clearly not the acquisition of a fresh piece of information, yet, as the paragraph in *The Claim of Reason* containing the proposal of "the education of grownups" emphasizes, there is learning that is not comprehensible as acquiring new facts; perhaps it can be thought of as learning further what kind of thing can be a fact, for example, that humans are mortals. One could call this learning rethinking, except that this may suggest clarifying (say, giving explanations), which may pass by the essential idea that you *already* know what you keep from yourself.

In my paragraph claiming that philosophy is the study of this further education, two main steps are taken: one step is to introduce a number of concepts new to my text—for example, knowing how to go on, the light in which something is seen, natural growth opposed by a change called conversion, a matter that entails anxiety and calls up the idea of rebirth. The other step is to cite four greatly famous figures in the history of philosophical imagination who exemplify the thinking that demands and guides the turnaround that characterizes human adulthood or, say, its claim to autonomy.

Each of these thinkers to my mind bears some intimate connection with thoughts in *Philosophical Investigations*, sometimes an intimacy in particular concepts, sometimes especially, I suppose, a general connection with Wittgenstein's incessant realization, beginning with his preface, that what he has to say is at once wholly clear yet difficult in a way unaccustomed, even indescribable, to those for whom he means to be writing.

Augustine is an obvious figure to cite, as Wittgenstein opens his *Investigations* by quoting Augustine's *Confessions*. There Wittgenstein launches his new mode of questioning against a question and an answer that have motivated philosophers forever, namely, the question of how language reveals the world and the obvious answer that it must happen by words naming or denoting particular things. No other philosophers I think of, however, have begun by taking up the question from the point of view of the infant, the one faced with learning (names).

And a narrower relation between Augustine and Wittgenstein shows, or should show, in their common emphasis on the restlessness of the human being. In the opening section of Augustine's *Confessions*, it is a restlessness deriving from our distance from God, with whom alone there is peace; in Wittgenstein's text it is a restlessness—Wittgenstein calls it a torment—deriving from our being driven to philosophy, to keep philosophizing (evidently an essential character of the human), for which Wittgenstein claims to discover a road to peace (*Ruhe*, rest), however momentary.[4] This claim is plainly not of new information but of the discovery of a new "method," one requiring endless practice.

I cite Rousseau, although Wittgenstein does not mention him, in order to highlight Wittgenstein's observation that in philosophizing pictures hold us "captive,"[5] a thought as old as Plato's myth of our everyday, our customary, that is to say, our present lives, spent as if we are chained in a cave watching shadows on a wall, but in Rousseau it is presented as if we should be able read this fact directly upon being told it and opening our eyes: "Man is born free and is everywhere in chains." Because I am one of mankind, this must be true of me, hence the truth must be open to me to entertain. That is, if I do not understand this of myself, I do not understand it at all. For Wittgenstein, you come to understand it in particular instances, cases where you face your own captivity, perhaps by coming to feel the emptiness, not to say boredom, in perpetually insisting (to whom?), for example, that if you *know* then you *cannot* be wrong, and that because you cannot *have* the feelings of another, you cannot *know* the feelings of another. Then the question becomes: how do I come to understand myself, recognize my boredom or emptiness or insistence in the ways I think? The paragraph of *The Claim of Reason* that is in principal question here (rethinking the idea of "the education of grownups") speaks of conversion, say, turning toward oneself. Turning is distinctly figured in Plato's myth of the cave, in which, as a first movement toward freedom, a prisoner "turns around" in order to walk up the path out of the cave.

Well, but then how can philosophy get you to, cause you to, suspect your captivity and turn to yourself, and turn around, and begin to walk on your own? I think the first condition here is for philosophy to suspect itself of wishing to be omnipotent, anyway inhumanly potent, as when it demands of itself that it provide "reasons" to get people, or cause people, to act in certain ways. But if conversion, and all that may imply, is a human capacity, the opportunity for it must present itself repeatedly (given health and a day). Then philosophy's first task is to show us to ourselves, revealing our (captivating) repetitions. This is how I understand Wittgenstein's saying: "We must do away with all *explanation*, and description alone must take its place."[6]

About the relations of Luther and Thoreau to the thought of philosophy and/as education, I shall be even briefer. In them, the relation to the *Investigations* is not with specific concepts so much as in their constant demand, or caution, that a turnaround or conversion is in store. Luther says: "For all our life should be baptism, and the fulfilling of the sign, or sacrament, of baptism; we have been set free from all else and given over to baptism alone, that is, to death and resurrection. This glorious liberty of ours, and this understanding of baptism have been carried captive in our day."[7] Baptism signifies rebirth, hence conversion. But such a remark is itself doubtless understood only under conversion. (Which, in my case, usually means that I have to suspect my various senses of liberation. It may be that I assume too great a familiarity with the idea of a transformation and freeing of experience, because I spent my first six years living in a house with—by today's standards—a large family, mostly of musicians, including two professional virtuosi, one of them my mother, where time out of mind I was granted touchstones of what it means to be transported instantaneously and entirely into a wordlessly enlightened, cleansed, world.)

The connection with Thoreau on this occasion became unavoidable to me when in looking up this past week, for other reasons, a passage in my *The Senses of Walden*,[8] my eye fell on the following sentence, at roughly the middle of my book: "For the child to grow he requires family and familiarity, but for a grownup to grow he requires strangeness and transformation, i.e., birth." I was astounded to find there the virtually literal occurrence of the core thought of the paragraph in question here from *The Claim of Reason*, which appeared the better part of a decade later. (My astonishment, but not at all my pleasure, largely subsided when I recollected that I wrote the three lectures making up *The Senses of Walden* in the same year, while on sabbatical leave in 1971, that I rewrote and extended part 1 of *The Claim of Reason*. That part ends on page 125 and was completed in 1971, and it is in fact that last page of part 1 on which occurs the thought that repeats almost verbatim the passage in *The Senses of Walden*. The material that was new in the appearance of *The Claim of Reason* in 1979 is solely part 4, beginning on page 329 or, strictly, 327, written in the summers of 1976 and 1977.) The pleasure for me in this simultaneity lies in discovering/remembering that the passage in *The Senses of Walden* puts its thoughts in conjunction with thoughts of America, specifically with thoughts of the danger that its public language or, say, the memory of its short history, of its extravagant promises to itself, keep becoming unintelligible, to it and for it. Nor do I regard it as accidental that, still more generally, my book on *Walden* describes Thoreau's book as declaring itself to be a scripture, which prompts me to take, or confirms me in taking seriously, Wittgenstein's tip to one of his students to consider his *Investigations* "from a religious point of view." This captures part of my sense of what I sometimes call the "transcendental" in Wittgenstein's view of our ordinary language, the pains he takes to show that our concepts (the motions of our words) remain in principle open to the future, to certain forms of change, one sense in which we perpetually mean beyond what we can say, something out of our control. For some of us, this is a happy dream, for others a nightmare.

A final word about why it is that I wish to show a significant connection between Wittgenstein's *Investigations* and central moments in the history of philosophical thinking. Unlike the work of every other major philosopher in the tradition of so-called analytic or analytical philosophy, Wittgenstein's *Investigations*, while joining in the criticism of earlier philosophy, makes clear, if one wishes to see it, that he continues philosophy's originating search to criticize, while continuing, the philosophical impulse and above all to demonstrate that its signature mode of criticism is one that is simultaneously turned toward oneself and toward one's contribution to the communal. To demonstrate, in a word, that it is philosophy itself that becomes the motive of education.

Notes

INTRODUCTION

Paul Standish and Naoko Saito

1. Stanley Cavell, *The Claim of Reason* (Oxford: Oxford University Press, 1979), 125.

2. Which it did at the Philosophy of Education Society Annual Meeting, in Cambridge, Massachusetts, when the topic was discussed, in a panel with René Arcilla, Stanley Cavell, Hilary Putnam, Naoko Saito, and Paul Standish.

3. Henry D. Thoreau, *Walden*, in *Walden and Resistance to Civil Government*, ed. William Rossi (New York: W. W. Norton & Company, 1992), 74. Quoted in Stanley Cavell, *The Senses of Walden* (Chicago: University of Chicago Press, 1992), 48.

4. Stanley Cavell, *Die Unheimlichkeit des Gewöhnlichen und andere philosophische Essays*, ed. Davide Sparti and Espen Hammer (Frankfurt am Main: Fischer Taschenbuch Verlag, 2002).

5. Hilary Putnam, "Philosophy as the Education of Grownups: Stanley Cavell and Skepticism," in *Reading Cavell*, ed. Alice Crary and Sanford Shieh (London: Routledge, 2005), 117.

6. Interview with Stanley Cavell by Naoko Saito, July 6, 2004; Paul Standish and Naoko Saito, "Stanley Cavell to *Walden* no Sekai: Nihon no Dokusha heno Izanai" ("Stanley Cavell's *Walden*: An Introduction to Japanese Readers"), in *Sensu obu Woruden* (the Japanese translation of *The Senses of Walden*), trans. Naoko Saito (Tokyo: Hosei University Press, 2005), 214.

7. Cavell, *The Senses of Walden*, 5.

8. Our conversation with Cavell in Cambridge, Massachusetts, April 13, 2008.

9. John Dewey, *Experience and Nature*, in *The Later Works of John Dewey*, ed. Jo Ann Boydston (Carbondale: Southern Illinois University Press, 1981), 1:186.

10. Ibid., 185.

11. See Richard Shusterman, *Pragmatist Aesthetics: Living Beauty, Rethinking Art* (Lanham, Md.: Rowman & Littlefield Publishers, Inc., 1997).

12. Our conversation with Putnam in Cambridge, Massachusetts, April 13, 2008.

13. Putnam, "Philosophy as the Education of Grownups," 223.

14. Thoreau, *Walden*, 66.

15. Walter Benn Michaels, "Walden's False Bottom," in *Walden and Resistance to Civil Government*, ed. William Rossi (New York: W. W. Norton & Company, 1992), 417.

16. Thoreau, *Walden*, 220. Quoted in Cavell, *The Senses of Walden*, 76.

17. Stanley Cavell, "Stanley Cavell and the Education of Grownups," at the Annual Meeting of Philosophy of Education Society (Cambridge on April 13, 2008).

18. Our conversation with Putnam, in Cambridge, Massachusetts, March 18, 2009.

19. Our conversation with Cavell, in Cambridge, Massachusetts, on April 13, 2008.

20. Cavell, "Stanley Cavell and the Education of Grownups."

21. Stanley Cavell, *A Pitch of Philosophy: Autobiographical Exercises* (Cambridge, Mass.: Harvard University Press, 1994).

22. Putnam, "Philosophy as the Education of Grownups," 120.

23. Ludwig Wittgenstein, *Philosophical Investigations*, trans. G. E. M. Anscombe (Oxford: Basil Blackwell, 1978), #217.

24. Stanley Cavell, *Themes of Our School: Effects and Causes* (Chicago: University of Chicago Press, 1984), 32.

25. Stanley Cavell, *Conditions Handsome and Unhandsome: The Constitution of Emersonian Perfectionism* (Chicago: University of Chicago Press, 1990), 7.

26. Ibid. The pertinence of Plato's phrase, whose significance reverberates through Cavell's work, is, of course, made most explicit in his title *Cities of Words: Pedagogical Letters on the Moral Life* (Cambridge, Mass.: The Belknap Press of Harvard University Press, 2004).

27. Stanley Cavell, *Philosophy the Day After Tomorrow* (Cambridge, Mass.: The Belknap Press of Harvard University Press, 2005), 212–235.

28. Cavell, *Conditions Handsome and Unhandsome*, 31.

29. "Knowing and Acknowledging," in Stanley Cavell, *Must We Mean What We Say? A Book of Essays* (Cambridge: Cambridge University Press, 1976), 238–266. This is an expansion of comments, given in a colloquium at the University of Rochester in 1966, in response to a paper by Norman Malcolm.

30. Ralph Waldo Emerson, *Ralph Waldo Emerson*, ed. Richard Poirier (Oxford: Oxford University Press, 1990), 131.

CHAPTER ONE
PHILOSOPHY AS THE EDUCATION OF GROWNUPS
Stanley Cavell

1. Ludwig Wittgenstein, *Philosophical Investigations*, ed. G. E. M. Anscombe and R. Rhees, trans. G. E. M. Anscombe (Oxford: B. Blackwell, 1976), §1.

2. Ibid.

3. Ibid.

4. Ibid., §90.

5. Ibid., §371.

6. Ibid., §122.

7. Ludwig Wittgenstein, *The Blue Book*.

8. Andrew Norris, ed., *The Claim to Community: Essays on Stanley Cavell and Political Philosophy* (Stanford, Calif.: Stanford University Press, 2006).

9. See "Performative and Passionate Utterance," in Stanley Cavell, *Philosophy the Day After Tomorrow* (Cambridge, Mass.: Harvard University Press), 155–191.

10. Wittgenstein, *Philosophical Investigations*, §25.

11. Ibid., §23.

12. J. L. Austin, *Philosophical Papers*, 3rd ed., 185.

CHAPTER TWO
THE FACT/VALUE DICHOTOMY AND ITS CRITICS
Hilary Putnam

1. Stanley Cavell, *The Claim of Reason: Wittgenstein, Skepticism, Morality, and Tragedy* (Oxford: Oxford University Press, 1979), 125.

2. Hilary Putnam, *The Collapse of the Fact/Value Dichotomy and Other Essays* (Cambridge, Mass.: Harvard University Press, 2002).

3. Ibid., 7.

4. Lionel Robbins, *An Essay on the Nature and Significance of Economic Science* (London: Macmillan, 1932), 132.

5. P. A. Samuelson, *Foundations of Economic Analysis* (Cambridge, Mass.: Harvard University Press, 1947), 219–220.

6. A. J. Ayer, *Philosophical Essays* (London: Macmillan, 1954), 237.

7. An important exception is Cora Diamond, "Losing Your Concepts," *Ethics* 98 (January 1988): 255–277.

8. Charles Stevenson, *Ethics and Language* (New Haven, Conn.: Yale University Press, 1944).

9. See especially ibid., 252–254.

10. Ibid., 2.

11. Ibid., 13.

12. I criticize this assumption in Hilary Putnam, *Ethics Without Ontology* (Cambridge, Mass.: Harvard University Press, 2004), 75–78.

13. Stevenson, *Ethics and Language*, 136.

14. Ibid., 113.

15. Cavell, *The Claim of Reason*, 253.

16. Ibid., 254.

17. Putnam, *Ethics Without Ontology*, 76.

18. Cavell, *The Claim of Reason*, 260.

19. Morton White, *Towards Reunion in Philosophy* (Cambridge, Mass.: Harvard University Press, 1956).

20. For an explanation and criticism of this rather unclear view, see Hilary Putnam, "What Theories Are Not," in *Philosophical Papers*, vol. 1: *Mathematics, Matter, and Method* (Cambridge, Mass.: Harvard University Press, 1975), 215–227.

21. Rudolf Carnap, *The Unity of Science* (London: Kegan Paul and Trench, Trubner, and Co, 1934), 26.

22. C. G. Hempel, "Problems and Changes in the Empiricist Criterion of Meaning," *Revue Internationale de Philosophie* 4 (1950): 41–63.

23. Rudolf Carnap, "The Foundations of Logic and Mathematics" in *The International Encyclopedia of Unified Science*, vol. 1, pt. 1, ed. Otto Neurath, Rudolf Carnap, and Charles W. Morris (Chicago: The University of Chicago Press, 1939), 198–211.

24. Rudolf Carnap, "On the Methodological Character of Theoretical Concepts," in *Minnesota Studies in the Philosophy of Science*, vol. 1: *The Foundations of Science and the Concepts of Psychology and Psychoanalysis*, ed. Herbert Feigl and May Brodbeck (Minneapolis: University of Minnesota Press, 1956), 38–76.

25. W. V. Quine, "Two Dogmas of Empiricism," *Philosophical Review* 60 (1951): 20–43.

26. W. V. Quine, "Carnap and Logical Truth," in *The Philosophy of Rudolf Carnap*, ed. P. A. Schilpp (LaSalle: Open Court, 1963), 406.

27. Vivian Walsh, "Philosophy and Economics," in *The New Palgrave: A Dictionary of Economics*, ed. J. Eatwell, M. Milgate, and P. Newman (London: Macmillan, 1987), 3:862.

28. For details of these attempts, see chapter 8 of Putnam, *The Collapse of the Fact/Value Dichotomy.*

29. Nelson Goodman, "The New Riddle of Induction," chapter 3 of his *Fact, Fiction, and Forecast* (Cambridge, Mass.: Harvard University Press, 1955).

30. Iris Murdoch, *The Sovereignty of "Good" Over Other Concepts* (Cambridge: Cambridge University Press, 1967).

31. Putnam, *The Collapse of the Fact/Value Dichotomy.*

32. John McDowell, "Non-Cognitivism and Rule-Following," in *Mind, Value, and Reality* (Cambridge, Mass.: Harvard University Press, 1998), 198–218. Originally published in *Wittgenstein: To Follow a Rule*, ed. Steven H. Holtzman and Christopher M. Leich (London: Routledge, 1981), 141–172.

33. Ibid., 200–201.

34. Ibid., 201.

35. Ibid., emphasis added.

36. Stanley Cavell, *Must We Mean What We Say? A Book of Essays* (Cambridge: Cambridge University Press, 1976.)

37. Plato, *Euthyphro*, trans. F. J. Church and R. D. Cumming (New York: The Library of Liberal Arts, The Liberal Arts Press, 1956), 9.

38. Cavell, *The Claim of Reason*, 264–265.

39. Bernard Williams reports that "the idea that it might be impossible to pick up an evaluative concept unless one shared its evaluative interest is basically a Wittgensteinian idea. I first heard it expressed by Philippa Foot and Iris Murdoch in a seminar in the 1950s." Bernard Williams, *Ethics and the Limits of Philosophy* (Cambridge, Mass.: Harvard University Press, 1985), 218.

40. Cavell, *The Claim of Reason*, 269.

41. Ibid., 265.

42. Ibid., 241.

43. Stevenson, *Ethics and Language*, 252.

44. Ibid., 251.

45. Cavell, *The Claim of Reason*, 287–288.

46. Hilary Putnam and Vivian Walsh, "A Response to Dasgupta," in *Economics and Philosophy* 23, no. 3 (November 2007): 359–364.

47. Carnap, *The Unity of Science*, 26.

CHAPTER THREE
ENCOUNTERING CAVELL: THE EDUCATION OF A GROWNUP
Russell B. Goodman

1. Ludwig Wittgenstein, *Philosophical Investigations*, trans. G. E. M. Anscombe (New York: Macmillan, 1953), 213.

2. Ibid., §90.

3. Stanley Cavell, *Must We Mean What We Say? A Book of Essays* (New York: Cambridge University Press, 1976), 65.

4. Wittgenstein, *Philosophical Investigations*, §133.

5. Ibid.

6. Cavell, *Must We Mean What We Say?*, 67.

7. Wittgenstein, *Philosophical Investigations*, §109.

8. Ibid., §128.

9. Cavell, *Must We Mean What We Say?*, 71.

10. Wittgenstein, *Philosophical Investigations*, §309.

11. Stanley Cavell, *The Senses of Walden* (Chicago: University of Chicago Press, 1992), 34.

12. Ibid., 103–104.

13. Ibid., 104.

14. Stanley Cavell, *The Claim of Reason: Wittgenstein, Skepticism, Morality, and Tragedy* (New York: Oxford University Press, 1979), 437.

15. Stanley Cavell, *In Quest of the Ordinary: Lines of Skepticism and Romanticism* (Chicago: University of Chicago Press, 1988), 53.

16. Ibid., 46.

17. William James, *Writings 1902–1910* (New York: Library of America, 1987), 502.

18. Cavell, *The Senses of Walden*, 126.

19. John Dewey, "Emerson—The Philosopher of Democracy," in *The Middle Works of John Dewey*, vol. 3, ed. Jo Ann Boydston (Carbondale: Southern Illinois University Press, 1977).

20. Russell B. Goodman, ed., *Pragmatism: Critical Concepts in Philosophy* (London: Routledge, 2005), 2:44.

21. Cavell, *The Senses of Walden*, 5.

22. Ibid., 12.

23. Ibid., 152.

24. Russell B. Goodman, *American Philosophy and the Romantic Tradition* (Cambridge: Cambridge University Press, 1990); *Wittgenstein and William James* (Cambridge: Cambridge University Press, 2003).

25. Ralph W. Emerson, *Collected Works of Ralph Waldo Emerson*, ed. Robert Spiller et al. (Cambridge, Mass.: Harvard University Press, 1971), 2:82.

26. Ibid., 2:87.

27. Ralph Barton Perry, *The Thought and Character of William James* (Boston: Little, Brown, and Company, 1935), 1:100.

28. William James, *The Principles of Psychology* (1890; repr. Cambridge, Mass.: Harvard University Press, 1981), 935.

29. William James, *The Correspondence of William James*, ed. Ignas K. Skrupskelis and Elizabeth M. Berkeley (Charlottesville: University of Virginia Press, 1994), 3:324.

30. Mathias Girel, "Les Angles de L'acte, Usages d'Emerson dans la Philosophie de William James," *Cahier Charles V* 37 (2004): 207–245.

31. Frederic I. Carpenter, "William James and Emerson," *American Literature* 11, no. 1 (1939): 43.

32. Russell B. Goodman, "Cavell and American Philosophy," in *Contending with Stanley Cavell*, ed. Russell B. Goodman (Oxford: Oxford University Press, 2005), 100–117.

33. James, *Writings 1902–1910*, 509.

CHAPTER FOUR

SKEPTICISM, ACKNOWLEDGMENT, AND

THE OWNERSHIP OF LEARNING

Paul Standish

1. See Paul Standish, "Data Return: The Sense of the Given in Educational Research," *Journal of Philosophy of Education* 35, no. 3 (2001): 497–518.

2. Ludwig Wittgenstein, *On Certainty*, ed. G. E. M. Anscombe and G. H. von Wright, trans. D. Paul and G. E. M. Anscombe (Oxford: Blackwell, 1977).

3. Stanley Cavell, *Disowning Knowledge in Six Plays of Shakespeare* (Cambridge: Cambridge University Press, 1987), 95–96.

4. William Shakespeare, *King Lear*, 1.1.50–55.

5. Ibid., 1.1.87–88.

6. Ibid., 4.2.49–50.

7. Stanley Cavell, *Contesting Tears: The Hollywood Melodrama of the Unknown Woman* (Chicago: University of Chicago Press, 1996), 13–14.

8. Stanley Cavell, *The Claim of Reason: Wittgenstein, Skepticism, Morality, and Tragedy* (Oxford: Oxford University Press, 1979), 454.

9. For a critical discussion, see Paul Standish, "Fetish for Effect," in *Education at the Interface: Philosophical Questions Concerning On-line Education*, ed. Nigel Blake and Paul Standish (Oxford: Blackwell, 2000): 151–168.

10. Martin Heidegger, *Discourse on Thinking*, trans. J. M. Anderson and E. H. Freund (1959; repr. New York: Harper and Row, 1969).

11. Martin Heidegger, *Being and Time*, trans. J. Macquarrie and E. Robinson (1927; repr. Oxford: Blackwell, 1962). In *Being and Time*, Heidegger avoids using the term "man" or "human being" on the grounds that these have become irrevocably burdened with the assumptions of modern metaphysics, preferring the term *Dasein*, which literally means being-there or there-being.

12. Ibid., 68.

13. Heidegger, *Discourse on Thinking*, 48–49.

14. That is, the context of Germany in the first half of the twentieth century. Heidegger was briefly a member of the Nazi party (in 1933), though he subsequently distanced himself from this. In the years after the war, however, he never fully acknowledged the extent or implications of his involvement.

15. Martin Heidegger, "Building Dwelling Thinking," in *Poetry, Language, Thought* (1952; repr. New York: Harper and Row, 1975).

16. Stanley Cavell, "Thoreau Thinks of Ponds, Heidegger of Rivers," in *Philosophy the Day After Tomorrow* (Cambridge, Mass.: The Belknap Press of Harvard University Press, 2005): 213–235.

17. See Paul Standish, "In Her Own Voice: Convention, Conversion, Criteria," *Educational Philosophy and Theory* 36, no. 1 (2004): 91–106.

18. Cavell, *The Claim of Reason*, 23.

19. Ibid., 454.

CHAPTER FIVE

SENSUAL SCHOOLING: ON THE AESTHETIC
EDUCATION OF GROWNUPS

Gordon C. F. Bearn

1. Alfred North Whitehead, *Science and the Modern World* (1925; repr. New York: The Free Press, 1967), 196.

2. Alfred North Whitehead, "Immortality," in *The Philosophy of Alfred North Whitehead*, ed. P. A. Schilpp (Evanston, Ill.: Northwestern University Press, 1941), 691.

3. Whitehead, *Science and the Modern World*, 196–197.

4. Whitehead, "Immortality," 670. And on the same page: "We shall never understand the history of exact scientific knowledge unless we examine the relation of this feeling 'Now we know' to the types of learning prevalent in each epoch. In some shape or other it is always present among the dominant group who are preserving and promoting civilized learning. It is a misapplication of that *sense of success* which is essential for the maintenance of any enterprise" (emphasis added).

5. This passage comes from the Whiteheadian opening of N. Lawrence, "Time Represented as Space," *The Monist* (July 1969): 447–456; reprinted in Wilfrid Sellars and Eugene Freeman, *Basic Issues in the Philosophy of Time* (La Salle, Ill: Open Court, 1971), 123.

6. Whitehead, *Science and the Modern World*, 198.

7. Ibid., 199.

8. Ibid., 198.

9. Ibid., 199.

10. Ibid., 200.

11. Ibid.

12. Ibid.

13. Whitehead, "Immortality," 696.

14. Whitehead, *Science and the Modern World*, 87–88.

15. See Russell B. Goodman, "James on the Nonconceptual," *Midwest Studies in Philosophy* 28 (2004): 137–148. Whitehead wanted to recover the power of Bergson and James and Dewey but absent the charge of anti-intellectualism. See Alfred North Whitehead, *Process and Reality*, corrected ed. (1929; repr. New York: Free Press, 1978), xii, 209.

16. Alfred North Whitehead, *Adventures of Ideas* (1933; repr. Cambridge: Cambridge University Press, 1943), 290–291.

17. Ibid., 315.

18. Whitehead, *Science and the Modern World*, 169–170. Whitehead and Bergson share the view that we are unable to complete the description of an actual occasion by means of concepts. In Whitehead, this is because such a description could never stop (it's infinite); in Bergson, this is because such a description could never start (pure duration is subrepresentational). In this paper, I use Bergsonian metaphysics to support a Whiteheadian philosophy of education, namely sensual schooling.

19. Whitehead, *Adventures of Ideas*, 370.

20. Henri Bergson, *Laughter* (1900; repr. Baltimore, Md.: The Johns Hopkins University Press, 1980), 159.

21. Whitehead, *Adventures of Ideas*, 365.

22. Stanley Cavell, *The Claim of Reason: Wittgenstein, Skepticism, Morality, and Tragedy* (Oxford: Oxford University Press, 1979), 125.

23. Ibid.

24. Ludwig Wittgenstein, *Philosophical Investigations*, ed. G. E. M. Anscombe and R. Rhees, trans. G. E. M. Anscombe (Oxford: B. Blackwell, 1976), §30. Hereafter, references to this book will appear this way: (*Investigations*, §30) or (*Investigations*, 200), the first referring to *paragraphs* in part 1, the second referring to *pages* in English in part 2).

25. For the importance of the notion of a "series of examples" that can be "broken off" in Wittgenstein's writing, see Wittgenstein, *Philosophical Investigations*, §133.

26. Wittgenstein, *Philosophical Investigations*, §31.

27. Ibid.

28. Stanley Cavell, "The *Investigations'* Everyday Aesthetics of Itself," in *The Cavell Reader*, ed. Stephen Mulhall (Oxford: B. Blackwell, 1996), 385.

29. Augustine, in Wittgenstein, *Philosophical Investigations*, §89.

30. Wittgenstein, *Philosophical Investigations*, §89.

31. On the position of seriousness in Cavell's reading of Derrida's discussion of Austin, especially Cavell's distinction between a (criticized) sacramental and a (defended) testamental interpretation of seriousness, see Stanley Cavell, *A Pitch of Philosophy: Autobiographical Exercises* (Cambridge, Mass.: Harvard University Press, 1994), esp. 124–127. In another place, Cavell tells us he found that his consideration of Derrida on Austin had "become something like a study of seriousness." Cavell, "The *Investigations'* Everyday Aesthetics of Itself," 371. For critical consideration of Cavell's reading of Derrida, see my "Sounding Serious: Cavell and Derrida," *Representations* 63 (Summer 1998): 65–92.

32. Stanley Cavell, "Something out of the Ordinary," in *Philosophy the Day After Tomorrow* (Cambridge, Mass.: The Belknap Press of Harvard University Press, 2005), 11–12.

33. Ludwig Wittgenstein, *The Blue Book and Brown Books*, ed. R. Rhees (New York: Harper Torchbooks, 1958), 1; Wittgenstein, *Philosophical Investigations*, §1.

34. Wittgenstein, *The Blue Book*, 1.

35. Ludwig Wittgenstein, "Philosophy," from *The Big Typescript* (1933), in Ludwig Wittgenstein, *Philosophical Occasions*, ed. J. C. Klagge and E. Nordmann (Indianapolis, Ind.: Hackett, 1993), 165.

36. Wittgenstein, *The Blue Book*, 47; compare Wittgenstein, *Philosophical Investigations*, §109.

37. Wittgenstein, *Philosophical Investigations*, §94.

38. Wittgenstein, *The Blue Book*, 30.

39. Wittgenstein, *Philosophical Investigations*, 232. For more on the neurological turn, see P. M. S. Hacker and M. R. Bennett, *Philosophical Foundations of Neuroscience* (Oxford: Blackwell, 2003).

40. Wittgenstein, *The Blue Book*, 27.

41. Ludwig Wittgenstein, *Culture and Value*, ed. G. H. von Wright, in collaboration with H. Nyman, trans. P. Winch (Chicago: University of Chi-

cago Press, 1980), 30. Compare Wittgenstein, *Philosophical Investigations*, §112.

42. Wittgenstein, *The Blue Book*, 1.

43. Wittgenstein, *Philosophical Investigations*, §122.

44. G. Baker and P. M. S. Hacker, *An Analytical Commentary on the Philosophical Investigations*, vol. 1: *Understanding and Meaning* (Chicago: University of Chicago Press, 1980), esp. 541–545.

45. G. Baker, "*Philosophical Investigations* §122: Neglected Aspects" (1991), reprinted in his *Wittgenstein's Method: Neglected Aspects*, ed. K. J. Morris (Oxford: B. Blackwell, 2004), esp. 37–46.

46. Cavell, "The *Investigations'* Everyday Aesthetics of Itself," 385.

47. Cavell, *The Claim of Reason*, 124–125.

48. Wittgenstein, *Philosophical Investigations*, §238. Cavell discusses this passage in *The Claim of Reason*, 122.

49. Wittgenstein, "Philosophy," from *The Big Typescript*, 175.

50. Cavell, *The Claim of Reason*, 73.

51. Ibid., 133–134.

52. Ibid., 73.

53. Ibid., 77.

54. Cavell, "The *Investigations'* Everyday Aesthetics of Itself," 209–210.

55. Wittgenstein, *Philosophical Investigations*, §122. See Baker, "*Philosophical Investigations* §122: Neglected Aspects," 38: Wittgenstein "focused his attention not so much on accumulating data on 'the use of our words' as on confronting more general prejudices or preconceptions which stand in the way of our making effective use of these data."

56. Cavell, *The Claim of Reason*, 78.

57. Ibid., 79.

58. Ibid., 7.

59. In brief, the difference between Baker and Hacker's interpretation of criteria and the interpretation identified by Cavell as the Malcolm-Albritton view is that for Malcolm-Albritton, criteria answer the skeptic with certainty, and for Baker and Hacker, criteria answer the skeptic with defeasible evidence. Both, however, unlike Cavell, use criteria to answer the skeptic, not to reveal the truth in skepticism. See G. Baker and P. M. S. Hacker, *Scepticism Rules and Language* (Oxford: B. Blackwell, 1984), esp. "Internal Relations and Criteria," 106–115. Their commentary on the *Investigations* makes frequent use of a semitechnical notion of criteria as "something that is *a priori*, defeasible evidence for something else." Baker and Hacker, *An Analytical Commentary on the Philosophical Investigations*, 7.

60. Cavell, *The Claim of Reason*, 79.

61. Ibid., 83.

62. Ibid., 84.

63. Ibid., 124–125.

64. Stanley Cavell, *Conditions Handsome and Unhandsome: Constitution of Emersonian Perfectionism* (Chicago: The University of Chicago Press, 1990), 71: "Call Wittgenstein's passage (at §217) his scene of instruction."

65. Wittgenstein, *Philosophical Investigations*, §217.

66. Stanley Cavell, "The Wittgensteinian Event," in *Philosophy the Day After Tomorrow*, 204.

67. Ibid., 209. (Why intellectual? Why not simultaneously volitional?)

68. I am thankful here for Cavell's impromptu reading of *Philosophical Investigations*, §133, which he provided in response to a cruder version of the argument of this paper on October 27, 2006 (at the Cavell Colloquium on October 27–29, 2006).

69. Here I am grateful for comments that Hilary Putnam made, once again on October 27, 2006 (at the Cavell Colloquium on October 27–29, 2006), after a cruder version of this paper. He pointed out that the questions that call for the education of grownups include more kinds of crisis-inducing questions than we find in the *Investigations*.

70. Cavell, *The Claim of Reason*, 125.

71. Cavell, "The *Investigations*' Everyday Aesthetics of Itself," 379.

72. Cavell, "The Wittgensteinian Event," 385, 209–210.

73. Wittgenstein, *Philosophical Investigations*, §31.

74. Cavell, "The *Investigations*' Everyday Aesthetics of Itself," 385.

75. Cavell, *The Claim of Reason*, 125.

76. Ibid.

77. At *Investigations*, §133, Wittgenstein tells us that the "real discovery is the one that makes me capable of stopping doing philosophy when I want to." This is to be distinguished from stopping doing philosophy when philosophy wants to, when it is finished, as at the end of the first *Critique*, where Kant imagined it would be finished by about 1800. And since the verb that Anscombe translates "stopping" is, more literally, to break off (*abbrechen*), it follows that philosophy, which can be broken off, can also be picked up again. That is perhaps the spirit in which to take Wittgenstein's otherwise conflicting crack, "You know I said I can stop doing philosophy when I like. That is a lie! I can't." R. Rhees, ed., *Ludwig Wittgenstein, Personal Recollections* (Totowa, N.J.: Rowman and Littlefield, 1981, 219.

78. Cavell, "The Wittgensteinian Event," 209.

79. Wittgenstein, *Philosophical Investigations*, §133.

80. Cavell, *A Pitch of Philosophy*, 153: "the world is successfully, if momentarily, called back from its skeptical annihilation."

81. G. E. Moore, "Wittgenstein's lectures in 1930–33" [1954–1955], in Ludwig Wittgenstein, *Philosophical Occasions*, ed. James C. Klagge and Alfred Nordmann (Indianapolis, Ind.: Hackett, 1993), 114.

82. Cavell, *The Claim of Reason*, xiii.

83. Wittgenstein, *Philosophical Investigations*, §78.

84. Ibid., 202.

85. Ibid., 200.

86. Wittgenstein, *The Blue Book*, 19.

87. Wittgenstein, *Philosophical Investigations*, §436.

88. Cavell, "The Wittgensteinian Event," 205.

89. Wittgenstein, *Philosophical Investigations*, §153.

90. Ibid., 181.

91. Ibid.

92. Whitehead, *Process and Reality*, 12.

93. Ibid.

94. Ibid., 11.

95. Ibid., 25.

96. Alfred North Whitehead, *Symbolism, Its Meaning and Effect* (1927; repr. New York: Fordham University Press, 1995), 83–84.

97. Wittgenstein, *Philosophical Investigations*, 183. See Ludwig Wittgenstein, *Remarks on the Philosophy of Psychology*, vol. 1, ed. G. E. M. Anscombe and G. H. von Wright, trans. G. E. M. Anscombe (Chicago: University of Chicago Press, 1980), §339.

98. Wittgenstein, *Philosophical Investigations*, §154.

99. Compare ibid., §145: "the effect of any further *explanation* depends on his *reaction*."

100. Wittgenstein, "Philosophy," from *The Big Typescript*, the title of paragraph 86, in *Philosophical Occasions*, 161.

101. William James, *Some Problems of Philosophy* (1911; repr. Cambridge: Harvard University Press, 1979), 45. Thanks once more to the published work of Russell Goodman.

102. Guy Debord, "Theory of the Dérive" (1958), reprinted in K. Knabb, ed., *Situationist International: Anthology* (Berkeley, Calif.: The Bureau of Public Secrets, 1995), 50, emphasis added.

103. Alfred North Whitehead, *Aims of Education* (1929; repr. New York: Mentor Books, 1949), 28.

104. Ibid., 29.

105. Ibid.

106. Ibid., 28–29.

107. See Jonathan Bennett "On Translating Locke, Berkeley, and Hume Into English," *Teaching Philosophy* 17 (1994): 261–269.

108. On coins and concrete attention in general, see Robert Brumbaugh, *Whitehead, Process Philosophy, and Education* (Albany, N.Y.: SUNY Press, 1982), and his *Ancient Greek Gadgets and Machines* (New York: Thomas Crowell, 1966).

109. Whitehead, *Science and the Modern World*, 196.

110. Ibid., 199.

111. The finish of this paper is, in large part, due to the attentions of Erin K. Seeba.

CHAPTER SIX

VOICE AND THE INTERROGATION OF PHILOSOPHY:
INHERITANCE, ABANDONMENT, AND JAZZ
Vincent Colapietro

1. Stanley Cavell, *A Pitch of Philosophy: Autobiographical Exercises* (Cambridge, Mass.: Harvard University Press, 1994), 47. Of course, he is acutely aware of the extent to which he is, in making this claim, cutting against the grain: "For philosophy, speaking for oneself [all the more, speaking *of* oneself] is, let us say too personal." Ibid., 4, emphasis added. See also Vincent Colapietro, "The Question of Voice and the Limits of Pragmatism: Emerson, Dewey, and Cavell," *Metaphilosophy* 32, nos. 1–2 (2004): 178–201; "Experience Ceded and Negated," *Journal of Speculative Philosophy* 22, no. 2 (2008): 118–126.

2. Cavell, *A Pitch of Philosophy*, 38. In *Remarks on the Philosophy of Psychology*, Wittgenstein asks us to imagine "a child who for a long time had been unable to learn how to speak and who suddenly used the expression 'I dread . . .' which it had heard from adults, and its face and the circumstances and the consequences make us say: He really meant it. (For one could always say: One fine day the child starts using the words. I choose the case of a child because what is happening to him is stranger to us than it would be with an adult. What do I know—I'm inclined to say—about the background for the words 'I dread . . .'? Does the child suddenly let me look into him?" Ludwig Wittgenstein, *Remarks on the Philosophy of Psychology*, vol. 2, ed. G. H. von Wright and Heikki Nyman, trans. C. G. Luckhardt and M. A. E. Aue (Chicago: University of Chicago Press, 1980), §171. In this connection, it is illumi-

nating to recall Ray Monk's depiction of the child who was father to the man: "For much of his childhood, he [Ludwig Wittgenstein] was considered one of the dullest of this extraordinary brood of siblings. He exhibited no precocious musical, artistic or literary talent, and, indeed, did not even start speaking until he was four years old." Ray Monk, *Ludwig Wittgenstein: The Duty of Genius* (New York: Penguin, 1990), 12.

3. Cavell, *A Pitch of Philosophy*, 51, emphasis added.

4. Ludwig Wittgenstein, *Philosophical Investigations*, trans. G. E. M. Anscombe (Malden, Mass.: Blackwell, 2001), §217. See Cavell, *A Pitch of Philosophy*, 14; and Stanley Cavell, *Conditions Handsome and Unhandsome: The Constitution of Emersonian Perfectionism* (Chicago: University of Chicago Press, 1990), 70.

5. Cavell, *A Pitch of Philosophy*, 51.

6. In *This New yet Unapproachable America*, Cavell goes so far as to assert: "The figure of the child is present in this portrait of civilization more prominently and decisively than in any other work of philosophy I think of." Stanley Cavell, *This New yet Unapproachable America: Lectures After Emerson After Wittgenstein* (Albuquerque, N.M.: Living Batch Press, 1989), 60. It may, however, be the case that a figure could be prominently and decisively present but in a quiet and muted way. In any event, my own sense is that it would be best to say that the child is decisively but unobtrusively present in the *Investigations* (not that he or she is "prominently and decisively present"). Regarding *On Certainty*, see Ludwig Wittgenstein, *On Certainty*, trans. D. Paul and G. E. M. Anscombe (New York: Harper & Row, 1972), §106, 107, 128, 143, 144, 160, 233, 374, 472, 476, 527, 534, 536, 538.

7. Cavell, *A Pitch of Philosophy*, 21.

8. Ibid., 33.

9. On my reading, though apparently not on Cavell's, *King Lear* concerns the inevitable (in a sense, "natural") yet impossible demands individuals make upon those whom they love or are expected to love.

10. Cavell, *A Pitch of Philosophy*, 22. We should not pass over in silence that Wittgenstein as a schoolteacher in Otterthal was physically abusive to several of his students. He returned to this village later "to apologize personally to the children whom he had physically hurt" (Monk, *Ludwig Wittgenstein*, 370). At least one of these individuals, remembering how as a girl Wittgenstein "had pulled her by the ears and by the hair in such a violent fashion that, on occasion, her ears had bled and her hair had come out" (ibid., 371), in effect refused to accept this apology. In recalling these events here, I am not suggesting a reductivist reading of the *Philosophical Investiga-*

tions, only presenting materials for a psychoanalytically inflected and historically informed interpretation.

11. In one place, Cavell notes: "The *Investigations* [of Wittgenstein] is a work that begins with a scene of inheritance, the child's inheritance of language; it is an image of a culture as an inheritance, one that takes place, as is fundamental to Freud, in the conflict of voices and generations" (*This New yet Unapproachable America*, 60). But, in being a work commencing with a scene of inheritance, it is at the same time one beginning with the task of initiation. And the focus is on the initiate, the one being initiated into language and, more generally, into culture. "The figure of the child is," Cavell goes on to remark, "present in this portrait of civilization more prominently and decisively than in any other work of philosophy you can think of (with the exception . . . of Emile)." He goes so far as to assert that Wittgenstein's *Investigations* "discovers or rediscovers childhood for philosophy (the child in us), as Emerson and Nietzsche and Kierkegaard discover youth, the student, say adolescence, the philosophical audience conscious that its culture demands consent; youth may never forgive the cost of granting it, or of withholding it. The child demands consent of its culture, attention from it; it may never forgive [or forget] the cost of exacting it, or of failing to" (ibid.).

12. Cavell, *A Pitch of Philosophy*, 51, emphasis added.

13. Ibid.

14. Salman Rushdie, "Out of Kansas" [A Critic at Large], *New Yorker* (May 11, 1992): 93.

15. Ibid., 103, emphasis added. Cf. Rushdie's own wonderful attempt to be the storytelling magician in *Haroun and the Sea of Stories* (New York: Penguin, 1991).

16. This impulse is one that Cavell connects with skepticism: "I say this struggle with Skepticism, with its threat or temptation, is endless; I mean to say that it is human, it is the human drive to transcend itself, which should not end until, as in Nietzsche, the human is over." *This New yet Unapproachable America*, 57.

17. In this regard, it is important to recall such essays of his as "Imaginary Homelands," "'In God We Trust,'" "In Good Faith," and "Is Nothing Sacred?" (Salman Rushdie, *Imaginary Homelands: Essays and Criticism, 1981–1991* [New York: Penguin Books, 1991]).

18. Rushdie, "Out of Kansas," 103.

19. Ibid.

20. Ibid., 103.

21. Cavell, *A Pitch of Philosophy*, 30.

22. Cavell, *Conditions Handsome and Unhandsome*, 13.

23. In "Forms of Life: Mapping the Rough Ground" (an essay to be considered later in this paper), Naomi Scheman criticizes Cavell's understanding of home. The basis of her critique is, ironically, what she shares with Cavell—what Cavell calls his "diaspora sensibility" (*A Pitch of Philosophy*, 11) and what Scheman calls "Disapora identity." Naomi Scheman, "Forms of Life: Mapping the Rough Ground," in *Cambridge Companion to Wittgenstein*, ed. Hans Slug and David G. Stern (Cambridge: Cambridge University Press, 1996), 404. She notes that in contrast to those who are strangers to a form of life, thus ones who find its practices "abhorrent," there are those who are "native to those practices . . . [and, thus, who are] unlikely to find them anything other than natural: 'we do what we do'" (ibid., 403). But there are still others "who are neither stranger nor native, who for the widest range of reasons, within and beyond their own choosing, live somewhere other than at the centers of the forms of life they inhabit" (ibid.). Especially cultures or societies such as our own "have within them members who are not truly at home there, who see with the eyes of the 'outsider within.'" (ibid., 403–404). On my reading, however, Cavell is just such a figure. His role in the all-black swing band is emblematic, in various senses, of "the outsider within." His presence at Harvard University and his relationship to analytic philosophy are also indicative of this. He sees Emerson as a "Jew" (Stanley Cavell, "An Apology for Skepticism" [Interview with Giovanna Borradori], in *The American Philosopher: Conversations*, ed. Giovanna Borradori [Chicago: University of Chicago, 1994], 136), an interpretation made plausible in *A Pitch of Philosophy* by his understanding of Emerson's concept of abandonment (for he takes this "to name a spiritual achievement . . . expressed as a willingness to depart from all settled habitation, all conformity of meaning, the human as immigrant" (ibid., 144), as wayfarer. The figure of the philosopher might itself be configured as "the hobo of thought" (*This New yet Unapproachable America*, 116).

24. Cavell, *A Pitch of Philosophy*, 30.

25. Michael Wood, "Why Praise Astaire?" *London Review of Books* 27, no. 20 (October 20, 2005): 14–15.

26. Ibid.

27. Cavell, *A Pitch of Philosophy*, 25–26.

28. Rushdie, "Out of Kansas," 93.

29. Stanley Cavell, *In Quest of the Ordinary: Lines of Skepticism and Romanticism* (Chicago: University of Chicago Press, 1988), 75.

30. Ibid., 73. This observation is made in the context of an essay entitled "Texts of Recovery (Coleridge, Wordsworth, Heidegger)." The immediate context in which the quoted texts appear concerns siding with Wordsworth against Coleridge: "I take it amiss that Coleridge refuses to try to determine why Wordsworth calls the child a philosopher" (Ibid.). The words quoted in the body of my essay are Cavell's endeavor to determine why Wordsworth granted the child this title. At the same time, however, William Wordsworth also questions the truth value of childhood experience as he as an adult is trying to "part/The shadow from the substance" in order to recognize "things . . ./In their true Dwelling." William Wordsworth, *The Prelude*, book 4, in *The Norton Anthology of English Literature*, vol. 2, ed. M. Abrams et al., 6th ed. (New York: Norton, 1993), 239.

31. Cavell, *In Quest of the Ordinary*, 73–74; emphasis added. "Putting aside childish things becomes," Cavell notes, "the achievement of intellect. It is the only path away from the sack of nostalgia, which we might think of, in opposition to remembering childhood, as the eternal reenactment (what Freud calls 'acting-out') of the past." In this connection, Cavell is emphatic in warning of a spiritual danger intertwined with this human necessity: "Childish things can be put aside vengefully, which is not giving something over. The way recommended [by Wordsworth and others], so far as I understood it . . . lies in forgoing the grief and anger in abandoning" childish things. Ibid., 74.

32. In "Studies in Hysteria" (1895), Freud and Breuer, in a remark addressed to patients about the efficacy of their therapy, said: "much will be gained in transforming your misery into common unhappiness. With a mental life that has been restored to health you will be better armed against that unhappiness." Sigmund Freud and Josef Breuer, "Studies in Hysteria" (1895), in Sigmund Freud, *The Standard Edition of the Complete Psychological Works of Sigmund Freud*, vol. 2, ed. and trans. James Strachey (London: Hogarth Press, 1999), 351. This might nonetheless be identified as a version of eudaemonism, if only an extremely minimalist version!

33. In *The Ego and the Id*, Freud suggests: "To the ego . . . living means the same as being loved." Sigmund Freud, *The Ego and the Id*, trans. Joan Riviere, rev. James Strachey (New York: W. W. Norton & Co., 1960), 61. Cf. Jonathan Lear, *Love and Its Place in Nature* (New Haven, Conn.: Yale University Press, 1999).

34. Cavell, *In Quest of the Ordinary*, 75.

35. One of the most important revelations, *for children* (at least for my own self), of *The Wizard of Oz* is that there are good witches, beautiful as

well as benevolent. Dorothy's surprise is, in this instance, as in so many other ones, representative of the children watching the movie.

36. At the conclusion of an interview, responding to why he does not more emphatically acknowledge his distinctively Jewish sensibility, Cavell resolutely defends his disposition to characterize himself in terms of Emerson rather than, say, Buber. After just claiming to have made Emerson into "the philosopher of immigrancy," after being challenged by the interviewer for explaining himself in terms of Christ and Emerson rather than Jewish figures and authors, Cavell explains: "Yes, because he [Emerson] is the philosopher who contradicts Heidegger's effort to dwell by saying you have to leave. Abandonment is for me the first door. You abandon the word you write, the house you live in, your father and mother. You have to leave when the kingdom of heaven calls you. But what's the kingdom of heaven? Emerson pictures it as writing, which in turn he will abandon only for thinking. So, in this sense of abandoning things and moving on, Emerson is a Jew, Thoreau is a Jew, and I'm a Jew. Or at least I would like to become one." Cavell, "An Apology for Skepticism," 136.

37. This has nowhere been more forcefully noted by Emerson in a justly famous passage from "Nature" (1836): "Nature is a setting that fits equally well a comic or a mourning piece. In good health, the air is a cordial of incredible virtue. Crossing a bare common, in snow puddles, at twilight, I am glad to the brink of fear." Ralph W. Emerson, *Selected Essays*, ed. Larzer Ziff (New York: Penguin, 1982), 38.

38. In *The New yet Unapproachable America*, Cavell asserts: "Philosophy begins in loss, in finding yourself at a loss, as Wittgenstein more or less says. Philosophy that does not so begin is so much talk" (114).

39. To cite but one representative text, consider what Cavell writes in *This New yet Unapproachable America*, 32–40. This section is tellingly entitled "Everydayness as Home."

40. Cavell, "An Apology for Skepticism," 126.

41. Alexis Tocqueville, *Democracy in America*, trans. George Lawrence, ed. J. P. Mayer (Garden City, N.Y.: Doubleday, 1969). Cf. Cavell, "An Apology for Skepticism," 123. Thomas Jefferson: "The question, whether one generation of men has a right to bind another, seems never to have been started either on this or our side of the water." But he considered it "self-evident" that "the earth belongs to the living" and that "the dead have neither rights nor power over us." Thomas Jefferson, "Letter to James Madison (Sept. 6, 1789)," in *The Writings of Thomas Jefferson*, ed. Andrew Lipscomb and Albert Ellery Bergh, memorial ed. (Washington, D.C.: Thomas Jefferson

Memorial Association, 1905), 7:459). He maintained further, "Each generation is as independent of the one preceding, as that was of all which had gone before." Jefferson, "Letter to Samuel Kercheval (July 12, 1816)," in *The Writings of Thomas Jefferson*, 15:42). At least as insistently, Emerson proclaimed the autonomy of his newly emerging generation, especially in the spheres of religion and, more generally, culture: "The foregoing generations beheld God and nature face to face; we, through their eyes. Why should not we also enjoy an original [rather than a traditional, an intuitive rather than mediated] relation to the universe? Should not we have a poetry and philosophy of insight and not of tradition, and a religion by revelation to us, and not the history of theirs?" Emerson, "Nature," in *Selected Essays*, 35. In *Walden*, Henry. D. Thoreau in turn bid his readers to "settle ourselves, and work and wedge our feet downward through the mud and slush of opinion, and prejudice, and tradition, and delusion, and appearance, that alluvion which covers the globe . . . till we come to hard bottom and rocks in place, which we can call *reality*, and say, This is, and no mistake." Henry, D. Thoreau, *Walden and Resistance to Civil Government*, ed. William Rossi (New York: W. W. Norton & Company, 1992), 66. Cf. Vincent M. Colapietro, "Tradition: First Steps Toward a Pragmatistic Clarification," in *Philosophy in Experience*, ed. Richard E. Hart and Douglas R. Anderson (New York: Fordham University Press, 1997), esp. 22–40.

42. Stanley Cavell, "Reflections on a Life of Philosophy [Interview with Stanley Cavell]," *Harvard Review of Philosophy* 7:26 (1999), emphasis added.

43. Ibid., emphasis added. Some critics (e.g., Douglas Anderson) contend that Cavell's preoccupation is with words, not experience. Douglas R. Anderson, "American Loss in Cavell's Emerson," *Transactions of the Charles S. Peirce Society* 29, no. 1 (1993): 69–89; reprinted in Douglas R. Anderson, *Philosophy Americana: Making Philosophy at Home in American Culture* (New York: Fordham University Press, 2006), 206–220. But this does not seem fair, because Cavell is concerned with both probing our *experience* of language and improvising a mode of writing in which the demands and disclosures of experience are given their due. He *shows*, in detail, the ramification of Wittgenstein's claim in the *Zettel*: "How words are understood is not told by words alone." Ludwig Wittgenstein, *Zettel*, trans. G. E. M. Anscombe (Berkeley: University of California Press, 1970), §144.

44. Cavell, *Philosophy the Day After Tomorrow*, 82.

45. Ibid., emphasis added. See also Colapietro, "Experience Ceded and Negated."

46. T. S. Eliot, "The Dry Salvages," II, in *Four Quartets* [1943] (New York: Harvest Books, 1971), 39.

47. Patricia Hampl contends: "For we do not, after all, simply *have* experience; we are entrusted with it. We must do something—make something—with it. A story, we sense, is the only possible habitation for the burden of our witnessing." But the having of it might entail what is in effect the process of being entrusted with something seemingly quite ordinary, though the treatment of the ordinary as the negligible or insignificant is almost certainly a self-denigration as much as a self-nullification. Patricia Hampl, *I Could Tell You Stories: Sojourns in the Land of Memory* (New York: W.W. Norton & Co., 2000), 18.

48. This is derived from at least a twofold source, as Scheman makes explicit: "I have in the past frequently responded to Cavell's writing out of an uneasy discrepancy I felt between the subject position in which the text placed me as a philosopher and my sense of myself as a woman. In the present instance I was struck by what seemed to me the same sort of discrepancy, but the identity in terms of which I felt it was that of a Diasporic Jew." Scheman, "Forms of Life," 401–402. What is immediately in the foreground here is Cavell's reliance on Kierkegaard's texts to explicate the meaning of home and homelessness. Cf. Cavell, "An Apology for Skepticism," 136.

49. Scheman, "Forms of Life," 401–402. See esp. 402–405.

50. Ibid., 401.

51. Ibid., 399; cf. Alessandra Tanesini, *Wittgenstein: A Feminist Introduction* (Cambridge: Polity, 2004).

52. Ibid., 401.

53. In the *Book on Adler; or, A Cycle of Ethico-Religious Essays*, Kierkegaard asserts: "Most men live in relation to their own self as if they were constantly out, never at home. . . . Spiritually and religiously understood, perdition consists in journeying into a foreign land, in being 'out.'" Søren Kierkegaard, *On Authority and Revelation: The Book on Adler; or, A Cycle of Ethico-Religious Essays*, trans. Walter Lowrie (Princeton, N.J.: Princeton University Press, 1955), 154–155. (The road to perdition seems, on this account, to be the road itself, the journey away from home.) Cavell quotes and apparently appropriates this in *This New yet Unapproachable America*—and it is to this that Scheman is reacting in "Forms of Life."

54. Scheman, "Forms of Life," 402.

55. "There are," Scheman adds, "no other homes for our words than the ones we create in and through our practices, nor any predetermined ways of specifying what it is to have gotten those practices right, but that does not mean that there is no sense to the idea that we might not be going on as we should be." Scheman, "Forms of Life," 402. But the words we are able to

create only in and through our practices enjoy a fateful involvement with inherited practices. Questions of creativity thus cannot be taken up in abstraction from questions of inheritance, and it is precisely the task and indeed fate of being inheritors to which Cavell is calling our attention or, better, in which he is eliciting our co-participation.

56. Ibid., 402–403.

57. Ibid., 403.

58. Cf. Cavell, *Conditions Handsome and Unhandsome*, 73–74.

59. Cavell, "An Apology for Skepticism," 133.

60. Cavell, *This New and Yet Unapproachable America*, 114.

61. This very expression might seem out of place in this context, and in a sense it truly is. For instance, Archie Shepp would designate jazz as black music (more fully, black music played on Western or European instruments). The etymology and meaning of jazz are, unquestionably, controversial. But, however variously understood or named, improvisation seems to be integral to this form of music. And that is my principal point.

62. William Shakespeare, *Hamlet*, 3.1, in *The Complete Works of Shakespeare*, ed. David Bevington (Glenville, Ill.: Scott, Foresman & Co, 1980), 1094. Cf. Timothy Gould, "The Name of Action," in *Stanley Cavell*, ed. Richard Eldridge (Cambridge: Cambridge University Press, 2003), 48–78.

63. Gould, "The Name of Action," 48. For a different dimension of human action, see Cavell, *A Pitch of Philosophy*, 25–26. When Stanley Goldstein as a sixteen-year-old undertook legally to change his name to Stanley Cavell, he learned he would have to undergo having this intention "published in a newspaper every day for some weeks" (ibid., 25). He learned in the course of this petition how important it is for a society "to serve notice that identifiable actions, deeds, the works of human beings, are the source of identity, and consequently constitute identity through accusation—all doing known as wrongdoing" (ibid., 26).

64. Cavell, *A Pitch of Philosophy*, 30.

65. Ibid., 32.

CHAPTER SEVEN
PERFECTIONISM'S EDUCATIONAL ADDRESS
René V. Arcilla

1. Stanley Cavell, *Conditions Handsome and Unhandsome: The Constitution of Emersonian Perfectionism* (Chicago: The University of Chicago Press, 1990), 4.

2. Ibid.

3. Ibid., xxxi–xxxii.

4. Ibid., xxxii.

5. J. D. Salinger, *Raise High the Roofbeam, Carpenters, and Seymour—An Introduction* (New York: Little, Brown and Company, 1963), 111.

6. Cavell's most sustained examination of the problem of skepticism may be found in Stanley Cavell, *The Claim of Reason: Wittgenstein, Skepticism, Morality, and Tragedy* (Oxford: Oxford University Press, 1979).

7. Plato, *Meno*, trans. W. K. C. Guthrie, in *The Collected Dialogues of Plato, Including the Letters*, ed. Edith Hamilton and Huntington Cairns (Princeton, N.J.: Princeton University Press, 1963), 363.

8. Cavell, *Conditions Handsome and Unhandsome*, xxxii.

9. Stanley Cavell, *Cities of Words: Pedagogical Letters on a Register of the Moral Life* (Cambridge, Mass.: Harvard University Press, 2004), 251.

10. Ralph Waldo Emerson, "The Divinity School Address," in *Essays and Lectures*, ed. Joel Porte (New York: Literary Classics of the United States, 1983), 79.

11. Cavell, *Conditions Handsome and Unhandsome*, xxx.

12. Ibid., 20.

13. See Cavell, *Conditions Handsome and Unhandsome*, 5.

14. See Stanley Cavell, *The World Viewed: Reflections on the Ontology of Film*, enlarged ed. (Cambridge, Mass.: Harvard University Press, 1979), 108–118.

15. Michael Oakeshott, "The Study of 'Politics' in a University: An Essay in Appropriateness," in *Rationalism in Politics and Other Essays* (Indianapolis, Ind.: Liberty Press, 1991), 187.

16. See Stanley Cavell, "An Emerson Mood," in *The Senses of Walden* (Chicago: University of Chicago Press, 1992); and Stanley Cavell, *Pursuits of Happiness: The Hollywood Comedy of Remarriage* (Cambridge, Mass.: Harvard University Press, 1981).

17. Cavell, *Conditions Handsome and Unhandsome*, 6–7.

18. See Hans Blumenberg, *The Legitimacy of the Modern Age*, trans. Robert M. Wallace (Cambridge, Mass.: The MIT Press, 1983), 227–453.

19. See ibid., 123–226.

20. See Oakeshott, "The Study of 'Politics' in a University," for a helpful account of the differences between these three kinds of education.

CHAPTER EIGHT

THE GLEAM OF LIGHT: INITIATION, PROPHESY,
AND EMERSONIAN MORAL PERFECTIONISM
Naoko Saito

1. Stanley Cavell, *The Senses of Walden* (Chicago: University of Chicago Press, 1992), 42. The first edition of *The Senses of Walden* was published in

1972. An expanded edition appeared in 1981 from North Point Press, and then, in 1992, from the University of Chicago Press. In the present discussion, the 1992 edition is used as a text for reference. Roman numerals in Cavell's quote indicate chapters, and Arabic numerals paragraphs, of Thoreau's *Walden*.

2. Ralph Waldo Emerson, *Ralph Waldo Emerson*, ed. Richard Poirier (Oxford: Oxford University Press, 1990), 134.

3. Henry D. Thoreau, *Walden and Resistance to Civil Government*, ed. William Rossi (New York: W. W. Norton & Company, 1992), 145.

4. Stanley Cavell, *Conditions Handsome and Unhandsome: The Constitution of Emersonian Perfectionism* (Chicago: University of Chicago Press, 1990), 12.

5. Ibid., xxxiv.

6. Emerson, *Ralph Waldo Emerson*, 134.

7. Ibid., 41.

8. Cavell, *Conditions Handsome and Unhandsome*, 27.

9. Ibid., 26.

10. Ibid., 29.

11. Ibid., 51.

12. Ibid., 11.

13. Ibid., 10–11.

14. Emerson, *Ralph Waldo Emerson*, 49.

15. Stanley Cavell, *Philosophical Passages: Wittgenstein, Emerson, Austin, Derrida* (Oxford: Blackwell, 1995), 26–27.

16. Cavell, *Conditions Handsome and Unhandsome*, 58–59. The theme of friendship in Emersonian moral perfectionism is discussed in Naoko Saito, "Leaving and Bequeathing: Friendship, Emersonian Moral Perfectionism, and the Gleam of Light," in *Emerson and Thoreau: Figures of Friendship*, ed. John T. Lysaker and William Rossi (Bloomington: Indiana University Press, 2010), 172–185.

17. Cavell, *Conditions Handsome and Unhandsome*, 16, 30.

18. Ibid., 59.

19. Ralph Waldo Emerson, "Friendship," in *The Essential Writings of Ralph Waldo Emerson*, ed. Brooks Atkinson (New York: The Modern Library, 2000), 209.

20. Cavell, *Conditions Handsome and Unhandsome*, 31.

21. Ibid., xxxii.

22. Ibid., 32.

23. Ibid., 8, 12.

24. Stanley Cavell, "The Politics of Interpretation (Politics as Opposed to What?)," in *Themes out of School: Effects and Causes* (Chicago: University of Chicago Press, 1984), 49, 50.

25. Cavell, *The Senses of Walden*, 63.

26. Cavell, *Conditions Handsome and Unhandsome*, 27.

27. Cavell, *The Senses of Walden*, 15.

28. Ibid.; Thoreau, *Walden*, 68.

29. Cavell, *The Senses of Walden*, 16.

30. Stanley Cavell, *The Claim of Reason: Wittgenstein, Skepticism, Morality, and Tragedy* (Oxford: Oxford University Press, 1979), 112.

31. Cavell, *The Claim of Reason*, 124–125.

32. Ibid., 115.

33. Ibid., 124.

34. Cavell, *Conditions Handsome and Unhandsome*, 76.

35. Cavell, *The Claim of Reason*, 125.

36. Cavell, *The Senses of Walden*, 32.

37. Ibid., 28–29.

38. Ibid., 12.

39. Ibid, p. 34.

40. Ibid., 32.

41. Ibid., 59.

42. Nel Noddings, *Caring: A Feminine Approach to Ethics* (Berkeley: University of California Press, 1984), 33–34.

43. Cavell, *The Senses of Walden*, 65.

44. Emerson, *Ralph Waldo Emerson*, 218.

45. Cavell, *The Senses of Walden*, 55.

46. Ibid., 106–107.

47. Ibid., 107–108. This idea is reframed in *Conditions Handsome and Unhandsome*: "we are from the beginning, that is from the time we can be described as having a self, a next, knotted" (12).

48. Cavell, *The Senses of Walden*, 102.

49. Emerson, "Friendship," 204.

50. Stanley Cavell, *In Quest of the Ordinary: Lines of Skepticism and Romanticism* (Chicago: University of Chicago Press, 1988), 101.

51. Cavell, *Conditions Handsome and Unhandsome*, 12.

52. Cavell, *The Senses of Walden*, 60.

53. Ibid., 48, 141–142.

54. Paul Standish discusses alterity in Thoreau and Cavell mainly as an *"internal* alterity" and as a "latent strangeness *within* ourselves" (italics mine). (Paul Standish, "Who Is My Neighbor? Scepticism and the Claims of Alterity," paper presented at the biennial meeting of the International Network for the Philosophers of Education [August 2006].) In Thoreau and Cavell, otherness is intertwined in the relationship between the outside and inside, as I have tried to show. The emphasis I put in this paper, by acknowledging this "internal alterity," is on how the outside other as a friend can influence the inside otherness of the self.

55. Henry D. Thoreau, *Great Short Works of Henry David Thoreau*, ed. Wendell Glick (New York: Harper & Row, 1982), 172.

56. Cavell, *Themes out of School*, 53.

57. Ibid.

58. Ibid., 54.

59. Stanley Cavell, *Philosophy the Day After Tomorrow* (Cambridge, Mass.: The Belknap Press of Harvard University Press, 2005), 218.

60. Emerson, *Ralph Waldo Emerson*, 166.

61. Ibid., 131. See also Naoko Saito, *The Gleam of Light: Moral Perfectionism and Education in Dewey and Emerson* (New York: Fordham University Press, 2005).

62. Paul Standish, "Solitude, Silence, Listening," in Nigel Blake, Paul Smeyers, Richard Smith, and Paul Standish, *Education in an Age of Nihilism* (London: Routledge/Farmer, 2000), 151.

63. Thoreau, *Great Short Works*, 178.

64. Cavell, *The Senses of Walden*, 54.

65. Ibid., 71.

66. Ibid., 119.

67. Ibid., 160.

68. Emerson, "The Law of Compensation," in *The Essential Writings*, 156.

69. Cavell, *The Senses of Walden*, 136, 137.

70. This is a remark made by Stanley Cavell at the Cavell Colloquium (October 27–29, 2006).

71. Emerson, *Ralph Waldo Emerson*, 131.

72. This is a remark made by Stanley Cavell at the Cavell Colloquium (October 27–29, 2006).

73. Cavell, *Themes Out of School*, 53.

74. Emerson, *Ralph Waldo Emerson*, 131. Thoreau also refers in *Walden* to the "outward and visible sign of an inward and spiritual grace" (47).

CHAPTER NINE

THE ORDINARY AS SUBLIME IN CAVELL, ZEN, AND NISHIDA:
CAVELL'S PHILOSOPHY OF EDUCATION IN EAST-WEST
PERSPECTIVE

Steve Odin

1. This paper is a modified version of my presentation at the Ninth East-West Philosopher's Conference held in the East West Center at the University of Hawaii from May 20 to June 10, 2005. For this occasion, I organized a panel on "Stanley Cavell's Philosophy of Education in East-West Perspective," including presentations by Naoko Saito, from Kyoto University in Japan, and Paul Standish, from the Institute of Education, University of London, in the United Kingdom, as well as my own presentation.

2. See notes 17 and 18 by Jeffery S. Cramer in Henry D. Thoreau, *Walden*, ed. Jeffery S. Cramer (New Haven, Conn.: Yale University Press, 2004), 130.

3. Wei-Ming Tu, *Centrality and Commonality: An Essay on Confucian Religiousness* (Albany, N.Y.: SUNY Press, 1989), 16.

4. Ibid., 132, n. 34.

5. Roger T. Ames and David Hall, *Focusing on the Familiar: A Translation and Philosophical Interpretation of the Zhongyong* (Honolulu: University of Hawaii Press, 2001), 43.

6. Ibid., 46.

7. Wei-Ming Tu, *Centrality and Commonality*, 113.

8. Van Meter Ames, *Zen and American Philosophy* (Honolulu: University of Hawaii Press, 1962), 13.

9. Ibid., 70.

10. Ibid.

11. Stanley Cavell, *The World Viewed: Reflections on the Ontology of Film* (Enlarged edition) (Cambridge, Mass.: Harvard University Press, 1979), 160.

12. Alan Watts, *The Way of Zen* (New York: Vintage Books, 1985), 181.

13. Shunryu Suzuki, *Zen Mind, Beginner's Mind* (1970; repr. New York: Weatherhill, 2003), 118–119.

14. Ibid., 57.

15. Shunryu Suzuki, *Not Always So: Practicing the True Spirit of Zen* (New York: HarperCollins/Quill, 2002), 59.

16. Ibid.

17. Eishin Nishimura, ed., *Mumonkan* (Tokyo: Iwanami Shoten, 2002), 87.

18. Kitarō Nishida, *An Inquiry Into the Good*, trans. Masao Abe and Christopher Ives (New Haven, Conn.: Yale University Press, 1990).

19. Kitarō Nishida, "The Logic of *Topos* and the Religious Worldview," trans. Michiko Yusa, *Eastern Buddhist* 19, no. 2 (1986): 1–29; 20, no. 1 (1986): 81–119.

20. Kitarō Nishida, *Last Writings: Nothingness and the Religious Worldview*, trans. David A. Dilworth (Honolulu: The University of Hawaii Press, 1987).

21. Kitarō Nishida, *Nishida Kitarō Zenshu* [Collected Works of Nishida Kitarō], 2nd ed. (Tokyo: Iwanami Shoten, 1965), 11:424.

22. Ibid., 454.

23. Ibid.; see also Nishida, *Last Writings*, 115.

24. Nishida, *Nishida Kitarō Zenshu*, 426; see also Nishida, *Last Writings*, 115.

25. Kōun Yamada, *The Gateless Gate: The Classic Book of Zen Koans*, trans. KōunYamada (Boston: Wisdom Publications, 2004), 11.

26. Philip B. Yampolsky, trans. *The Zen Master Hakuin: Selected Writings* (New York: Columbia University Press, 1971), 13.

27. Ibid., 13, 144–146.

28. Michel Mohr, "Emerging from Nonduality: Kōan Practice in the Rinzai Tradition Since Hakuin," in *The Kōan: Texts and Contexts in Zen Buddhism*, ed. Steven Heine and Dale S. Wright (Oxford: Oxford University Press, 2000), 266.

CHAPTER TEN

PHILOSOPHY AS EDUCATION

Stanley Cavell

1. Ludwig Wittgenstein, *Philosophical Investigations*, eds. G. E. M. Anscombe and R. Rhees, trans. G. E. M. Anscombe (Oxford: B. Blackwell, 1976), §109.

2. Ibid., §126.

3. Ibid., §109.

4. Ibid., §133.

5. Ibid., §115.

6. Ibid., §109.

7. This text appears as an epigraph to *The Senses of Walden*.

8. Stanley Cavell, *The Senses of Walden* (Chicago: University of Chicago Press, 1992), 60.

Bibliography

Ames, Roger T., and David Hall. *Focusing on the Familiar: A Translation and Philosophical Interpretation of the Zhongyong.* Honolulu: University of Hawaii Press, 2001.

Ames, Van Meter. *Zen and American Philosophy.* Honolulu: University of Hawaii Press, 1962.

Anderson, Douglas R. "American Loss in Cavell's Emerson." *Transactions of the Charles S. Peirce Society* 29, no. 1 (1993): 69–89. Reprinted in Anderson, Douglas R., *Philosophy Americana: Making Philosophy at Home in American Culture.* New York: Fordham University Press, 2006, 206–220.

Austin, J. L. 1970. *Philosophical Papers.* 3rd ed. Oxford: Oxford University Press.

Ayer, A. J. 1954. *Philosophical Essays.* London: Macmillan.

Baker, G. "Philosophical Investigations §122: Neglected Aspects" [1991]. In *Wittgenstein's Method: Neglected Aspects*, ed. K. J. Morris. Oxford: B. Blackwell, 2004.

Baker, G., and P. M. S. Hacker. *An Analytical Commentary on the Philosophical Investigations.* Vol. 1: *Understanding and Meaning.* Chicago: University of Chicago Press, 1980.

———. *Scepticism, Rules, and Language.* Oxford: B. Blackwell, 1984.

Bearn, Gordon C. F. "Sounding Serious: Cavell and Derrida," *Representations* 63 (Summer 1998): 65–92.

Bennett, Jonathan. "On Translating Locke, Berkeley, and Hume Into English." *Teaching Philosophy* 17 (1994): 261–269.

Bergson, Henri. *Laughter* [1900]. Baltimore, Md.: Johns Hopkins University Press, 1980.

Blumenberg, Hans. *The Legitimacy of the Modern Age.* Trans. Robert M. Wallace. Cambridge, Mass.: The MIT Press, 1983.

Brumbaugh, Robert. *Ancient Greek Gadgets and Machines.* New York: Thomas Crowell, 1996.

————. *Whitehead, Process Philosophy, and Education*. Albany, N.Y.: SUNY Press, 1982.

Carnap, Rudolf. "The Foundations of Logic and Mathematics." In *The International Encyclopedia of Unified Science*, vol. 1, pt. 1., ed. Otto Neurath, Rudolf Carnap, and Charles W. Morris, 198–211. Chicago: The University of Chicago Press, 1939.

————. "On the Methodological Character of Theoretical Concepts." In *Minnesota Studies in the Philosophy of Science*, vol. 1: *The Foundations of Science and the Concepts of Psychology and Psychoanalysis*, ed. Herbert Feigl and May Brodbeck, 38–76. Minneapolis: University of Minnesota Press, 1956.

————. *The Unity of Science*. London: Kegan Paul and Trench, Trubner, and Co., 1934.

Carpenter, Frederic I. "William James and Emerson." *American Literature* 11, no. 1 (1939): 39–57.

Cavell, Stanley. "An Apology for Skepticism" [interview with Giovanna Borradori]. In *The American Philosopher: Conversations*, ed. Giovanna Borradori, 118–136. Chicago: University of Chicago Press, 1994.

————. *Cities of Words: Pedagogical Letters on a Register of the Moral Life*. Cambridge, Mass.: Harvard University Press, 2004.

————. *The Claim of Reason: Wittgenstein, Skepticism, Morality, and Tragedy*. Oxford: Oxford University Press, 1979.

————. *Conditions Handsome and Unhandsome: The Constitution of Emersonian Perfectionism*. Chicago: University of Chicago Press, 1990.

————. *Contesting Tears: The Hollywood Melodrama of the Unknown Woman*. Chicago: University of Chicago Press, 1996.

————. *Disowning Knowledge in Six Plays of Shakespeare*. Cambridge: Cambridge University Press, 1987.

————. *In Quest of the Ordinary: Lines of Skepticism and Romanticism*. Chicago: University of Chicago Press, 1988.

————. "The Investigations' Everyday Aesthetics of Itself." In *The Cavell Reader*, ed. Stephen Mulhall, 369–389. Oxford: B. Blackwell, 1996.

————. *Must We Mean What We Say? A Book of Essays*. Cambridge: Cambridge University Press, 1976.

————. *Philosophical Passages: Wittgenstein, Emerson, Austin, Derrida* (Oxford: Blackwell, 1995).

————. *Philosophy the Day After Tomorrow*. Cambridge, Mass.: The Belknap Press of Harvard University Press, 2005.

————. *A Pitch of Philosophy: Autobiographical Exercises*. Cambridge, Mass.: Harvard University Press, 1994.

———. *Pursuits of Happiness: The Hollywood Comedy of Remarriage*. Cambridge, Mass.: Harvard University Press, 1989.

———. "Reflections on a Life of Philosophy" [Interview with Stanley Cavell]. *Harvard Review of Philosophy* 7 (1999): 19–28.

———. *The Senses of Walden*. Chicago: University of Chicago Press, 1992.

———. *Themes out of School: Effects and Causes*. Chicago: University of Chicago Press, 1984.

———. *This New yet Unapproachable America: Lectures After Emerson After Wittgenstein*. Albuquerque, N.M.: Living Batch Press, 1989.

———. *Die Unheimlichkeit des Gewöhnlichen und andere philosophische Essays*. Ed. Davide Sparti and Espen Hammer. Frankfurt am Main: Fischer Taschenbuch Verlag, 2002.

———. *The World Viewed: Reflections on the Ontology of Film*. Enlarged ed. Cambridge, Mass.: Harvard University Press, 1979.

Colapietro, Vincent M. "Experience Ceded and Negated." *Journal of Speculative Philosophy* 22, no. 2 (2008): 118–126.

———. "The Question of Voice and the Limits of Pragmatism: Emerson, Dewey, and Cavell." *Metaphilosophy* 32, nos. 1–2 (2004): 178–201.

———. "Tradition: First Steps Toward a Pragmatistic Clarification." In *Philosophy in Experience*, ed. Richard E. Hart and Douglas R. Anderson, 14–45. New York: Fordham University Press, 1997.

Debord, Guy. "Theory of the Dérive" [1958]. In 1995. *Situationist International: Anthology*, ed. K. Knabb, 50–54. Berkeley, Calif.: The Bureau of Public Secrets, 1995.

Dewey, John. "Emerson—The Philosopher of Democracy." In *The Middle Works of John Dewey*, vol. 3, ed. Jo Ann Boydston. Carbondale: Southern Illinois University Press, 1977.

———. *Experience and Nature*. In *The Later Works of John Dewey*, vol. 1, ed. Jo Ann Boydston. Carbondale: Southern Illinois University Press, 1981.

Diamond, Cora. "Losing Your Concepts." *Ethics* 98 (January 1988): 255–277.

Doty, Mark. *Dog Years*. New York: Harper, 2007.

Eliot, T. S. *Four Quartets* [1943]. New York: Harvest Books, 1971.

Emerson, Ralph Waldo. *Collected Works of Ralph Waldo Emerson*, vol. 2, ed. Robert Spiller et al. Cambridge, Mass.: Harvard University Press, 1971.

———. *Essays and Lectures*, ed. Joel Porte. New York: Literary Classics of the United States, 1983.

———. *The Essential Writings of Ralph Waldo Emerson*, ed. Brooks Atkinson. New York: The Modern Library, 2000.

———. *Ralph Waldo Emerson*. Ed. Richard Poirier. Oxford: Oxford University Press, 1990.

————. *Selected Essays.* Ed. Larzer Ziff. New York: Penguin, 1982.

Freud, Sigmund. *The Ego and the Id.* Trans. Joan Riviere. Rev. James Strachey. New York: W. W. Norton & Co., 1960.

Freud, Sigmund, and Josef Breuer. "Studies in Hysteria" [1895]. In Sigmund Freud, *The Standard Edition of the Complete Psychological Works of Sigmund Freud,* vol. 2, ed. and trans. James Strachey. London: Hogarth Press, 1999.

Girel, Mathias. "Les Angles de L'acte, Usages d'Emerson dans la Philosophie de William James." *Cahier Charles V* 37 (2004): 207–245.

Goodman, Russell B. *American Philosophy and the Romantic Tradition.* Cambridge: Cambridge University Press, 1990.

————. "Cavell and American Philosophy." In *Contending with Stanley Cavell,* ed. Russell B. Goodman, 100–117. Oxford: Oxford University Press, 2005.

————. "James on the Nonconceptual." *Midwest Studies in Philosophy* 28 (2004): 137–148.

————. "The New Riddle of Induction." In *Fact, Fiction, and Forecast,* chap. 3. Cambridge, Mass.: Harvard University Press, 1955.

————. *Wittgenstein and William James.* Cambridge: Cambridge University Press, 2003.

Goodman, Russell B., ed. *Pragmatism: Critical Concepts in Philosophy.* London: Routledge, 2005.

Gould, Timothy. *Hearing Things: Voice and Method in the Writing of Stanley Cavell.* Chicago: University of Chicago Press, 1998.

————. "The Name of Action." In *Stanley Cavell,* ed. Richard Eldridge, 48–78. Cambridge: Cambridge University Press, 2003.

Hacker, P. M. S., and M. R. Bennett. *Philosophical Foundations of Neuroscience.* Oxford: B. Blackwell, 2003.

Hampl, Patricia. *I Could Tell You Stories: Sojourns in the Land of Memory.* New York: W. W. Norton & Co., 2000.

Hempel, C. G. "Problems and Changes in the Empiricist Criterion of Meaning." *Revue Internationale de Philosophie* 4 (1950): 41–63.

Heidegger, Martin. *Being and Time* [1927]. Trans. J. Macquarrie and E. Robinson. Oxford: Blackwell, 1962.

————. "Building Dwelling Thinking" [1952]. In *Poetry, Language, Thought.* New York, Harper and Row, 1975.

————. *Discourse on Thinking* [1959]. Trans. J. M. Anderson and E. H. Freund. New York: Harper and Row, 1969.

James, William. *The Correspondence of William James.* Vol. 3. Ed. Ignas K. Skrupskelis and Elizabeth M. Berkeley. Charlottesville: University of Virginia Press, 1994.

————. *The Principles of Psychology* [1890]. Cambridge, Mass.: Harvard University Press, 1981.

————. *Some Problems of Philosophy* [1911]. Cambridge, Mass.: Harvard University Press, 1979.

————. *Writings 1902–1910*. New York: Library of America, 1987.

Jefferson, Thomas. *The Writings of Thomas Jefferson*. Ed. Andrew Lipscomb and Albert Ellery Bergh. Memorial ed. Washington, D.C.: Thomas Jefferson Memorial Association, 1905.

Kierkegaard, Søren. *On Authority and Revelation: The Book on Adler; or, A Cycle of Ethico-Religious Essays*. Trans. Walter Lowrie. Princeton, N.J.: Princeton University Press, 1955.

Lawrence, N. "Time Represented as Space." *The Monist* (July 1969): 447–456. Reprinted in Sellars, Wilfrid, and Eugene Freeman. *Basic Issues in the Philosophy of Time*. LaSalle, Ill.: Open Court, 1971.

Lear, Jonathan. *Love and Its Place in Nature*. New Haven, Conn.: Yale University Press, 1999.

McDowell, John. "Non-Cognitivism and Rule-Following." In *Mind, Value, and Reality*, 198–218. Cambridge, Mass.: Harvard University Press, 1998. Originally published in *Wittgenstein: To Follow a Rule*, ed. Steven H. Holtzman and Christopher M. Leich, 141–172. London: Routledge (1981).

Michaels, Walter Benn. "Walden's False Bottom." In *Walden and Resistance to Civil Government*, ed. William Rossi. New York: W. W. Norton & Co., 1992.

Mohr, Michel. "Emerging from Nonduality: Kōan Practice in the Rinzai Tradition Since Hakuin." In *The Kōan: Texts and Contexts in Zen Buddhism*, ed. Steven Heine and Dale S. Wright. Oxford: Oxford University Press, 2000, 244–279.

Monk, Ray. *Ludwig Wittgenstein: The Duty of Genius*. New York: Penguin, 1990.

Moore, G. E. "Wittgenstein's Lectures in 1930–33" [1954–1955]. In Ludwig Wittgenstein, *Philosophical Occasions*, ed. James C. Klagge and Alfred Nordmann. Indianapolis, Ind.: Hackett, 1993, 46–114.

Murdoch, Iris. *The Sovereignty of "Good" Over Other Concepts*. Cambridge: Cambridge University Press, 1967.

Nishida, Kitarō. *An Inquiry Into the Good*. Trans. Masao Abe and Christopher Ives. New Haven, Conn.: Yale University Press, 1990.

————. *Last Writings: Nothingness and the Religious Worldview*. Trans. David A. Dilworth. Honolulu: The University of Hawaii Press, 1987.

————. "The Logic of Topos and the Religious Worldview." *Eastern Buddhist* 19, no. 2 (1987): 1–29; 20, no. 1 (1987): 81–119.

————. *Nishida Kitarō Zenshu* [NKZ/Collected Works of Nishida Kitarō]. Vol. 11. 2nd ed. Tokyo: Iwanami Shoten, 1965.

Nishimura, Eishin, ed. *Mumonkan*. Tokyo: Iwanami Shoten, 2002.

Noddings, Nel. *Caring: A Feminine Approach to Ethics*. Berkeley: University of California Press, 1984.

Norris, Andrew, ed. *The Claim to Community: Essays on Stanley Cavell and Political Philosophy*. Stanford, Calif.: Stanford University Press, 2006.

Oakeshott, Michael. *Rationalism in Politics and Other Essays*. Indianapolis, Ind.: Liberty Press, 1991.

Perry, Ralph Barton. *The Thought and Character of William James*. Vol. 1. Boston: Little, Brown, and Company, 1935.

Plato. *Euthyphro*. Trans. F. J. Church and R. D. Cumming. New York: The Library of Liberal Arts, The Liberal Arts Press, 1956.

————. *Meno*. In *The Collected Dialogues of Plato, Including the Letters*, ed. Edith Hamilton and Huntington Cairns. Princeton, N.J.: Princeton University Press, 1963.

Putnam, Hilary. *The Collapse of the Fact/Value Dichotomy and Other Essays*. Cambridge, Mass.: Harvard University Press, 2002.

————. *Ethics Without Ontology*. Cambridge, Mass.: Harvard University Press, 2004.

————. "Philosophy as the Education of Grownups: Stanley Cavell and Skepticism." In *Reading Cavell*, ed. Alice Crary and Sanford Shieh. London: Routledge, 2005.

————. "What Theories Are Not." In *Philosophical Papers*, vol. 1: *Mathematics, Matter, and Method*, 215–227. Cambridge, Mass.: Harvard University Press, 1975.

Putnam, Hilary, and Vivian Walsh. "A Response to Dasgupta." *Economics and Philosophy* 23, no. 3 (November 2007): 359–364.

Quine, W. V. "Carnap and Logical Truth." In *The Philosophy of Rudolf Carnap*, ed. P.A. Schilpp, 385–406. LaSalle, Ill.: Open Court, 1963.

————. "Two Dogmas of Empiricism." *Philosophical Review* 60 (1951): 20–43.

Rhees, R., ed. *Ludwig Wittgenstein, Personal Recollections*. Totowa, N.J.: Rowman and Littlefield, 1981.

Robbins, Lionel. *An Essay on the Nature and Significance of Economic Science*. London: Macmillan, 1932.

Rushdie, Salman. *Haroun and the Sea of Stories*. New York: Penguin, 1991.

————. *Imaginary Homelands: Essays and Criticism, 1981–1991*. New York: Penguin, 1991.

———. "Out of Kansas" [A Critic at Large]. *New Yorker* (May 11, 1992): 93–103.

Saito, Naoko. *The Gleam of Light: Moral Perfectionism and Education in Dewey and Emerson*. New York: Fordham University Press, 2005.

———. "Leaving and Bequeathing: Friendship, Emersonian Moral Perfectionism, and the Gleam of Light." In *Emerson and Thoreau: Figures of Friendship*, ed. John T. Lysaker and William Rossi, 172–185. Bloomington: Indiana University Press, 2009.

Salinger, J. D. *Raise High the Roofbeam, Carpenters and Seymour—An Introduction*. New York: Little, Brown and Company, 1963.

Samuelson, P. A. *Foundations of Economic Analysis*. Cambridge, Mass.: Harvard University Press, 1947.

Scheman, Naomi. "Forms of Life: Mapping the Rough Ground." In *Cambridge Companion to Wittgenstein*, ed. Hans Sluga and David G. Stern, 383–410. Cambridge: Cambridge University Press, 1996.

Shakespeare, William. *Hamlet*. In *The Complete Works of Shakespeare*, ed. David Bevington. Glenville, Ill: Scott, Foresman & Co, 1980.

Shusterman, Richard. *Pragmatist Aesthetics: Living Beauty, Rethinking Art*. Lanham, Md.: Rowman & Littlefield, 1997.

Standish, Paul. "Data Return: The Sense of the Given in Educational Research." *Journal of Philosophy of Education* 35, no. 3 (2001): 497–518.

———. 2000. "Fetish for Effect." In *Education at the Interface: Philosophical Questions Concerning On-line Education*, ed. Nigel Blake and Paul Standish, 151–168. Oxford: Blackwell, 2000.

———. "In Her Own Voice: Convention, Conversion, Criteria." *Educational Philosophy and Theory* 36, no. 1 (2004): 91–106.

———. "Solitude, Silence, Listening." In *Education in an Age of Nihilism*, ed. Nigel Blake, Paul Smeyers, Richard Smith, and Paul Standish. London: Routledge/Farmer, 2000, 143–162.

———. "Who Is My Neighbor?: Scepticism and the Claims of Alterity." Paper presented at the biennial meeting of the International Network for the Philosophers of Education, August 2006.

Standish, Paul, and Naoko Saito. "Stanley Cavell to *Walden* no Sekai: Nihon no Dokusha heno Izanai" ("Stanley Cavell's *Walden*: An Introduction to Japanese Readers"). In *Sensu obu Woruden* (the Japanese translation of *The Senses of Walden*), trans. Naoko Saito. Tokyo: Hosei University Press, 2005, 213–240.

Stevenson, Charles. *Ethics and Language*. New Haven, Conn.: Yale University Press, 1944.

Suzuki, Shunryu. *Not Always So: Practicing the True Spirit of Zen*. New York: Harper-Collins/Quill, 2002.

———. 2003. *Zen Mind, Beginner's Mind* [1970]. New York: Weatherhill, 2003.

Tanesini, Alessandra. *Wittgenstein: A Feminist Introduction*. Cambridge: Polity, 2004.

Thoreau, Henry David. *Great Short Works of Henry David Thoreau*. Ed. Wendell Glick. New York: Harper & Row, 1982.

———. *Walden*. Ed. Jeffery S. Cramer. New Haven, Conn.: Yale University Press, 2004.

———. *Walden and Resistance to Civil Government*. Ed. William Rossi. New York: W. W. Norton & Co., 1992.

Tocqueville, Alexis. *Democracy in America*. Trans. George Lawrence. Ed. J. P. Mayer. Garden City, N.Y.: Doubleday, 1969.

Tu, Wei-Ming. *Centrality and Commonality: An Essay on Confucian Religiousness*. Albany, N.Y.: SUNY Press, 1989.

Walsh, Vivian. "Philosophy and Economics." In *The New Palgrave Dictionary of Economics*, ed. J. Eatwell, M. Milgate, and P. Newman, 3:861–869. London: Macmillan, 1987.

Watts, Alan. *The Way of Zen*. New York: Vintage Books, 1985.

White, Morton. *Towards Reunion in Philosophy*: Cambridge, Mass.: Harvard University Press, 1956.

Whitehead, Alfred North. *Adventures of Ideas* [1933]. Cambridge: Cambridge University Press, 1943.

———. *Aims of Education* [1929]. New York: Mentor Books, 1949.

———. "Immortality." In *The Philosophy of Alfred North Whitehead*, ed. P. A. Schilpp, 682–700. Evanston, Ill.: Northwestern University Press, 1941.

———. *Process and Reality* [1929]. Corrected ed. New York: The Free Press, 1978.

———. *Science and the Modern World* [1925]. New York: The Free Press, 1967.

———. *Symbolism: Its Meaning and Effect* [1927]. New York: Fordham University Press, 1995.

Williams, Bernard. *Ethics and the Limits of Philosophy*. Cambridge, Mass.: Harvard University Press, 1985.

Wittgenstein, Ludwig. *The Blue and Brown Books*. Ed. and trans. R. Rhees. New York: Harper Torchbooks, 1958.

———. *Culture and Value*. Ed. G. H. von Wright, in collaboration with H. Nyman. Trans. P. Winch. Chicago: University of Chicago Press, 1980.

———. *On Certainty*. Trans. D. Paul and G. E. M. Anscombe. New York: Harper & Row, 1972.

———. *On Certainty*. Ed. G. E. M. Anscombe and G. H. von Wright. Trans. D. Paul and G. E. M. Anscombe. Oxford: Blackwell, 1977.

———. *Philosophical Investigations*. Trans. G. E. M. Anscombe. New York: Macmillan, 1953.

———. *Philosophical Investigations*. Ed. G. E. M. Anscombe. Trans. G. E. M. and R. Rhees. Oxford: B. Blackwell, 1976.

———. *Philosophical Investigations*. Trans. G. E. M. Anscombe. Oxford: Basil Blackwell, 1978.

———. *Philosophical Investigations*. Trans. G. E. M. Anscombe. Malden, Mass.: Blackwell, 2001.

———. 1933/1993. "Philosophy" [1933], from *The Big Typescript*. In *Philosophical Occasions*, by Ludwig Wittgenstein. Ed. J. C. Klagge and E. Nordmann. Indianapolis, Ind.: Hackett.

———. *Remarks on the Philosophy of Psychology*. 2 vols. Ed. G. E. M. Anscombe and G. H. von Wright. Trans. G. E. M. Anscombe. Chicago: University of Chicago Press, 1980.

———. *Zettel*. Trans. G. E. M. Anscombe. Berkeley: University of California Press, 1970.

Wood, Michael. "Why Praise Astaire?" *London Review of Books* 27, no. 20 (October 20, 2005): 14–15.

Wordsworth, William. *The Prelude*. In *The Norton Anthology of English Literature*, vol. 2., ed. M. Abrams et. al, 6th ed. New York: Norton, 1993.

Yamada, Kōun. *The Gateless Gate: The Classic Book of Zen Koans*. Trans. Kōun Yamada. Boston: Wisdom Publications, 2004.

Yampolsky, Philip B., trans. *The Zen Master Hakuin: Selected Writings*. New York: Columbia University Press, 1971.

Contributors

René Arcilla is a Professor of Philosophy of Education at New York University's Steinhardt School. He is the author of numerous articles and the book *For the Love of Perfection: Richard Rorty and Liberal Education* (1995); he also co-edited, with David T. Hansen and Mary Erina Driscoll, *A Life in Classrooms: Philip W. Jackson and the Practice of Education* (2007). His most recent book is *Mediumism: A Philosophical Reconstruction of Modernism for Existential Learning* (2010). His current research focuses on questions at the intersection of liberal learning, modernist art, existentialist philosophy, and cultural politics.

Gordon C. F. Bearn is a Professor of Philosophy at Lehigh University. He has published a book on Nietzsche and Wittgenstein, *Waking to Wonder: Wittgenstein's Existential Investigations* (1997). His affection for Cavell's reading of Wittgenstein has never cooled, even though he was drawn away from the fold, first by Derrida and then by Deleuze. In addition to papers that track those movements, he is completing a Deleuzoid manuscript on making your life beautiful, *Life Drawing: An Aesthetics of Existence*. He has recently become fascinated with the unfortunate way that Grice's William James Lectures marginalized the revolutionary power of the appeal to what we would say, and he enjoys imagining what analytic philosophy might have become had Grice's arguments been answered on time. Some of those historical ideas are appearing in words if not yet in print.

Stanley Cavell, who taught at Harvard University for four decades, is the Walter M. Cabot Professor of Aesthetics and the General Theory of Value, emeritus, and former president of the American Philosophical Association. His major interests center on the intersection of the analytical tradition (especially the work of Austin and Wittgenstein) with moments of the continental tradition (for example, Heidegger and Nietzsche), with American philosophy (especially Emerson and Thoreau), with the arts (for example, Shakespeare, film, and opera), and with psychoanalysis. His memoir, *Little Did I Know: Excerpts from Memory,* was published in 2010. His other books include *Must We Mean What We Say? A Book of Essays* (1976); *The Claim of Reason: Wittgenstein, Skepticism, Morality, and Tragedy* (1979); *Pursuits of Happiness: The Hollywood Comedy of Remarriage* (1981); *Conditions Handsome and Unhandsome: The Constitution of Emersonian Perfectionism* (1990); *The Senses of Walden* (1992); *A Pitch of Philosophy: Autobiographical Exercises* (1994); *Contesting Tears: The Hollywood Melodrama of the Unknown Woman* (1996); *Emerson's Transcendental Etudes* (2003); *Disowning Knowledge: In Seven Plays of Shakespeare* (2004); *Cities of Words: Pedagogical Letters on a Register of the Moral Life* (2004); and *Philosophy the Day After Tomorrow* (2005).

Vincent Colapietro is a Liberal Arts Research Professor in the Department of Philosophy at Pennsylvania State University (University Park Campus). While his principal area of historical research is classical American pragmatism (especially Peirce, James, and Dewey), he has wide and varied scholarly interests. They range from literature, film, and music (above all, jazz) to semiotics, poststructuralism, and psychoanalysis. He is the author of *Peirce's Approach to the Self: A Glossary of Semiotics* (1989) and of *Fateful Shapes of Human Freedom* (2003), as well as scores of articles. The main focus of his current research is the intersections between pragmatism and psychoanalysis. In his efforts to explore questions regarding voice, identity, and inheritance, he has found no author more suggestive or insightful than Stanley Cavell.

Russell Goodman is Regents Professor in the Philosophy Department at the University of New Mexico. He is the author of *American Philosophy and the Romantic Tradition* (1990/2008) and *Wittgenstein and William James* (2002/2007). He edited *Contending with Stanley Cavell* (2005), *Pragmatism: Critical Concepts in Philosophy* (2005), and *Pragmatism: A Contemporary Reader* (1995). He has been a fellow at the Institute for Advanced Study in the Humanities at the University of Edinburgh and a Fulbright senior lecturer at the University of Barcelona. In 2003, he directed a National Endowment for the Humanities summer institute on Ralph Waldo Emerson, and in 2005 and 2007 he directed NEH seminars on Emerson and pragmatism.

Steve Odin teaches Japanese philosophy and East-West comparative philosophy in the Department of Philosophy at the University of Hawaii. Some of his areas of specialization include American philosophy, Whitehead's process metaphysics, aesthetics, environmental ethics, and phenomenology. His published books include *Process Metaphysics and Hua-Yen Buddhism* (1982), *The Social Self in Zen and American Pragmatism* (1996), and *Artistic Detachment in Japan and the West* (1996).

Hilary W. Putnam is Cogan University Professor *Emeritus* in the Department of Philosophy at Harvard University. Before joining the faculty of Harvard, he was a professor of the philosophy of science at the Massachusetts Institute of Technology. He has also taught at Northwestern University and Princeton University. He is a past president of the American Philosophical Association (Eastern Division), the Philosophy of Science Association, and the Association for Symbolic Logic. He is a fellow of the American Academy of Arts and Sciences, the American Philosophical Society, a corresponding fellow of the British Academy and the French Académie des Sciences Politiques et Morales, and holds a number of honorary degrees. Putnam has written extensively on issues in philosophy of science, philosophy of mathematics, philosophy of language, and philosophy of mind, as well as on pragmatism and on the relations of ethics and economics. His *Ethics Without Ontology* (2004) deals with many of these topics.

Naoko Saito is Associate Professor at the Graduate School of Education, University of Kyoto. Her area of research is American philosophy and pragmatism and its implications for education. She writes in Japanese and English, with a commitment to crossing cultural borders. She is the author of *The Gleam of Light: Moral Perfectionism and Education in Dewey and Emerson* (2005) as well as numerous articles. In collaboration with Paul Standish, she has co-authored *Democracy and Education from Dewey to Cavell* (2012) and has co-edited the collection *Education and the Kyoto School of Philosophy* (2011). She is the translator of *The Senses of Walden* (2005), the first book of Cavell's to be published in Japanese, and is the author of *Uchinaru Hikari to Kyoiku: Pragmatism no Sai-Kochiku* (2009), an adaptation of *The Gleam of Light.*

Paul Standish is Professor and the Head of Philosophy of Education at the Institute of Education, University of London. His books include *Beyond the Self: Wittgenstein, Heidegger, and the Limits of Language* (1992) and, in various collaborations with Nigel Blake, Paul Smeyers, and Richard Smith, *Thinking Again: Education After Postmodernism* (1998), *Education in an Age of Nihilism* (2000), *The Therapy of Education* (2006), and the edited collection *The Blackwell Guide to Philosophy of Education* (2003). With Naoko Saito, he has co-authored *Democracy and Education from Dewey to Cavell* (2012) and co-edited *Education and the Kyoto School of Philosophy* (2011). For the past ten years, he has been editor of the *Journal of Philosophy of Education.*

Index

AMERICAN PHILOSOPHY
Douglas R. Anderson and Jude Jones, series editors

Kenneth Laine Ketner, ed., *Peirce and Contemporary Thought: Philosophical Inquiries.*

Max H. Fisch, ed., *Classic American Philosophers: Peirce, James, Royce, Santayana, Dewey, Whitehead, second edition.* Introduction by Nathan Houser.

John E. Smith, *Experience and God, second edition.*

Vincent G. Potter, *Peirce's Philosophical Perspectives.* Ed. by Vincent Colapietro.

Richard E. Hart and Douglas R. Anderson, eds., *Philosophy in Experience: American Philosophy in Transition.*

Vincent G. Potter, *Charles S. Peirce: On Norms and Ideals, second edition.* Introduction by Stanley M. Harrison.

Vincent M. Colapietro, ed., *Reason, Experience, and God: John E. Smith in Dialogue.* Introduction by Merold Westphal.

Robert J. O'Connell, S.J., *William James on the Courage to Believe, second edition.*

Elizabeth M. Kraus, *The Metaphysics of Experience: A Companion to Whitehead's "Process and Reality," second edition.* Introduction by Robert C. Neville.

Kenneth Westphal, ed., *Pragmatism, Reason, and Norms: A Realistic Assessment—Essays in Critical Appreciation of Frederick L. Will.*

Beth J. Singer, *Pragmatism, Rights, and Democracy.*

Eugene Fontinell, *Self, God, and Immorality: A Jamesian Investigation.*

Roger Ward, *Conversion in American Philosophy: Exploring the Practice of Transformation.*

Michael Epperson, *Quantum Mechanics and the Philosophy of Alfred North Whitehead.*

Kory Sorrell, *Representative Practices: Peirce, Pragmatism, and Feminist Epistemology.*

Naoko Saito, *The Gleam of Light: Moral Perfectionism and Education in Dewey and Emerson.*

Josiah Royce, *The Basic Writings of Josiah Royce.*

Douglas R. Anderson, *Philosophy Americana: Making Philosophy at Home in American Culture.*

James Campbell and Richard E. Hart, eds., *Experience as Philosophy: On the World of John J. McDermott.*

John J. McDermott, *The Drama of Possibility: Experience as Philosophy of Culture.* Edited by Douglas R. Anderson.

Larry A. Hickman, *Pragmatism as Post-Postmodernism: Lessons from John Dewey.*

Larry A. Hickman, Stefan Neubert, and Kersten Reich, eds., *John Dewey Between Pragmatism and Constructivism.*

Dwayne A. Tunstall, *Yes, But Not Quite: Encountering Josiah Royce's Ethico-Religious Insight.*

Josiah Royce, *Race Questions, Provincialism, and Other American Problems, Expanded Edition.* Edited by Scott L. Pratt and Shannon Sullivan.

Lara Trout, *The Politics of Survival: Peirce, Affectivity, and Social Criticism.*

John R. Shook and James A. Good, *John Dewey's Philosophy of Spirit, with the 1897 Lecture on Hegel.*

Gregory Fernando Pappas, ed., *Pragmatism in the Americas.*

Donald J. Morse, *Faith in Life: John Dewey's Early Philosophy.*

Josiah Warren, *The Practical Anarchist: Writings of Josiah Warren.* Edited and with an Introduction by Crispin Sartwell.